D1565446

SIGNS
OF THE
LITERARY
TIMES

SUNY Series, The Margins of Literature
Mihai I. Spariosu, editor

BOOKS BY WILLIAM O'ROURKE

The Harrisburg 7 and the New Catholic Left (1972)
The Meekness of Isaac (1974)
On the Job: Fiction About Work by Contemporary
  American Writers, Editor (1977)
Idle Hands (1981)
Criminal Tendencies (1987)

Signs
OF THE
Literary
Times

Essays,
Reviews,
Profiles
1970 - 1992

William
O'Rourke

STATE UNIVERSITY OF NEW YORK PRESS

Published by
State University of New York Press, Albany

For information, address State University of New York Press,
State University Plaza, Albany, N.Y., 12246

The Acknowledgments on page xv are an extension of the copyright page.
Cover photo of William O'Rourke by James K. Ruhl

Production by Marilyn P. Semerad
Marketing by Lynne Lekakis

Library of Congress Catloging-in-Publication Data

O'Rourke, William.
    Signs of the literary times : essays, reviews, profiles 1970-1992
/ William O'Rourke.
        p.   cm. — (SUNY series, the margins of literature)
    Includes index.
    ISBN 0-7914-1681-X (hard). — ISBN 0-7914-1682-8 (pbk.)
    I. Title. II. Series.
PS3565.R65S54 1993
814'.54—dc20   92-43027
                                                                CIP

10 9 8 7 6 5 4 3 2 1

To
Teresa and Joseph

CONTENTS

PREFACE

Writing any sort of Preface to a book such as this is a risky thing, akin to asking a delicate question a second time after the right answer has already been given: Will you marry me? Yes. Would you like to reconsider? It's an invitation to gaucherie. You are, after all, holding the book in your hands.

Signs of the Literary Times makes available the lion's share of disparate pieces of nonfiction of varying lengths (and one interloping short story) that I have published over the last twenty-two years. They all represent occasions where I had something to say and had the opportunity to say it, a condition not always easily brought about. At times I had to track down an editor and publication the way an ornithologist searches jungles for a species of bird thought to be extinct. Writing this sort of nonfiction (like the publishing of most literary short stories) was not an activity that would have been self-supporting.

It was suggested by sympathetic, but less adventuresome editors elsewhere that I do a collection of solely political articles or solely literary pieces, that a mix more "thematically linked" was preferred—but it is just such an "unlinked" mix that I want to present.

Signs of the Literary Times is my second book of nonfiction; it has been twenty years since my first was published. I did not necessarily intend such a long span to intervene. Two years after my 1972 book, *The Harrisburg 7 and the New Catholic Left* (an account of one of the last Nixon-era, anti-Vietnam war conspiracy trials) was published, I was offered a good deal of money to write a book on the Patty Hearst kidnapping and metamorphosis, then in progress. One author, it had been reported, was secured to write on the case for a half-million; it was deemed that I was worth easily 10 percent of that amount, since my Harrisburg book had been, at least, a success of esteem. But, I declined, foolishly, doubtless; I didn't want to write another "trial" book (I presumed there would be a trial, eventually). And I was finishing my first novel, *The Meekness of Isaac*—that is, when I wasn't working at some menial job to keep a roof over my head. (I had not yet landed a teaching job.)

In one of the pieces collected here (written a number of years after the Hearst case came and went) I write, "When young writers-to-be are growing up they actually imagine that their literary lives will take the shape of the generation of writers before them; whereas, in most cases (save those where wealth will purchase any fantasy), their literary lives are formed by contemporary forces they haven't yet been able to identify." And by 1974, I only had begun to identify the contemporary forces that certainly were shaping my generation's literary life.

An agent I spoke with back then suggested I "delay my gratification" and take the Hearst deal offered. I had told her I wanted to finish my novel and saw myself as primarily a novelist. I was lost in the thrall of an earlier generation's dream, and, paradoxically, just as Norman Mailer and Truman Capote were awakening from it, abdicating the throne of fiction for the ringside seat of journalism, new or used, I wanted to dream on, have my own coronation, even though I was spending more time doing construction work in the South Bronx than shaping sentences in my one-room apartment in Greenwich Village.

I suppose I thought one first had to publish a novel before one could write "novelistic nonfiction." I had somehow gotten it backwards, and I wanted to correct the sequence (or, at least, achieve a sequence: it took Tom Wolfe a couple of decades to achieve his sequence). Of course, most of what I was contemplating in the very early seventies was drenched in the rather ordinary callowness of youth. What I clearly didn't understand then, I nonetheless had to grapple with daily: how was I going to finance my budding writing career?

Though I did not comprehend the social forces shaping me and my generation of young writers, I had been readily surfing their waves. When I applied to Columbia University's new MFA creative writing program in 1968, my "writing sample" was six poems; I knew then that the audience for poetry was likely to be only other poets, even though in 1968 the *New York Times* still published poetry on its editorial page, surrounded by the letters to the editors. I remember this well, since I sent the *Times* some poems and had them returned with a memorable rejection note. The poems themselves came back stuck together with spilled liquor and accompanied by an unsigned note, scrawled on a torn piece of paper: "I don't think we can use these."

I promptly switched to prose and the *Times* shortly dropped poetry from its pages. I didn't foresee, though, that the audience for most serious novelists would soon become other serious fiction writers. The current situation is a result of numbers, but not, as is often cited, because of the increase in the number of graduate writing programs. They are an effect, not a cause. A fact I refer to in a couple of the essays collected here deserves further exploration. In 1978 the number of first novels published was roughly that of the number of first novels published in 1962 (*Library Journal* has been keeping count): slightly more than a hundred. During the sixties the number of people in institutions of higher learning increased dramatically: it tripled. That period (from the early sixties to the end of the seventies) was, in many ways, the last golden age of readers for serious fiction. There were many more readers being educated during those years, while the number of novels being published remained constant. Now more than three hundred first novels are published each year. Obviously, that increase is a result of tripling the number of people who went on to some form of higher education during the sixties. But, there is no longer that happy surplus of freshly minted readers, though their presence in my "formative" years certainly illuminated my dreams.

As one finds in the larger economy, in the literary economy the rich are getting richer, and the poor, poorer. Here, too, the middle class of novelists is being squeezed. The situation my generation (and younger writers) face resembles the economics of a lottery: the greater the number of participants, the larger the reward for the few. This doesn't dissuade people from participating; far from it—it actually increases the desire. The more writers writing and publishing, the bigger the payoff for the handful of writers who get lucky. Everyone is a gambler. Of course, this has very little to do with literary quality or sound judgments. And, it accounts for one reason why the notion of generation as a category has become passé: critical attention, both academic and popular, chases the bright lights exploding over the big city.

Scarce resources—the amount of attention any one novel or volume of poetry is likely to get (or, for that matter, any book at all), whether published by large press or small—engender a system of rationing and hand over even more concentrated power to those who dispense attention. Here, trickle-down theory does work: a cataract of attention from Manhattan does saturate the rest of the country.

Even though, one is informed testily often enough, there is an overabundance of writers of fiction (and, by implication, that the duty of the marketplace is to thin them out), on the nonfiction side, an additional (and antithetical) contemporary complaint needs addressing: the so-called death of the "public intellectual," the dearth of literary journalists of the Edmund Wilson stripe, a lament I allude to in the last of the N.E.A. pieces reprinted here.

Though I also disagree with that conventional wisdom, I do have a sense of what absence those commentators are decrying. (It is that "golden age" period I described that is nevermore.) But their whips are lashing the wrong backs. As I point out in an N.E.A. article, it is not a supply-side problem, as they would have it, the result of a "decline of literary journalism" and a rise of so many academics speaking and writing gibberish, holed up in colleges and universities, without, as one typical complaint puts it, "any experience or knowledge of anything outside the university, least of all working-class life." Quite the opposite: the sixties did place any number of individuals from decidedly untraditional backgrounds (women, for one) in universities, a change as large for the professoriate as, say, the GI bill made in the overall university population after World War II.

There are so many public intellectuals these days, one might notice that there is also an equal number of publics. It is not impossible to imagine Edmund Wilson on the *This Week with David Brinkley* show (after all, John Leonard, the former editor of the *New York Times Book Review*, is on the CBS *Sunday Morning* show), but I don't think it would be quite the same.

What the complainers would prefer is not more "public" intellectuals; I suspect that they themselves would like to become "privatized" intellectuals, or corporate intellectuals, those glittering few who are brought into millions of livingrooms by the good grace of Ted Turner or Time Warner.

One of the reasons I have done (and still do) journalistic pieces, both literary and general, is to secure the haphazard captive audiences the variety of publications provides. Novels do not have captive audiences; periodicals, however eccentric, do. And what one writes for regional publications stands the chance of escaping locality by being bound into a book; but it should be pointed out that volumes of, say, previously published short stories do not lure their authors into mea culpas about why their very slightly used goods are being offered in book form, though even writers of a more brand name sort than mine feel compelled to offer some explanation for their impertinence when they collect previously published nonfiction. Yet in either case (fiction or nonfiction), the books need to chase down an audience, since there is no longer a captive one available.

As noted earlier, my youthful apprehension of what being a person of letters entailed was a bit old fashioned. And I am not the first or the last to point out how economic forces impact literary pursuits. During the Age of Reagan aesthetic questions became overwhelming issues of value and control. What's it worth and who decides? The old American axiom has gone from a half-joke to a surly charge: if you're so smart, why aren't you rich? Cash aesthetics are seductive. Everywhere the audience for literature is fragmenting and dispersing. At times, the whole of it can be summoned to pay attention, but only by forces so powerful and costly that they are the equivalent of Noah summoning livestock to the ark.

The surplus, given the demand, of serious fiction writers is being subsidized (the writing, at least—teaching is work) by colleges and universities throughout the land. The paradox is that as the numbers of writers increased, the perceived ability of the next generation to read and write well declined, since that generation matured in a much more thoroughly postliterate culture (television, etc.) than did mine. Now, even in Greenwich Village, bookstores have disappeared, and video stores have replaced them; in libraries throughout the land, video budgets rival, if not outstrip, book budgets.

The next generation of writers is not likely to have the beckoning harbor of the university to take them in; at least, not until the present generation retires. The growth period is over. A goodly portion may have to do something else, and what that turns out to be might be good for all of us, if not immediately for them. In our culture, *academic* is not a synonym for *intellectual*, which is why there seems to be such an abundance of the former and such a deficit of the latter.

Nothing much has been done to the individual articles, beyond attempting to correct typos and removing a few repetitions and inadvertencies. By way of an afterword, I supply brief comments on the individual selections; essays, reviews and profiles are all genres: what the afterword contains is ex genre, out-of-the-genre comments. The remarks are various, the "afterword" truly afterwords: matters of publication, reservations about content, second thoughts generally, my current feelings on the subject. Since the material covers over two decades, some things have changed—though never as much as one would think, or wish.

South Bend, Indiana
    September 1992

ACKNOWLEDGMENTS

I would like to thank the following periodicals, editors, and publishers for permission to reprint my work from the source of its original publication.

American Book Review: Review of *Lunar Attractions* and *Passage Through Gehenna*, vol. 2, no. 2, Oct. 1979, p. 24. © 1979 by The American Book Review.

American Rag: Jury, vol. 1, no. 2-3, 1980, pp. 34-38. © 1980 by Frederick Douglass Creative Arts Center, Inc.

Another Chicago Magazine: "Letters to Editors: The N.E.A. and the Loyalty Oafs," no. 24. © 1992 by Left Field Press.

Arts Indiana: "Of Judges and G-strings," vol. 13, no. 3, April 1991, pp. 28-30. © 1991 by Arts Indiana, Inc.

Bookreview, a service of American Booksellers Association: Review of *Like Father*, vol. 1, no. 3, Sept. 24, 1979, p. 15. © 1979 by Booksellers Publishing, Inc.

Boston Phoenix: Review of *A Month of Sundays*, sec. 2, Mar. 5, 1975, p. 8. © 1975 by The Boston Phoenix.

Chicago Tribune: Review of *Lying Together*, July 15, 1990, sec. 14, p. 5. Review of *A Stranger in the Kingdom*, *Chicago Tribune*, Nov. 9, 1989, sec. 3, p. 3. Review of *Mr. Field's Daughter* and *Winter Losses*, July 2, 1989, sec. 14, pp. 3, 7. Review of *Mischief Makers*, May 15, 1989, sec. 2, p. 3. Review of *The Turkey War*, Nov. 13, 1988, sec. 14, p. 5. Review of *The Book and the Brotherhood*, Feb. 7, 1988, sec. 14, p. 3. Review of *Loving Little Egypt*, Feb. 22,

1987, sec. 14, pp. 1, 8. Review of *The Tidewater Tales*, June 7, 1987, sec. 14, p. 3. Review of *Peru*, Feb. 2, 1986, pp. 37-38. Review of *Famous People I Have Known*, Nov. 17, 1985, p. 47. Review of *The Tree of Life*, Oct. 27, 1985, pp. 10-11. Review of *Difficult Women* and *Minor Characters*, Mar. 6, 1983, sec. 7, p. 3. Review of *Beyond the Pale* and *Watching Me, Watching You*, Feb. 14, 1982, sec. 7, p. 3. © 1982, 83, 85, 87, 88, 89, 90 *Chicago Tribune*.

Chronicle of Higher Education: "Artists Should Accept Grants from the Arts Endowment," vol. 36, no. 40, June 20, 1990, p. A48 © 1990 The Chronicle of Higher Education, Inc.

Commonweal: Review of *Prince of Peace*, vol. 111, no. 22, Dec. 14, 1984, pp. 694-96. Review of *On Becoming a Novelist* and *Panic Among the Philistines*, vol. 111, no. 1, Jan. 13, 1984, pp. 24-26. Review of *In Such Dark Places* and *The Offering*, vol. 105, no. 14, July 21, 1978, pp. 467-77. Review of *The Voice: Life at the Village Voice*, vol. 104, no. 14, July 8, 1977, pp. 444-46. © 1977, 1978, 1984 Commonweal Publishing Co.

Indiana University Press: "The Literature of Place and No Place," in *Where We Live: Essays About Indiana*, edited by David Hoppe, Indiana University Press, Indianapolis, 1989, pp. 73-81. © 1989 Indiana Humanities Council.

Los Angeles Times: Review of *Foggage*, pt. 5, Dec. 15, 1983, p. 44. © 1983 Times Mirror Co.

Mulch: Review of *Turkey Hash*, 8-9, vol. 3, no. 4/vol. 4, no. 1, Spring-Summer 1976, pp. 193-95. © 1976 by Mulch Press.

Nation: Reviews, "Book Marks," vol. 211, no. 5, Aug. 31, 1970, pp. 156-57. Reviews, "Book Marks," vol. 210, no. 16, Apr. 27, 1970, pp. 508-9. Review of *The Company of Women*, vol. 232, no. 6, Feb. 28, 1981, pp. 245-46. "Protesting NEA," vol. 250, no. 25, June 25, 1990, pp. 880-81. Article, "Nudity and Free Speech: Will the Court Bare All?" vol. 252, no. 24, June 24, 1991, pp. 846-47. © 1970, 1981, 1990, 1991 by The Nation Company, Inc.

New Catholic World: "Catholics Coming of Age: The Literary Consequences," vol. 228, no. 1366, July-Aug. 1985, pp. 148-52. © 1985 by the Missionary Society of St. Paul the Apostle in the State of New York.

New York Times Book Review: Review of *The Bodyguard*, Nov. 7, 1971, p. 41. © 1971 by The New York Times Company. Reprinted by Permission.

Poets & Writers Magazine: "The Night the Ghost Didn't Get In," vol. 16, no. 1, Jan.-Feb. 1988, pp. 7-12. © 1988 Poets & Writers, Inc.

Politicks & other human interests: "From CIA to Riverside Coffin Aims for the Top," vol. 1, no. 5, Jan. 3, 1978, pp. 25-26. © 1977 Morgan Publishing Co.

Review of Contemporary Fiction: "The Causes of Immortal Conceptions," vol. 11, no. 1, Spring 1991, pp. 107-16. © 1991 The Review of Contemporary Fiction.

Rights: "Notes on the Question of Amnesty: Remembering to Forget," vol. 20, no. 3 & 4, May-June 1974, pp. 3-14. Review of *Freedom at Risk*, vol. 37, no. 2, July-Aug. 1991, pp. 8-10.

Salem Press: "Saturday Night" reprinted from *Masterplots II: Short Story Series*, pages 2025-28. By permission of the publisher, Salem Press, Inc. © 1986 by Frank N. Magill.

Salmagundi: "Response to Charles Newman's 'The Post-Modern Aura,'" *Salmagundi*, no. 67, Summer 1985, pp. 183-85. © 1985 *Salmagundi* (Skidmore College).

San Francisco Review of Books: "Edward Dahlberg: On the Occasion of the First Anniversary of His Death," *San Francisco Review of Books*, vol. 3, no. 1, March 1978, pp. 23-24. © 1978 The San Francisco Review of Books.

Soho Weekly News: "Michael Harrington . . . Beyond Watergate, Sixties, and Reform," vol. 3, no. 6, Nov. 13, 1975, pp. 6-7. Review of *The Olive of Minerva*, vol. 3, no. 40, July 8, 1976, p. 22. © 1975, 1976 The Soho Weekly News.

South Bend Tribune: Review of *Trombone*, Aug. 23, 1992, sec. F, p. 8. Review of *Cooler by the Lake*, June 28, 1992, sec. F, p. 9. Review of *Vineland* and *Thomas Pynchon: A Bibliography of Primary and Secondary Materials*, May 20, 1990, sec. C, p. 9. Review of *Disco Frito* and *All You Can Eat*, Jan. 1, 1989, sec. C, p. 7. Review of *Learning About God*, Nov. 27, 1988, sec. C, p. 9. Review of *John Cheever: A Biography*, July 17, 1988, sec. B, p. 11. Review of *My Father in Dreams*, June 25, 1989, sec. E, p. 9. Review of *Cal, Michiana Magazine*, Jan. 13, 1985, p. 13. © 1985, 1988, 1989, 1990, 1992 The South Bend Tribune Corp.

Transatlantic Review: "The Maggot Principle" reprinted from *On the Job: Fiction about Work by Contemporary American Writers* (Random House,

1977). First published in *Transatlantic Review* 44, 1972. © 1972, 1977 by William O'Rourke.

TriQuarterly: "Reminiscence," vol. 19, Fall 1970, pp. 74-78. © 1970 by Tri-Quarterly, a publication of Northwestern University.

Village Voice: Review of *The Wages of Expectation: A Biography of Edward Dahlberg*, vol. 24, no. 15, April 16, 1979, p. 91. Review of *The Geek*, vol. 20, no. 44, Nov. 3, 1975, p. 54. © 1975, 1979 The Village Voice.

I

EDWARD DAHLBERG
TIMES 5

EDWARD DAHLBERG, TEACHER*

*Kansas City is a vast inland city, and its marvelous river,
the Missouri, heats the senses.*
—Because I Was Flesh

*But he said unto them, All men cannot receive this saying,
save they to whom it is given.*
—Matt. 19:11

Kansas City was never vast to me, and, since I knew neither shelf of the continent, *inland* had no meaning. The river Missouri was reported as a suicide ditch; the newspaper carried inky photos of police with malignant grappling hooks. The city and I shared the heavy wastrel days of my youth—the memories of childhood that are the phantom pains of the amputee. The Church was a gray proctor, but it gave me gold, frankincense, and myrrh. Kansas City is a market town with belligerent exhausts of monster trucks, battered ramps of loading docks, and the weak-colored, three-copy bill of lading. Most men's histories are written in bill receipts. Kansas City feels the waves of the nation around it, the tossed stone that does not cause the ripples but is impressed by them.

"Homer sang of many sacred towns in Hellas which were no better than Kansas City." Edward Dahlberg returned to the city of his youth to teach at the University of Missouri—Kansas City the spring of 1965; his audience were creative paupers, for I was one of them.

Women filled his classes. Cameoed dowagers with rouged jowls and red velvet capes, young brittle-lipped girls whose pens took notes nodding like steadfast crochet needles. A fluorescent insect hum came from the lighting

---

* First appeared in *TriQuarterly*, no. 19, Fall 1970.

fixtures in the large room, terraced with rows of chairs with wide spatula arms. The university had the charm of the nondescript. Originally a small private institution, it had a few simple sandstone buildings with red clay gable roofs— "pigeons had a universe in their eaves." I moved about the buildings with the vacant motions of a vagrant. My education has a Jesuitical residue, and at eighteen the difference between the Spanish Civil War and the Franco-American War (which I adopted from a can of spaghetti) was not yet clear.

The draft in the corridors raised the fabric around the wrist that February. Edward Dahlberg came into the room in a heavy umber coat, mounted a creaking pine dais, was introduced by the head of the English Department, who listed Dahlberg's books soon to be published. Patches of white hair lay across his head; above a frieze of mustache was the strong nose, as galling as the golden calf. Dahlberg announced that this would be no class of dry syntax; rather he would have us read truthful books that would quicken our pulses and dilate our sensibilities. These were not the regions where books were taken by the nervous nonce lives of his students. Taught as young critics, they demanded the incest of fiction. There is no misfortune esteemed as a novel—an image to a primitive people has more power than the life it represents. A man of strong parts will be shunned, whereas the thinnest fictions will pulse, transfused with the plasma of professors. Homer said the last song is always applauded the loudest; the students were in the din of the continual midst. The ancients and sages are considered the brackish past for the word *quote*, and its usage has become inhuman. It now denotes a bloodless severance. Phrases are put in quotation marks to disavow them in scorn or to allow the impasse to realize itself in print. We are provided with adages, truisms, and the gnomic line, but like the doubtful chiropractors they manage to crack our backs but do not give us spines. Edward Dahlberg partakes of the multiple rhythm of the blood of the writers who were as anonymous to his students as he was

Edward Dahlberg told his class if they would read *The Compleat Angler*, they would be more quiet. The masters' candidates were concerned with dredging up Faulkner, whom Dahlberg refused to discuss as "the literary figure of the Century," as one graduate student was wont to put it, because it was an ordeal to read his books. A lathy navy veteran asked him a bogus question about oriental art, its suggestive qualities and its relationship to our abstract painting. He paused to let the hiss of sophistry out between the words of his question, which contained the antithetical approach he considered Edward Dahlberg's prose to have. The class waited, alerted.

He answered that he did not know enough about oriental art to instruct the fellow, except that as Lao-tsu uses a slight linen manner and is in no way an elliptical mind so he believed their art to be. The filling-in the student allowed himself was the blending of his own empty spaces. He then told of an afternoon he spent with the painter Willem De Kooning in De Kooning's lower East Side apartment. The painter stood at a window that looked down upon an alley of corrugated ashcans, wet, unhealthy skin of cardboard, sunken cellar windows agape like severed lower jaws and exclaimed to the persons in the room: "Isn't it beautiful?" with a smeary sincerity.

Dahlberg showed simple horror at this and told De Kooning, "Children could not help but be maimed if they have such sights scratching across their memories," and quit his company.

Papers were read on novels we had selected that, as he advised us, were not sufficiently bad to be book publishers' forewords. The numbers in the room started to lessen; none returned with a green bough. Two wantons with yellow teeth and pants with brass zippers for their gentle central seam missed his classes because even they fell under a reproachment. The older women whose memories loosened as their vessels collapsed fell off from the front row where they commanded his gaze if not his imagination. But as I would pass out of the building I often saw him walking with a straight-limb girl who had always spoken in a soft manner. I never said a word to her, though during the recitations of student papers her bowed back eased my *rigor mortis* contemplations.

He recommended all of Sherwood Anderson, so a few papers were written on *Winesburg, Ohio* and *Poor White*. The night before, he told us, he visited a home where the child of the family kissed his hand. He was very moved, for he told it twice. A paper was then read by a boy on *Poor White* that was dim sociology. Dahlberg asked why he did not include the meaning of the seed, the machinery invented to harvest it, and the sterile seed the man delivered to his wife; The boy had not pondered this and was not concerned with how much love or "hot sperm" went into the making of a child. When Anderson's own lines were read, Edward Dahlberg would lean back, close his eyes, and say: "Yes, very good. Thank you."

Edward Dahlberg would nod his head while his thumbs muttered at his waist and thank the young person who would repeat such lines to let him dwell on and release their powers to his listeners.

In his creative writing class there were some two dozen students. Women in the special education division who took these courses so their wells of sensibility might be dipped into. One businessman was included who sat immobile in a corner chair with a suit the color of corrosion. His face had a translucent skin that showed catacombs of veins, red and periwinkle. He was auditing and seemed comfortable in this position. Throughout the semester he offered only the diction of pleasantries, and finally Edward Dahlberg asked him if he might do a paper. The men spoke and his awry face flamed:

"I've worked for my company twenty years and I have had eighteen electric shock treatments . . ."

He stopped and began grasping air with his mouth. Dahlberg sat at his desk in a plain of silence that followed whereon passed annals of intrusions of suffering. He said: "I am very sorry for you."

The man never reappeared.

Edward Dahlberg forsook a lecture only when he was in need of a physician. The head of the English Department announced this and called for remarks about the author in residence. After their objections he told the students Dahlberg was fond of using "inkhorn words," which was an enema synthesis they found a comfort.

The writing class had decomposed to a half-dozen. Another male, a speech teacher of twenty-four who needed the credits to get his master's degree in order to teach some hapless students the next year, and an assortment of female poets. Dahlberg sat with his legs crossed with gray exhaustion over his face and the tops of his unraveling many-colored socks exposed when a woman volunteered to read a children's book she had written. He had spoken against the children's dilutions of the classics before, but consented with alarm for there was no other offering during the period. She began: "Winnie was a puppy who looked like a mop and rode the elevators of downtown Kansas City until everybody knew his name . . ."

Edward Dahlberg, American artist, sat with his face shrouded by his hands.

She continued: "He would walk around the Plaza, for he lived with his master in an apartment . . ."

"Stop," he said, hardly audible. "Stop. Please."

The panes in the building's long windows were mottled and May filled these thin pools with color. Only after asking permission would Edward Dahlberg read from his own works and this late in the semester. He read from *The Sorrows of Priapus*: "Socrates described love as the sting of a tarantula. We see that desire dominates the old as well as youth; the senile forget to button their clothes, and leave the door of their trousers ajar . . ." He stopped and looked up at his class of housewives and the one young man, who "desperately wanted to have feelings."

"Why do you stop?" asked one of the mothers from the back of the room.

He hesitated, but turned the pages from the spot and replied: "You should be frank on paper, but I'll decline to read this passage aloud."

He had once before remarked on the Scottsboro case—the verdict of which I knew nothing about—saying, if he could be pardoned: "I would not use the washroom after the woman involved."

Justice was within that remark and, I thought, in the measure of his balance that knew a frank page and could find reason to leave it be.

In the larger class the navy veteran again asked a question with an impertinent unction on it, but quoted a line from the autobiography in doing so. After hearing his words come from the man's lips Edward Dahlberg said: "Since you remember what I have written, I have seeped into your soul, and it will take you quite a few years to realize what that means."

The veteran was silenced as were the others as he remained thrust out over his desk, the pine bending aloud while under his weight.

He often said, "Read my books, don't look to me." When someone would say an agreeable thing about him, he said, quoting Prince Myshkin, "Thank you very much for liking me." In the writing class delivered by a deux ex machina adviser there was the "Miss Missouri" of that year. She was the daughter of a talented family who would tour counties playing at fairs, livestock shows, and, in larger cities, nightclubs. Their traveling bus had large gleeful letters of advertisement on its side. She played more than one instrument and more than one at a time. She wrote a paper on *Madame Bovary* and defended Emma, which Dahlberg amended and reminded her it was Flaubert who said, "I am Madame Bovary." She had a peculiar way of standing that amounted to a contestant's at attention. Her smile was as ready as an opening curtain. She was absent frequently because of the family's raucous touring, and Dahlberg had been asking her to perform for the class if she refused to write more papers. He finally shamed her into doing a song, which she did in a timely up-temp fashion, tapping her thigh, standing forthrightly but without the aid of her silk "Miss Missouri" bandolier. She sat down after applause and the meager looks of the other women and asked Edward Dahlberg if he would sing—the same number, for it was an old one. He tipped back his chair, raised his jaw, and, making a rapids of his throat, sang. And he sang!—a slow original blues version of the tune. He often grieved he could no longer see the image of his mother before him. I grieve that I can't remember the simple verses of the song he sang before us.

When I last shook his hand I was sure of dropping out of school. I had his book, unread, *Alms for Oblivion*, which I asked him to inscribe. He did, bending low above the page, for his "sight is starved." I looked into his face then; the left eye had turned a robin's-egg blue and the other, which caught into you as he said: "I sympathize with your predicament, as you know I must, but you should stay in school lest you become entangled by Sears Roebuck."

All I knew was that he had seeped into my soul and I no longer could follow the shambles of his figure silently down the steps of that midland university.

He returned to Kansas City the following semester, I learned, and became ill; having no quickened students he left shortly after. A small editorial in the student newspaper complained of the money the English Department paid him, about half the price of a Chevrolet. In a public lecture he gave to Kansas City, he said that for those who did not read his books, "It was their loss."

He had given out a list of books that he wanted his students to read, not for the class but during their whole lives, for these were such books. His classes, too, were for his students' whole lives; but the stories of his friends Dreiser, Anderson, and Crane, his beloved Ford Madox Ford were only place-names to his listeners. "I sing of Oak, Walnut, Chestnut, Maple, and Elm Streets." Ford Madox Ford called it "jocund fate," but is this what returned Edward Dahlberg to Kansas City, a town that "nursed men, mules, and horses as famous as the asses of Arcadia"?

Edward Dahlberg was bleached in a town that is still green and meadowed; I too neglected him there, though I now know that Kansas City has its living region in Edward Dahlberg. It is he who has a vast inland city and the marvelous river that heats the senses.

DAHLBERG'S *THE OLIVE OF MINERVA**

Any writer who advances on four-score years does so at his peril; if not tucked into a bed of tenure or into a bucolic retreat protected by wise investment, what remains is to mimic Lear wild on the heath. Thomas Wolfe, like Edward Dahlberg, was born in 1900; Wolfe died at thirty-eight, leaving behind an eight-foot pile of manuscripts. Ernest Hemingway was born in 1899 and dispatched himself to kingdom come sixty-two years later. Publishers will preserve your corpus (if you bring them kingly rewards) better than Egyptian embalmers; such monuments of print, though, are as rare as the pyramids. Next to memory, age is our national scourge: we refuse to remember and we refuse to grow old. Dahlberg refutes both, aging and recollecting. And, at three-quarters of this century, we have a new book from him, an irascible plaint of decline, *The Olive of Minerva or The Comedy of a Cuckold*, and an omnibus volume of his fiction of the thirties, *Bottom Dogs, From Flushing to Calvary, Those Who Perish*.

I have had the great good fortune to have known Edward Dahlberg since 1965; and, though many take offense at those who review books written by friends, it is a dour truth that if you happen to know too many literary people, it is more likely your work will be "virtuously" passed-by. "Thank God for strangers," is a writer's benediction when he sees the aid provided by acquaintances.

This could easily go down the primrose path of remembrance; it is always easier to talk about Dahlberg's life than his work. It is difficult for me to review his book (not, certainly, because there isn't much to laud). Friendship does rust the critical edge regardless if you're trying to carve a figure of praise or damnation.

"All excuses are perjuries, O'Rourke," I can hear Dahlberg saying (all the way from California where he resides). His eighteen books have not gathered

---

* First appeared in the *Soho Weekly News*, vol. 3, no. 40, July 8, 1976.

him a large audience, though he is one of the handful of American authors who should be considered for the Nobel Prize. His novel-autobiography *Because I Was Flesh* is a masterpiece (and is still available after twelve years in a New Directions paperback). The publication of the omnibus volume of his "proletarian" novels (frequently mentioned by chroniclers but little read because of their scarcity) and *The Olive of Minerva* fix both poles of his life's work. He contains within himself most of the history of twentieth-century American literature; he has influenced at least two generations of writers, and he has managed to make enemies out of half of the literary establishment just because he detests cats. The other half he has made enemies of personally. None of his detractors, though, can compose a majestic sentence. From them there is supercilious sniping, such as a recent review of the novel in the *New Yorker*: "The reader's orbs extrude. The storm of words bedews his danksome brow . . ." Unable to parody Dahlberg, they parody themselves.

There is more laughter in *The Olive of Minerva* than malediction, and it does need to be read more than once to release all its humor, just as lyrics need to be sung a few times before they are understood, since music always obscures literalness. And Dahlberg's prose is belles lettres and therefore, alas, seems to be a foreign language. This comedy of a cuckold's mirth is sulphurous, but sustaining; it is narrated by Abel, who has a "starless sky in his veins," whose predicament is "himself and the rout. Character is indestructible, and one is worse for it as he grows older. . . ." This is a rare book, and young writers can blush at this volume since they cannot equal the energy that drives it.

The Olive of Minerva is a philosophic tale, a fable, but I'll let you—if possessed of enough courage—tend to its plot. And I'll let its author have the penultimate word.

> Abel sauntered through a grove of olives to quiet the maggots in his spirit. Man's noble faculties decline as he steps into the fag-end of his life, but as the olive decays, it is wise as Minerva. It is fabled that Menelaus came to Iberia and may have been the first to plant an olive tree in the Balearics. It is a seraphic legend, that one myth can obliterate bad luck . . .

It is a seraphic legend. And one book cannot obliterate bad luck, but if any could, it would be a book of Edward Dahlberg.

EDWARD DAHLBERG, 1900-1977*

The last time I spoke with Edward Dahlberg the circumstances were these: I had been living an economically immature existence, the most lucrative part of which saw me toiling as a laborer in the South Bronx. You learn only so much from poverty; it quickly becomes a redundant lesson. I was offered a university position and—always willing to have a new experience—I accepted and thereby turned into the kind of writer I (and Dahlberg) distrusted: an author of two books who had a full-time teaching position. My estimation of such an individual had been that he couldn't possibly be any good. Dahlberg asked me what my salary was, and I told him. He shouted into the phone: "No university has ever paid me $12,000!" and he slammed the receiver down. I hadn't expected those to be my private version of his last words, but they were. So now, in my own personal ossuary, Dahlberg's stone is etched:

EDWARD DAHLBERG,
AMERICAN AUTHOR 1900-1977

"No university has ever
paid me $12,000!"

In the summer of 1978, Crowell brought out his last novel, *The Olive of Minerva or The Comedy of a Cuckold*, and an omnibus volume of his thirties "Proletarian" novels: *Bottom Dogs, From Flushing to Calvary, Those Who Perish. The Olive of Minerva* was scored in the *New York Times Book Review* by some drone of the academy suffering from terminal snit. He quite fraudulently failed to mention (as did the obituary in the *Times* on February 28, 1977) Dahlberg's masterpiece, the novel-autobiography *Because I Was Flesh*.

I wrote a review of the new book that summer that I now see contained

---

* First appeared in the *San Francisco Review of Books*, vol. 3, no. 1, March 1978.

more eulogy than I intended; because I loved the man, it was a difficult task—
not, certainly, because there wasn't a good deal to laud.

A good many people had been waiting for him to die. A small cottage
industry has developed in the literary world of telling outrageous Dahlberg
tales: of offense taken and given, of majestic rudeness and sidereal insult. They
are of the variety that grows livelier from beyond the grave. The good stories,
alas, are often not interred with the bones. So, paraphrasing one of our contemporary heroes of the Reprint Pantheon, What can you say about a seventy-
seven-year-old author who has died?

Well, you can say that Edward Dahlberg was a Man of Letters, not of the
World. That he was party to no institution that wields power. That he was
quite crazy at times, from a combination of drugs and bodily ills. And, that he
was always kind to me, even kind enough to suggest that I had plagiarized
Because I Was Flesh.

In the final five years he began to mimic Lear wild on the heath. The last
night, he was up at three in the morning singing television jingles. He found a
way of dying quite unlike his life: quietly, in his sleep. Pulmonary conges-
tion. It would be a sour irony for him if he knew he died in such a Prufrockian
manner: "Till human voices wake us, and we drown."

His wife, Julia Lawlor, awoke and discovered him extraordinarily still;
she felt his hands and they were cold, and then she felt his feet and they were
warm. She did not know if he was dead or in a coma. An electric blanket had
kept the feet warm.

The last time I had visited him on East Ninety-first Street we ate Merit
Farm chicken, drank beer, and he would alternately rage at me and laugh with
me. He had begun to have the fierce precariousness of the old that leaves the
will and spirit strong, but the body weak. Rage becomes more terrifying
because it is apparent that the flesh can no longer endure it.

He fled the city for Ireland and I packed for him his two thousand pounds
of books, which was the stone he rolled before him on his travels up and down
mountains. I had always wanted a picture of us together, so I borrowed a cheap
camera from a friend, and Julia took one of us together dockside. I have the picture; it is two black shapes, one higher than the other. You cannot see his arm
around my shoulder.

Quitting Ireland he returned to New York, stayed in the Chelsea, then
rented an apartment, much to the distress of a representative of the hotel who
wanted him to remain there (hoping, doubtless, for another American author to
die under its roof). He abandoned the new place a week later, returned to Ireland, fled back again to the States and then settled in Santa Barbara, California,
where he died. I last saw him amidst the not-yet fading baronic splendor of the
Yale Club, where a patron had provided him with quarters. There we shared

more laughter and rage, Dahlberg enjoying himself more than he would admit ensconced in the Yale Club's version of WASP heaven. Then came the phone call and the testy ending; Dahlberg did not like simple goodbyes, which is why I'm still shocked that he died in his sleep.

In the preface to the omnibus volume of novels that appeared in 1976, he wrote:

> I have committed sundry moldy solecisms; yet I was not born to desecrate literature. Wood that has aged for a thousand years or more becomes charcoal; I have grown old as a result of centuries of sorrows and am just a writer. In a pragmatical era of the polypus that solely reflects its surroundings, I wonder which is more useful nowadays, coal or a good *boke*.

This is bitter business; and I am angry that a friend has to sing his praises, because it catches in my throat—for any author deserves to have strangers hail him. For whatever Dear Readers there are now, or are to come, Edward Dahlberg wrote eighteen books and one masterpiece that will endure; at the end of his long life he had fewer than six people he would have called "friend."

THE WAGES OF EXPECTATION*

Charles DeFanti's perceptive and engrossing rendering of the life of Edward Dahlberg (1900-77) is subtitled *A Biography*; but I believe it will be *the* biography—because of both merit and the fact that no one else will likely attempt one. Indeed, the major disadvantage that this biography carries is that Dahlberg, alas, did not leave a large audience waiting for it.

DeFanti had the great asset of knowing Dahlberg during the last tempestuous years, and the mutual exposure was a rewarding one: he displays the affection one might have for an eccentric relative, while still retaining a sharp, critical eye. Dahlberg's career was long (and he is a chief refutation that there are no second acts in American writers' careers). His fifty years as an author spanned changing currents in our literature and saw his own evolution from a social realist to a belletrist, ending with the myth-realization of his last volumes. (Dahlberg published nineteen volumes of fiction, poetry, criticism, and autobiography.)

But if Dahlberg was a bridge, he was a narrow one, somewhat dilapidated, which few travelers took, most forsaking him for the new interstates— Hemingway, Fitzgerald, Eliot. Dahlberg was the scenic route. And it is ironic, but fitting, that the most accessible introduction to Dahlberg's writing is his biography.

It was the midstream shift in Dahlberg's own style that makes *Wages of Expectation* so valuable. Dahlberg wrote autobiographically in his first novel, *Bottom Dogs* (1929), about his vagabond youth, his mother, the first three colorful decades of twentieth-century America. And he reused this same material for his masterpiece, published in his sixties, *Because I Was Flesh* (1964). But of the second half of his life—the radicalism, bohemian literary life, friendships with other writers—Dahlberg was an ineffectual chronicler. We have it in a

---

* First appeared in the *Village Voice*, vol. 24, no. 15, April 16, 1979. A review of *The Wages of Expectation* by Charles DeFanti.

number of books—*The Flea of Sodom* (1950), *The Olive of Minerva* (1976)—but it is used as fable and exaggerated to the point of being incomprehensible. The second volume of "straight" autobiography, *The Confessions of Edward Dahlberg* (1971), mixes fact and fancy to the degree that vituperation far overshadows the vignettes—though some are hilarious—and historic vigilance is abandoned.

Dahlberg led his life seemingly enunciating one state above all, that of the writer as pariah, the glorious nay-sayer unsullied by commerce, fashion, and vain success. DeFanti's biography exposes how ambivalent Dahlberg was about the pursuit of fame and fortune. In fact, it was a paltry fame and a dubious fortune—though he managed after forty years of age never to hold a job (excepting the occasional teaching post, which always ended in recriminations) and survive, if not in destitution, always in genteel poverty. Nonetheless, in literary circles, especially with members of his own generation, he was certainly Banquo's ghost, accusatory, making any of his contemporaries uneasy about whatever security their lives in art had provided them. Dahlberg still raged outside the gates of acceptability, never an elder statesman, never invited to the White House (what a thought!), never what all old men hope to be, a dignitary.

Dahlberg's bile was in direct proportion to the neglect he felt, which, of course, was enormous. Even if you produce a masterwork—which *Because I Was Flesh* surely is—you can be ignored, because literature plays little role in the life of the commonwealth. Dahlberg was absent of lucidity no more than Delmore Schwartz, but Dahlberg was twenty-five years older when he died and could not be remembered as nostalgically for a blazing youth as Schwartz, even though Dahlberg was far more productive—except in friendship—and important. Dahlberg had many more years to alienate all his friends, become in old age a burden, a man who could provide embarrassment more easily than pleasure. He finally became of little use to anyone, and, oh, how he hated not to be useful; he was just as well aware of the pitiful irony as I was when I (the apprentice) arranged a publisher for him, rather than he (the master) arranging one for me.

DeFanti's *Wages of Expectation* (a Dahlbergian phrase, but of DeFanti's coinage) tells the stories Dahlberg was unable to tell, and I found myself laughing out loud every other page at the marvelous human comedy DeFanti captures. It sounds like low praise, but Dahlberg never lost his sense of humor, even though it could entirely disappear at times. Dahlberg's moods were medieval, more like humors, and one would take over from the other completely; they would seldom commingle. One moment we would be sharing laughter over some wonderful absurdity or human failing, and the next he would pierce me with a look of the deepest unmitigated despair.

He was a hard man, but, unlike many, he did apply his own severe standards occasionally to himself. And DeFanti has finally unlocked the stuff of Dahlberg's life from the oppressive rococo cage, fit only for solitude (though Dahlberg did manage to capture seven wives) that he fashioned for himself. Truly Dahlberg was payed the wages of his own expectations: rejection, isolation, and the curse of superfluity.

DeFanti's revelatory biography anchors the life and, because of that, is most valuable; otherwise Dahlberg and his lovely books would likely be cast permanently adrift.

THE CAUSES OF
IMMORTAL CONCEPTIONS*

I've had a long, personal history with Edward Dahlberg's books—literally and figuratively. They almost killed me once. He and his last wife, Julia Lawlor, had returned to New York City from Ireland, and I, at the time (1969) a graduate student at Columbia University, was enlisted to retrieve the 150 or so cartons from the dock where they sat locked away in a shipping container. Dahlberg rented the van, which I picked up, a more than slightly masticated vehicle, its skin thoroughly chewed by the traffic mishaps it had already endured.

Dahlberg and Lawlor and a professor friend of theirs cabbed to the docks. My memory places them on Manhattan's East River, but more likely it may have been the West Side. Whichever, there was a long expanse of open wharf, sky, space, and air spicy with the mulch of the not-too-distant sea. It was a literary day, a Melvillean morning, dark, dreary, sometime after November. Dahlberg immediately ran into some custom problems and began jousting unsuccessfully with the functionaries. He turned to me and said, "You have to be a millionaire to be immune in this society."

That day there were no immunities from the bureaucracy, harassments, and so forth, but finally we were cleared to remove the books. The metal container sat a football field's length from where the van was parked. I sped off to it and midway discovered that the van had lost its brakes. Luckily, as I swiftly passed by the forlorn metal container, stuffed with ancient wisdom, there was another football field of open wharf beyond it and I was able to coast to a stop—the parking brake was busted, and the van had an automatic transmission. It took a while to walk back to where Lawlor and Dahlberg and the professor were waiting, shielded from the inclement weather.

* First appeared in the *Review of Contemporary Fiction*, vol. 11, no. 1, Spring 1991.

Dahlberg could easily become irate, but he was also given, at times, to a bemused stoicism. We all cabbed back to the apartment on Seventy-fifth Street, and arrangements were made to have professional movers later in the week cart the books to the apartment. That had been part of the subject of the earlier disputations at dockside: the brotherhood of stevedores wasn't used to the economies Dahlberg was attempting to practice, by having friends unload shipping containers. Teamsters (or their comradely equivalents) eventually did the job, and I was glad for that—and happy I wasn't driving the van loaded with thousands of pounds of learning on the West Side Highway when the van's brakes failed. WOULD-BE WRITER, I imagined the headline, CRUSHED BY RARE VOLUMES. Or, in tabloid style, ENTOMBED BY TOMES.

Though I didn't unpack that shipment, I helped repack it when Dahlberg once again decamped from New York to Florida. And I helped pack it again (though most of it had never been unpacked) when in 1974 he left his Ninety-first Street apartment to return to Ireland. He subsequently left Ireland much sooner than he had predicted, alone, without his wife, without, thank God, books. He took a room at the Chelsea Hotel and I helped him find an apartment on the east side, but before he moved in, he returned to Ireland and he and Julia from there moved to his final destination, Santa Barbara.

There would be dividends resulting from all the book packing and unpacking, beyond spending the hours it took with Dahlberg. He would observe my progress, criticize my technique, and occasionally hand over a volume he thought I should have, or that—more often the case—he no longer wanted.

I have these, most read by him and marked with his marginalia. It's an odd collection, some ancients (a volume, copiously marked, of Plato), some immediately contemporary at the time (a galley, hilariously annotated—"intellectual babyism"—of Norman Podhoretz's autobiography *Making It*, which Dahlberg was supposed to review for the *Washington Post*). Amongst the miscellany is the cause of these reminiscences, Alexander Theroux's first novel, *Three Wogs*, sent to Dahlberg by its publisher's publicity director.

> Dear Mr. Dahlberg:
> Enclosed is *Three Wogs*, a first novel by Alexander Theroux. The artist's subject is racial prejudice and his style, zany caricature. Any comments you would care to make on the work would be appreciated.
> Thank you very much.

Dahlberg tossed it my way without comment, and, since the novel was published in 1972, it must have been during the packing for Ireland from the Ninety-first Street apartment. Theroux, I surmised, had requested his publisher send a copy to Dahlberg, for that is usually how such things are done: the author supplies a list of literary figures one hopes will be receptive and might be induced to offer blurbs. From my perusal of the novel it was obvious to me why Theroux would want Dahlberg to see it and why he would, vainly it appeared, hope for a comment, or as Theroux would want to put it and Dahlberg would, an encomium.

So, I became aware of Alexander Theroux and "followed," as it is often put, his "career," more so than his more "successful" younger brother Paul's. *Three Wogs* was published the year my first book, *The Harrisburg 7 and the New Catholic Left*, was, and his second novel, *Darconville's Cat*, appeared the year my second novel, *Idle Hands*, was published, 1981. (And his third novel came out in 1987, as did mine.)

Doubleday published *Darconville's Cat* with some enthusiasm, which I wasn't entirely happy to see, insofar as Delacorte published *Idle Hands* with almost none. I would wander into many a New York City bookstore (and elsewhere) and see high stacks of *Darconville's Cat* but nary a copy of *Idle Hands*, and though Theroux's novel might not have been quickly exiting the store, my novel had never made it into the establishment. Doubleday promoted *Darconville's Cat* as a literary *tour de force*, with an example of the author's own portraiture on its cover, while Delacorte put a photograph of a young woman in high heels on my novel's dust jacket, wearing nothing else, beyond her footwear, but a lavender bath towel.

By 1981 Edward Dahlberg was dead four years, and Theroux's novel, alas, managed to bury him a bit deeper, even though Dahlberg lives on in Theroux's novel, unacknowledged. That might not seem to be much of a problem,. except that the novel is full of catalogs, acknowledgments of authors alluded to and quoted, and nowhere is Dahlberg or his work mentioned. It appears to me as if the omission is not entirely innocent, especially because the last line of the novel is Dahlberg's language and not Theroux's.

Now, a lot of literary people deliberately ignore Dahlberg. American intellectuals' most potent weapon is their ability to overlook. Since Dahlberg's death I have picked up dozens of books wherein I expected to find Dahlberg either mentioned or discussed, and, upon consulting the index, I find him there not at all. Intellectual discourse in this country is something of a bad joke, since literary folk make absolute claims ("no one does this better," "the best example of," etc.) based on an individual's meager portion of reading, and worse yet, deliberate omissions of the exceptions to the critic's view of things.

Why Theroux leaves Dahlberg out of *Darconville's Cat*, while making use of his learning and language, may be easier to understand than I am granting. There are simple reasons: Dahlberg did not respond to *Three Wogs*, perhaps earning Theroux's enmity, if not lessening Dahlberg's influence. Though

I doubt that was the specific cause; it more likely has to do with literary Oedipalism, the nagging nature of influence. And I suppose "influence" is a subject I want to explore regarding Dahlberg, Theroux, and myself.

In the past, I have often chafed at the suggestion that I was a "disciple" of Dahlberg, that he was my "mentor," that I chose to "emulate" his style, that I wanted to write like him. Such things have been said about me and to me, by friend and foe alike—mainly foe. I, of course, had, or have, another version of Dahlberg's influence. He *influenced* me all right, but he didn't do a whole lot to my prose style, except insofar as he directed me to books, including his own, and writers I wouldn't have come upon myself. Every writer wants to appear in the world full-blown from his or her own forehead. What, I thought, sparked Dahlberg's interest in me was that I had a talent for aphorism, a talent that was there before he entered my life. Influence obviously requires some similarity to start with: streams flow into rivers, rivers into lakes, gulfs, oceans.

But those who scornfully ascribe emulation, which is actually a description of unsuccessful influence, are usually enemies of that which they see as the influence, the influence itself. In other words, most people who mention Dahlberg when criticizing me are actually criticizing Dahlberg. Language in America in the 1990s (and 1980s) is so starved that rich prose like Dahlberg's is tolerated, if at all, as a florid aberration.

In simpleminded ways this fact is encountered endlessly. Witless critics often praise what they redundantly title "deceptively simple" prose styles. Such styles are indeed simple and often deceptive, but seldom are they deceptively simple, which implies the deception to be the agile work of the writer, who then places upon the reader, however strong-hearted he or she might be, the hard work of fashioning out of the writer's simplicity complexity. Often I think this taste for the simple comes from the fact that most critics, if not all, do not like to praise prose they cannot write themselves. ("I could do that," is the troubling echo of thunder I hear rumbling behind the bolts of hyperbole launched at so many "deceptively simple" authors.) In the 1920s, Thomas Wolfe and F. Scott Fitzgerald debated the merits of the "leaving out" and the "putting in" schools, which is, more or less, the same dispute. Today's English critics put it a bit differently. For instance, John Bayley reviewing a compatriot's novel (in the May 17, 1990 *New York Review of Books*), has this to say: "In modernism and postmodernism the writing is everything; that comfortable, verbally unselfconscious world created by Victorian writers soaked in Scott has disappeared, replaced by the mechanisms of writers who have been equally soaked in Joyce." His concern is more the story/antistory world, though the plain and fancy language question is pertinent, if unexplored.

Certainly, in the States there appear to be two camps out there, the deceptively simple and the others (the former much more populous than the latter).

Given that circumstance, I should be more of a fan of Alexander Theroux, since he is so much a member of the minority, my camp, the sort of writer I esteem, but I am not *entirely* a fan: I will attempt to explain my Theroux problem, which is not unrelated to my Dahlberg problem and many other problems besides.

"All great writing is anonymous," someone (perhaps Dahlberg) quoted to me, and the proof of the quote is that whoever said it is anonymous to me (though perhaps not to others). Regardless, I know what the remark is pointing to: there is something about language, about intelligence, that does separate the maker from the words, certain thoughts detach themselves from personality, become personality themselves, and join the legion of pithy insights, universally related, all gratefully orphaned by their makers, all happily expressed in majestic English—even if majestically translated—and therefore become anonymous, folded into the culture, where they have so much harmonious company.

The truth of the remark can be further seen by altering it a bit: all great novels are not anonymous, all great poems are not anonymous, and so on. Great works are authored, deconstructionists notwithstanding. But thoughts? God, who can claim a thought, say no other has ever had it? Ideas? The structure of DNA? Is it a matter of getting there first? Intellectual imperialism? Thought-grabbing, stakes driven, territory claimed. Did James Dickey, when he toiled in advertising, really coin the Coca-Cola slogan, "It's the real thing"? There are answers somewhere.

Theroux might agree with me. He has Darconville aver, "The greatest lines in English poetry are always the simplest." Anyway, when it comes to these smaller linkages of language, sentences, thoughts, it is harder to defend absolutely the concept of "originality," since so much caprice and so much otherness floats in the stream of anyone's intelligence, and just what does sift down onto the page? The silt of many styles builds up in all of us. I suppose that's where the monkeys-at-the-typewriter business comes from, but such randomness is just that, random, without content and context; whereas anyone claiming to think already has content and context along with randomness.

Which brings me back to Theroux and whether his liftings from Dahlberg are homage, or something else. Especially the last line of *Darconville's Cat*. Now, I have not read everything there is to read, so can I claim that Dahlberg writing in *The Confessions of Edward Dahlberg* (1971), "God sat shrouded in the ocean, which is His tear-bottle, for sorrow is the cause of immortal conceptions," is not himself harvesting another's language? The sentence is introduced by "It is fabled that water was:". Fabled? Where? By whom? So, when Theroux ends *Darconville's Cat* with the sentence "Sorrow is the cause of immortal conceptions," is he "quoting" Dahlberg or alluding to him or to some fable both he and Dahlberg have coincidentally stumbled upon? Well, I think he's quoting Dahlberg, since Dahlberg's language turns up a number of other times in the novel.

After my first book *The Harrisburg 7 and the New Catholic Left* (1972) appeared, Dahlberg requested of Charles DeFanti, his biographer-to-be, that DeFanti scour the volume to see where I had plagiarized Dahlberg. I had used an attributed line of Dahlberg's (from *The Confessions*) as an epigraph to a chapter—"I may not understand good and evil, but I know what pains me and, I pray, others"—in order to link myself to him, but nothing was lifted from him. But my book's first line, "In the logic of our time, it is better to have a bad experience that turns out well, than to have just a plain good one," was close enough to something Dahlberg, in an off moment, might have written that he sent DeFanti scurrying through the volume (which Charlie ceased doing as soon as he left Dahlberg's apartment). Looking at the line now, I suspect it probably had more to do with Camus than Dahlberg, but who knows? Dahlberg prized good writing and was often surprised when he found it in anything a friend had written, so much so that he quite naturally wanted to ascribe it to his own pen.

So, why does Theroux use Dahlberg at his novel's end and bits and pieces from Dahlberg's other books throughout? This brings me to the some-what less autobiographical subject *Darconville's Cat* inspires. Dahlberg would often look at the two-volume *OED* he kept by his side and say, "A million words, O'Rourke, that's philosophy." *Logophilia* is not a lovely neologism, but writers who take physical pleasure from language are often treated in our cul-ture as if they are practicing a reprehensible perversion. As cranks, show-offs, self-lovers, indulgers, fops. It might be a plot of sorts: language is the only thing that is free in our society, free for the taking—if one has learned how to read and write. All those words just sitting there. But we all know it is not a matter of vocabulary.

There are many subliterate volumes telling the unwary how to improve one's vocabulary. Software thesauruses abound now; electronic dictionaries are beneath our fingerpads. Computers will select possible words for use: mul-tiple-choice prose awaits. You, of course, improve your vocabulary by reading, and, along the way, you improve a lot of other things, your mind principally. Inkhorn words, "erudition," this sort of conspicuous consumption has always been pooh-poohed by the contemporary nouveaux poor language gurus.

And to realize who are the most well-known protectors of public lan-guage! William Safire, a political hack, speechwriter and PR person; Edwin Newman, a rumpled former TV commentator; James Kilpatrick, a dyspeptic newspaper columnist (though they all spread their language salvation in newsprint everywhere). Talk about the fox in the henhouse. What has occurred is not entirely Orwellian—there is something that Orwell overlooked: not so much the dumbing down of language, but the ultimate triumph of post-literacy. Newspeak under Reagan became mis-speak. A former CIA employee who now does cultural criticism—mainly TV reviewing—for the *New York Times* once sent me back something I had offered the Sunday *Times* "Arts and Leisure" section, dismissing along the way my "somewhat fancy prose style," while rejecting the piece. I might be inclined to read more politics into the argument between plain and fancy language, except that it is the neocons of the last decade who attempt to strut (or goose-step) their heavy-footed language across the page, wearing polished polysyllables like jackboots. There are obviously only two kinds of writing, good or bad, and any style can be done crudely or with grace.

For a number of years, I used to hear, never seeing it in print, the cliché "deathless prose" as "deafless prose," and it kept me wondering. Deafless? Why deafless? Then I thought it was "depthless," since the phrase was always used in derision, not respect, and "depthless" at least made some sense. Finally, I got it straight: deathless. It doesn't die. Right. Good writing is not only anonymous, it is immortal. Well, Shakespeare isn't anonymous—except for the folk who claim the work is all written by someone, anyone, else. The play's the thing: How much of *Darconville's Cat* is in danger of death after nearly a decade?

I suppose the first thing that jumps out in the Bush nineties is the fact that were the action of the novel to take place today, Darconville would be slapped with a sexual harassment suit and tossed out on his ear from the two-bit women's college where he teaches. A professor sleeping with a freshman! Oh, the good old days, as depicted by Theroux.

When the novel was published in 1981, at least one reviewer, one I usually disagree with, Benjamin DeMott, commented on Darconville's self-love; DeMott termed it "self-idolizing." After ten years that overripe scent is still redolent, cheesy. What other author loves himself so much that he does a portrait of his idealized self and has it serve as the book jacket?

And this Isabel creature that consumes Darconville! I know it is difficult to make the beloved materialize on the page, but to make this human vacuity the cause of all Darconville's strife is to reveal her as no cause at all, a cause uncaused, indeed.

In Darconville, Theroux builds himself a Frankenstein's monster of autobiographical bits and pieces; he makes him a brotherless orphan (wishful thinking?), that most romantic of male American protagonists, the man alone, albeit one with rich relatives—would that Darconville, this faux Ishmael, had taken to sea, rather than to Quinsy College!

Dahlberg used language as a vehicle of transformation. Theroux uses it as a vehicle, the same sort of costly purchase of singularity, that apartness-from-the-crowd that makes Theroux have Darconville drive an old Bentley. Dahlberg was not consumed with self-love; self-loathing, perhaps. Language was not a Joseph's coat of many colors for him, not display, or dance. Theroux's principal rhetorical device is the list, and the novel is full of them. The list, the catalog, might be the earliest written form: cuneiform-etched clay tablets listing how many chickens, how many vats of oil, and so forth. And in *Darconville's Cat* Theroux hasn't taken the evolution of the novel form much beyond the list. Nonetheless, he provides us in chapter 68 a catalog of "The Misogynist's Library," which may or may not be comprehensive, depending on your tastes. I have not counted the volumes. It is here that one of Dahlberg's volumes could have been quietly shelved, but Dahlberg is absent from this list. (Perhaps Theroux considers his absence a compliment, the hollow praise of not being mentioned.) He does include his brother—"Paul Theroux's *Girls at Play*"—as he put in his own *Three Wogs* in the list of essay topics Darconville's freshmen submitted at Quinsy.

The casual anti-Semitism in the novel is a bit gamey, too, though that is primarily given over to Darconville's alter ego, Dr. Crucifer: "it's like trying to rub the smell of nickels off a Jew's hands"; "As coins to Hebrews!"; "Feed her out of a lead footpan into which several Hassidic Jews have just vomited!"; "Feed her the gets of cupped and goitrous Jewgirls!" Since most of these come in the endless list of imagined tortures to be inflicted upon the hapless nitwit Isabel, the mixture of misogyny and anti-Semitism does especially curdle, since there is no other similar ethnic insult running at such a rate through Crucifer's rant. And Theroux's positively fey rapture over High Church trappings (the fussily planned marriage at Westminster Cathedral indeed!) makes the anti-Semitic remarks, by contrast, even more questionable. Prewar American fiction by non-Jewish writers is littered with such remarks, but after World War II they are no longer strewn about quite so unselfconsciously.

It would be hard not to call Dahlberg a "misogynist," but one must consider Dahlberg's mother, the lady barber and quack, immortalized in *Because I Was Flesh*. In Theroux's case, I don't know what or whom must be considered. There are all kinds of misogyny. Theroux's is a curious sort. In *Darconville's Cat* there is no female Darconville's intellectual equal—though that is not an uncommon failing in American male writers. The object of his obsession is, as depicted, a dunce. Theroux, at least, doesn't suffer from the reigning type of misogyny, the sort that gives no thought to women at all.

But what is Theroux and what is Darconville? I, doubtless, am of the I-am-Madame-Bovary school. All authors, I hold, are complicitous with their characters. You can create thoroughly evil characters, I suppose, or merely unpleasant ones; but when you do, you are also admitting some commonly shared human traits. Writing against one's self is an unsolvable problem. Back when Dahlberg was still alive, the novelist Craig Nova and I used to joke about this, about writing novels full of lovingly detailed violence, or some outrageousness, creating characters jam-packed with hateful (and taboo) traits. But, in order not to be charged with loving too much what we create, we would subtitle every work "A Vicious Attack," thereby showing our authorial remove. Theroux might not be misogynistic, and even less likely anti-Semitic, but *Darconville's Cat* has more than its fair share—and to what point?

What is good about *Darconville's Cat*? Well, quite a few things. Any novel that makes you laugh out loud a dozen times warrants its sacrificial trees. There might be a great thin novel fighting to get out of the fat one—though I presume Theroux presumed he could blunt criticism by giantism, not an unthoughtful position. Something grotesque usually stands to the side of normal analysis.

The college-life scenes at the dreadful women's college in the South are smartly done. In fact, that which seems most autobiographical has some bite. It is his inventions that I balk at: Dr. Crucifer (though his manservant is amusing), Darconville alone, and, saints forbid, *thinking*, the final, drawn-out death in Venice, to not coin a phrase. I believe Theroux does have a personal voice that frees itself from the guy wires, the ropy tethers of allusions and quotations, and lifts off majestically. Here are some examples (I need to pick the sentence up midstream): "the exact but brief animadversion in flawless Latin, dated 1584, in defense of the assassination of that goofball in the orange helmet, mouthy William the Silent of Dutchland." He does that at least a half-dozen times, the mixture of high and low culture being the most dominant strain of postmodern male literary fiction (Pynchon to Boyle, even Updike can do it). "That goofball" lets us know we are in the late twentieth century, not a bad thing to be reminded of when we read *Darconville's Cat*. "Not surprisingly, it was in just such small sheriffwicks and timber- and box-producing outbacks as Fawx's Mt.—the land of the piney-wood folk—that they set up their hate factories and bigotoriums"—"bigotoriums," that has sting, the tart mix of old and new.

The various descriptions of faculty parties and so on are funny, on target: the "predictable cast of poltroons, gum-beating fibsters, and others whose brains were kept in jars above the moon; to wit: the Funster with the double-jointed thumb which also serves—to everybody's dismay—as a finger-puppet; the Trendy Wife (always from California) wearing hoop earrings and a bandanna who's found the most *fantastic* recipe for sharksfin soup . . ." Not just because it is a world Theroux obviously knows, but because it is a world; the other landscape in the novel is his mind, still terra incognita, even, and especially, to him—at least during the composition of *Darconville's Cat*.

Throughout the novel there are lines of the sort Dahlberg would be attracted to and often use himself. His most common marginalia in the books he read would be the word *..se* and use such lines he did. Theroux: "Vinegar is the corpse of wine." Note that such a remark is about something, which lets it travel intact across time. Another: "Laurel was the first plant that grew after the Flood." There are a dozen or so more: "It was the kind of female voice that Juvenal somewhere naughtily describes as having fingers." These are liftings from learning, and Dahlberg would do it all the time, but this is the sort of prospecting any good writer does, finding precious nuggets after much sifting and reading. Writers drop them into their own books so the reader profits. Theroux has an eye for them, and when they turn up here and there they are satisfying, no matter what their parentage (and Dahlberg's books provide him with a few).

But, here is a longer selection of what I consider to be Theroux's best, truest, voice:

> These were the "hearties" of Fawx's Mt., not a great deal different, truth to tell, from the other wonderful sapsuckers down South that might be classified under *ordo squamata*: yomp heads, mountain boomers, rackensacks, hoopies, haw-eaters, snags, pot-wallopers, buckras, goober goopers, scataways, pee-willies, wool hats, pukes, raggeds, boondockers, dug downs, tackies, crackers, and no-lobes. It's a kind of club—300-pound dipshits, always named something like "Hawg," Kincaid, or Harley—who drink flask bourbon, have chigger-bites on their arms, and wear their hair either short or slicked back (the comb tracks are always visible) to reveal faces like those reversible *trompe-l'oeil* funheads you snip from the Sunday paper to fool someone with. They have no chins, are inclined to be goitral, and are always chewing down a blade of grass fiercely and absentmindedly. They are given to wearing suntans, white socks, work boots, and cheap acetate shirts, the sleeves of which are always rolled up to a point higher than the triceps brachii in tight little knots. They like whiskey with a good bead, respect Shriners, whistle a lot, drive with one hand, slide crotch-first onto barstools, and—just "funnin'"— love to hang around butt-slapping and goosing each other, punctuating certain remarks of course with that significant nudge just before they're going to fart.

The echoes of a lot of American male fictioneers of the late twentieth century can be heard here, but Theroux's portion of erudition and colloquial rhythms is different enough to make it his own voice. But, alas, only about a quarter of the novel has this voice energizing it. And this raises a not entirely uncommon quandary: if a quarter of the novel's writing is far superior to, and so much more enjoyable than, the entirety of dozens of overpraised, underwritten novels published each year, why not unreservedly applaud it, however "flawed"? Well, that's something we all need to chew on.

I wasn't happy that Dahlberg was left out of *Darconville's Cat*—which is some sort of backhanded compliment to Theroux's novel. And, finally, any discussion of Theroux, Dahlberg, and *Darconville's Cat* should acknowledge the fact that Dahlberg hated cats.

II

THE LITERARY LIFE AND HARD TIMES

THE LITERATURE OF PLACE
AND NO PLACE*

The town where I live, South Bend, Indiana, has an identity problem. Several, in fact. Some are geographic. The Chamber of Commerce uses a hyphenated label, South Bend-Mishawaka, as a name, as well as the term *Michiana*. Mishawaka is the town adjacent to South Bend, to the east. It has a number of distinctions, including a building boom of malls and car dealerships along Grape Road. (This Grape has many vines now, all of them bulging with ripe American shopping varietals.) "Michiana" is derived from the blending of state borders. Michigan is a stone's throw from South Bend.

The Michigan/Indiana conflicts—taxes, time zones, lotteries, and liquor sales—are other versions of South Bend's own town/gown split, between Notre Dame (itself a "town") and South Bend. During the 1988 NCAA basketball tournament, banners emblazoned "South Bend, Indiana" were replaced for a televised game with ones reading "Notre Dame, Indiana 46556," a sorry display of zip code jingoism.

Other sorts of identity problems are, perhaps, more serious. Some are economic. "Dying Rust Belt town" is a label that is used. Heavy manufacturing has been departing for quite a while. South Bend's population growth has stalled. The city's government has tried to attract new businesses to replace those that have left. Once famous for building Studebakers, South Bend is now a regional center of service industries: hospitals, banks, shopping.

The South Shore railroad still rolls from Chicago to South Bend. And, since South Bend is ninety miles by car from Chicago, it is under the gravitational sway of that large metropolis; it bends the orbits of South Bend residents in many varied ways. Those who live at the edges (of continents, of states) often find their communities hosting alien influences.

---

* First appeared in *Where We Live*, Indiana University Press, 1989.

An economist I know is of the opinion that the Midwest produces and the two coasts consume. This may well be the case, and it certainly is true when it comes to the production of middle America's writers and artists.

I consider myself a child of the Midwest. So much so, I declared it on the first page of my first novel, *The Meekness of Isaac*: "As a child of the Middle West there was nothing to do but leave it, for it is the center of the country and any direction in which you may go is away." Away I indeed went, repeating the same journey many American writers made throughout the twentieth century, from the center to the edge. What is different now, toward the end of the century, is that so many are returning, for reasons both profound and simple, reasons that I will attempt to sketch.

Being a "serious" writer in the late twentieth century means one of three things. You come from wealth or have married it, you struggle, or you teach. The modifier "serious" is a tricky one. It is now generally used to be the antonym of "commercial." Commercial implies that you make money by writing. Serious implies no such thing; if anything it implies just the opposite.

In 1981 Herbert Mitgang reported in the *New York Times* the results of a survey that showed that the average income (from writing) of half of American writers was less than $5,000 a year. Just what constitutes a writer was defined as "a contemporary American writer who had had at least one book published." This income figure is disputable, but if the survey had been limited to contemporary American novelists, the amount would not be doubted—though, perhaps, as a median figure, rather than an average. Stephen King and a few others would skew the numbers. Regardless, very few novels earn what they cost to write, if they are "serious." Most are bankrolled by trust funds, wealthy acquaintances, or the nonwriting toil of the writer. Universities are subsidizing a great many commercial publishers, since the writers who publish with them could not afford to write without the employment of teaching. This is both good and bad.

In my midwestern youth, the cliché—a paraphrase of G. B. Shaw—I grew up with (I was born in 1945) was, "If you can't do, teach." It is my contention that my generation of writers can do—and does—both. When I graduated from the University of Missouri-Kansas City in 1968 and took myself to New York for graduate school at Columbia University I had no idea that I was participating in one of the literary movements of my generation: the growth of graduate writing programs throughout the land. (Columbia's had just started.) This, too, was both good and bad.

In 1968 my generation had the experience of preceding generations to shape it—and whatever mythmaking about writers' lives that had been passed down over the years. One myth that was still potent was the writer as primitive, the self-educated man of experience. Doubtless the Beat Generation of the

1950s had something to do with this, except that many of the Beat Generation's primary figures had come from and had orbited around the same Columbia University I was attending in 1968. But the notion was hard to shake: writers somehow were educated by life, not in classrooms (either/or always, rather than the actual *both*). Even Thomas Wolfe—who had seemed to my younger self a representative primitive as I thought of them—had gone to graduate classes at Harvard (in playwriting!). Hemingway, one of the few twentieth century American writers of prominence without some college experience, was a doctor's son and most certainly could have gone to college.

The mushrooming of graduate writing programs during the seventies was something new. Though the Midwest has been associated with—and even responsible for—schools of writing (more literally than figuratively, because of the history of the Iowa Writing Workshop), until the end of the sixties there had been mainly migration. Young writers (to-be) would come from the coasts to the Midwest for instruction and the midwesterners would head for the coasts. In both cases, the *strangeness* was salubrious. Since the beginning of the seventies, writing programs have prospered everywhere (almost everywhere). The journey of the American writer is no longer just along the simple East-West axis but is determined by a more complicated vortex of destinations and departures.

There are a number of large cultural forces at work, as well as the more individual tensions of particular personalities at play, that fashion the current situation. America is moving, like it or not, into a postliterate age. The aural/visual culture is now more dominant than the print culture. We are presented with the paradox of a golden age—in terms of numbers—of writers, but it is no golden age of readers. At least fifty thousand "books" are published each year, but the ratio of readers to population—readers of certain sorts of literature—has become smaller. (The number of first novels published in 1958 was roughly that of the number published in 1978, according to *Library Journal*, a little more than a hundred. It is now a little more than three hundred.) Reading is a finite thing. It takes time to read, and all that competes for people's time and attention is remarkable.

The current dispute over certain changes in course reading lists at universities (like the case of Stanford's Western Civ: what constitutes a great book, etc.) is symptomatic of many things, but one uncontestable thing it points to is the fact that very few people read the same books. Many people see the same TV shows and movies. If there are now more books being published, the likelihood decreases that people will read the same ones. Excess can produce a babble even more efficiently than general ignorance. As the number of magazines and books increases, the one outlet of reading that declines is the number of newspapers available in any city. This situation benefits the status quo in a number of depressing ways: the overeducated are never speaking the same language to each other and the undereducated stand less of a chance of becoming well informed.

Writers may wonder where they are coming from, the effect of place on their work, but they also are concerned with where they are going, what sort of place their work might have in the culture.

The postliterate age is having definite effects on the subject of place. In the past, regional writers, in Tom McGuane's remark, were writers who collected "funny phrases." A regional writer these days can acquire uniqueness through his or her parochialism. If s/he only knows or chronicles one place, s/he is protected, safe down deep in the regional cellar from the cyclone of American homogenization. The paradox of our culture is the acquiring of sameness (the *malling* of the collective psyche) contending with the impulse toward eccentricity (territorial signs marking more limited kinships). Geography still holds dominion over some of this; individuals, chameleonlike, often want to blend into the landscape, regardless of the idiosyncrasies of region.

But the general situation in 1988 of the writer in these United States makes the "Indiana" writer a different sort of creature than s/he might have been in the not-too-distant past. In the reference volume *Indiana Authors and Their Books, 1967-1980*, the compiler, Donald E. Thompson, makes a number of salient points. The first concerns what is needed to qualify as an Indiana author: one must have been "born in Indiana or have lived in the state for at least twenty to twenty-five years." Given that criterion, I do not qualify, and will not, it seems, for at least another twelve years.

The accident of birth conveys inalienable rights, but the accruement of citizenship requires time served. No doubt this is to eliminate an infestation of intellectual carpetbagging (L. L. Bean-bagging?) by gypsy writers caravaning across the country. But what is interesting about such rules of entitlement (and they are common) is that they are completely antithetical in reasoning. They announce a kind of understanding of the power of chance and the power of hard work. You can be either lucky or steadfast. So a writer who is born in Indiana, but spends most—if not all—of his life elsewhere, is an Indiana author, whereas one who writes a number of books in Indiana over a span of, say, nineteen years is not. What such an irrational rule points to is a fact: we ascribe such a title not to a person so much as to an idea—our presumptions of what that idea is. So, if a future author is born in Indiana, Indiana-ness is in that writer's blood, or forebears (or transfused by the trauma of birth, if the parents happened to be driving through). It is a genuflection to the magical properties of being born. The other takes more sweat and tears, two decades for the necessarily humdrum, quotidian osmosis to occur.

Of course, there are other ways to classify writers. Again, the idea of *place* in literature is an old one; not a few volumes have been devoted to it.

What would Joyce be without Dublin? But there are plenty of unnameable Irish writers who have written about Dublin. What is wished for by proponents of place is that a writer of genius (or great talent) occupy and write about one. (And, by doing so, celebrate and honor the place—or, at least, bring it retroactive glory or notoriety.) When one wonders what northern Michigan (or Oak Park, Illinois) did to Hemingway, one is asking essentially psychological questions, as if one is raised by trees, by nature, by cement and brick. One is, in a manner of speaking—or writing.

Writers are often contradictory personalities. Opposing attributes are required for certain sorts of composition: you must be curious and adventurous, but also have the capacity to remain in one place and do solitary work. And many writers have found it impossible to write about the place they are presently in; perhaps this differs with genre. The poet John Matthias has described (in "Poetry of Place," in the *Southern Review*) why he hasn't written about the St. Joseph River, so close to hand, though he has written of three rivers in England: "I think the reason is that while the St. Joseph is rich with associations that might stimulate another poet . . . for me it is associated entirely with the kind of daily grind that prevents poetry from being written . . . It is the river I cross in my car to go to work." John Matthias would qualify as an Indiana poet, since he has lived in the state twenty years. (Though his depiction could describe a literature of anti-place, a not-uncommon genre for midwestern writers, most often practiced by novelists: one thinks of Sinclair Lewis, Sherwood Anderson, and Indiana's own Theodore Dreiser.) Ernest Sandeen, another true Indiana poet (over forty years in South Bend), finds it otherwise. His poetry is suffused with the sustenance of place: "It smelled of old secrets unearthed" (from "Gardening Through the Ages"). What Robert Frost was to New England, Sandeen is to our Midwest. Sonia Gernes, the poet and novelist, in residence for more than twelve years, has learned, she writes in her poem "Back Home in Indiana," the "passions of the landlocked heart." But Anthony Kerrigan, the poet and award-winning translator, likes to call this corner of Indiana where he has resided for nearly ten years "Siberia, U.S.A."

I have my own experience (as well as accounts of others), but with regard to fiction writers of a certain sort, leaving presents you with immediate perspective, the distance required to see clearly. One definition that can be employed to separate nonfiction and fiction is this: nonfiction is written from fact, fiction is written from memory. When one writes fiction, one is remembering, and the event takes place in one's head, not out one's window (though it may have taken place out the window some time before).

When I lived in New York City, I found it difficult to write fiction there. There were many reasons for that, doubtless. One was the contrast of the city itself, the great metropolis, its hulking heroic materialism, to my own work. I would leave my small apartment on Charles Street and see the twin towers of the World Trade Center looming. It was difficult not to let the fragile paragraphs of the day be crushed by such sights. New York City is more a place of performance than creation.

I wrote a great deal about New York City in my second novel, *Idle Hands*, but I wrote about it in South Hadley, Massachusetts. I did not begin the writing of my third novel, *Criminal Tendencies*, till I began teaching in Indiana at the University of Notre Dame. *Criminal Tendencies* is set in Key West, Florida. New York City is engraved in my memory; Key West, a place I visited on and off for a decade, is also similarly etched. (Though I cannot be a New York author, or a Florida author, either, since I have not lived in either place twenty years. I haven't lived anywhere twenty years yet, not an uncommon circumstance for writers of my generation. I was born in Chicago, but moved from there when I was four. Am I an Illinois writer?)

But I have found that where you write is as important as what you write about, because the great difficulty is the writing itself. *Does* the place permit you to write? That is, to me, more the *literature of place* than the usual conferred meaning of the term: not the place you write about, but the place that lets you write. New York City did many things for me, gave me ten years of full life and higher education, but I was able to write only short pieces there. The life was too difficult, too hectic. New York City breeds wonderful nonfiction, journalism; the novels, books of memory, not fact, tend to be written outside of it. (Thomas Wolfe, you remember, wrote in Brooklyn, looking homeward to North Carolina using the jagged skyline of New York City as a sharp spur to memory.)

Donald E. Thompson in *Indiana Authors* discusses remarks by R. E. Banta found in the first (1916) volume of the series, "one central theme is that Indiana has produced a proportionately larger number of writers than any other state in the union . . ." Indeed, the three reference volumes include 6,819 authors, quite a harvest. A current reference volume, *A Directory of American Poets and Fiction Writers 1987-1988* (with its own not too dissimilar criteria for inclusion—it leaves out the aspiring and the lightly published), includes the names and addresses of sixty contemporary poets and fiction writers living in Indiana. (Doubtless, an equal number could have been missed.)

The states with the highest numbers of poets and fiction writers might be guessable: New York State has more than nine hundred listed, though New York City alone accounts for more than half of that number. California is second with more than three hundred, followed by Massachusetts with somewhat less than two hundred. Though not necessarily an accurate count, the *Directory* provides what I take to be correct proportions, state by state. Of Indiana's neighbors, Ohio and Illinois have some twenty-five more listed than our state's sixty, Michigan a bit more, Kentucky far less. The proportion of writers one finds has something to do with the number of writing positions at institutions of higher learning in each state. Those with more will have more writers, for the reasons I've mentioned earlier, particularly the burgeoning of writing programs throughout the land during the past two decades, which allows states to keep the writers they have and lure others. Big cities play a role: writers will be found in Boston, San Francisco, Chicago, as well as in states with geographic attractions, coastlines, mountain ranges, charged landscapes and associations (New Mexico has more writers listed than Kansas).

Well, things have changed since 1816-1916, the period Banta was considering. We have moved into a postliterate era and the reasons why writers come and go, or go and come, have altered. But the Midwest tends to honor production, and it is not always clear to the population what writers produce. One reason Indiana has literary roots, Thompson points out, is Richard Cordell's observation about "the proximity of Cincinnati and Lexington as early periodical publishing centers and the later establishment of the Bobbs-Merrill Company in Indianapolis."

New York City tends to hold writers in somewhat higher regard because it is clear that even poets and fiction writers make money for the city's inhabitants. It is the publishing center of the country; all those concerned know what writers do. But elsewhere, where the industry is not so large (or nonexistent, especially for poetry and fiction), writers do not seem to be producers, or are not seen to be adding anything to the region, either good or bad. In South Bend, I am a professor at Notre Dame; everyone understands that. If I say I am a writer I am presented only with quizzical expressions and calls for explanation.

But, yet, a number of midwestern states have taken the time to honor their writers of late, though they are writers with enduring reputations and some decades dead. I was the first James Thurber writer at the Thurber House in Columbus, Ohio, in 1984, and a couple of years later was invited to speak at a Literary Heritage conference in Springfield, Illinois, where a reception was held at the poet Vachel Lindsey's house, which is open for public inspection. In Missouri there is Mark Twain's home in Hannibal, which I saw as a youth and which gave me the impression that writers could be held in esteem.

My connection to Indiana, whether or not I become an "Indiana" author (by virtue of residing here two decades), is already intricate. Though my most recent novel, *Criminal Tendencies*, is set in Key West, there are moments that owe their origin to the back roads around South Bend and Elkhart, Indiana, to the atmosphere engendered by the sight of satellite dishes squatting next to trailer homes on shaved plots of domesticated land surrounded by fields of corn and soybeans, to the loneliness of tree rows left standing as boundaries and windbreaks. The characters in *Criminal Tendencies* are transients, and I thought of one or two coming from this area, with these memories in their heads. A vividly painted van that a character drives in the novel is the vehicle of a man who lives on a county road I often traveled on my way into Elkhart.

There are other sights I will always identify as Indianaian, since I saw them, or noticed them, or associated them first with Indiana, like the ubiquitous, portable yellow sign or billboard, its top edge often arrow shaped, usually surrounded with an edging of illumination.

Highway 80, the "Main Street of America" as it boasts itself to be, I travel quite frequently; it is indeed a symbolic artery. The town of Gary, its various mills, is redolent with symbolism, too, as well as its own history of odors. I spent a day going through the Bethlehem Steel mill at Burns Harbor, Indiana, an experience, I trust, that won't be spared chronicling by me in fiction. Everyday the bounty of place stands revealed, often in unexpected ways, announcing improbable portents: pickup trucks with oversized tires, which I take to be testicular, swollen images of exaggerated masculinity. But these things are incremental, for a place does seep into you, as well as settle over you. Questions revolving around the literature of place often come down to this: Does the place claim you? Do you claim the place?

When I think of where I live, this topmost part of Indiana, its northernmost reach, I picture the whole state as a full water glass, a tumbler, which its shape does somewhat resemble. Into that glass someone has poured a powdery substance and has stirred it up. It has begun to settle: that is my image of where I live. Whatever I think Indiana is, whatever mysterious substances, unknowable essences, make up its mix, the thickest part of it gathers at the bottom of the state, the middle is cloudy, but not as dense, and at the top, where I live, it is almost clear, though not quite.

THE NIGHT THE GHOST
DIDN'T GET IN*

T he ringing phone finally awakened me. Bringing it to my ear I heard a
female voice say: "We have received a signal of unauthorized entry and
have called the police."

"What?" I said. The voice may or may not have repeated itself.

I put the phone down and tried to come to my senses. The ringing that
had roused me had ceased, but I began to hear another sound filling the darkness of the attic apartment: RAA-raa-Ra-AA-Raa-rA-rAA.

All was pitch black, except for a shaft of gray light coming in through the
attic's dormer window. It was not moonlight, but the spill from a high-intensity
streetlamp illuminating a used-car lot located at the end of the avenue that the
Thurber House was on.

I was spending my last night in the Thurber House, but it was officially
my first night. Though I was the inaugural writer-in-residence in the former
Columbus, Ohio, home of James Thurber's family and had been ensconced
for over two months, my last night happened to fall on the evening of the
Thurber House's official opening day, a Sunday concluding a weekend of cel-
ebrative events honoring one of Columbus's favorite sons.

The Thurber House was being restored to the condition it had been in
from 1914 to 1918, when the Thurber family had lived there while young
James attended Ohio State University, a half-hour streetcar ride away from
the Jefferson Avenue home.

The restoration work on the large old house was far from finished when
I arrived in the late fall of 1984. Happily, the attic was not being faithfully
restored but had been completely redone before I moved in. A modern apartment was the result; in some ways, too modern.

---

* First appeared in *Poets & Writers Magazine*, vol. 16, issue 1, Jan.-Feb. 1988.

On my first night, after unpacking, I reread the stories directly connected to the house, those in *My Life and Hard Times*: a good bit of the action of "The Night the Bed Fell" and "The Night the Ghost Got In" takes place in the very attic I was freshly occupying. The attic had been the sleeping quarters of Thurber's grandfather, the harassed and often indignant white-haired old man whose robust delusions, as Thurber depicted in those famous tales, lead to late-night encounters with squads of blustering Columbus constables.

I may have read the stories my first night in the attic, but on my last night they were being replayed: Ra-raa-AA-rA.

Approaching a half-awakened state, I clearly recognized the alarm siren; it sounded like World War III was a few minutes from commencement.

Bounding—as Thurber would have it—out of bed, wearing only the nightshirt I had been given to keep me warm on cold Columbus December nights, I started for the back stairs to descend the two flights to the kitchen, where the alarm system's control panel was located. I knew the sequence of numbers that, once punched into the alarm's memory, would silence the siren. The Thurber House's security system was state of the art, though it had been set off a number of times (but never in the middle of the night): by smoke generated by dull power blades used by carpenters; and by what seemed mere electrical whim. (The light fixtures leaking electricity, doubtless, as depicted by Thurber in his drawings for *My Life and Hard Times*.)

Only for a moment did I consider there might really be burglars in the house. There wasn't a great deal to steal as yet. The building next to the Thurber House was a dormitory for an art school and the students living there were raucous enough, or so I thought, to be a deterrent to mere burglars. The students carried on day and night during my two months, behaving like the late adolescents they were, suffering mildly psychotic episodes occasioned by alcohol and other intoxicants, which usually culminated, by the wee hours, in the throwing of glass beer bottles against the large brick wall of the Thurber House which faced them, blank and tempting as a squash court's.

In addition to the percussive *thromp* of the bursting bottles, I heard, at times, the thwap thwap thwap of a Columbus police helicopter, its searchlight falling on the house, sweeping in concentric circles above it. The helicopter was not threatening the students or attempting to curtail the throwing of beer bottles but making sure that no one was molesting the vehicles in the acre of used-car lot nearby.

I would pull the covers up to my chin, thinking of Thurber and all the ways life and hard times had changed. When he lived on Jefferson Avenue, it sported gas street lamps and horse-drawn carriages; but, by the time of my domiciling there, the carriage house in the rear only housed the offices of the not-for-profit agency that was overseeing the house's restoration.

But on this last night, the student dormitory was strangely silent. When I reached the bottom of the stairs (after turning on the second floor hall lights), the dining room I entered remained murky. I regretted not putting on my pants. A nightshirt, worn anywhere but in bed, is a ridiculous garment.

As I crossed the room, heading for the kitchen, the siren's wail suddenly quit. I stopped and then saw—and was simultaneously seen by—a figure lurking outside a window.

"There's one in the middle room," I heard the figure say urgently into its hand. Then a flashlight beam jumped through the window and its pillar of light careened around the room. When the white column fell on me I jumped back, realizing I had done the wrong thing. Since I had heard the voice, the voice should be able to hear me. I yelled: "Wait just a minute! I live here."

I raised my hands, pointing to the ceiling, to the attic above, where I, only a few minutes before, had been peacefully sleeping, and I realized I had made yet another mistake. I had lifted my hands in the attitude of surrender.

"I'll open the back door," I said, and gestured to the rear of the house, glad that the gray figure outside had only two hands: one for a walkie-talkie, the other for a flashlight. If human beings had three hands, I might have been shot.

Entering the kitchen, I flipped on the overhead fluorescent fixtures and light filled the room, empty of appliances except for the elaborate control board of the alarm. No need now to punch the secret numbers, since the siren had already ceased its apocalyptic screech. The kitchen's windows returned to opacity when I turned on the lights. I could no longer see outside, but I knew I could be easily seen.

I opened the door and in rushed three uniformed officers, three of Columbus's finest. I was taken aback, though, when I saw that all three were wearing what appeared to be brand-new uniforms, winter parkas covered with insignia, right out of a box, or costume shop. The three were some modern triptych advertising the fruits of affirmative action: two young white women and one black man. As Thurber's ethnic cops who invaded this house in the early part of this century were indicative of Columbus and the rest of the country then, so this trio was especially representative of our time.

The young man and one woman ran right past me, hardly giving me a glance. The other young female officer had, I now noticed, a flashlight in one hand and a walkie-talkie in the other. She confronted me; or, rather, I started talking.

"I live here. On the third floor," I said, elevating the garret apartment to an actual third floor, "and I was just awakened by a phone call from the security agency saying they had called you. Then I heard the alarm."

She stared at me—not exactly speechless, but skeptical. She looked to be in her late twenties, had short, curly red hair, pale skin, lightly freckled, and bore an unsettling resemblance to a nun who taught me when I was in fifth grade at St. Francis Xavier grammar school. But what did I appear to her? White male, short, in his late thirties, wearing bedclothes.

"Do you have any identification?" she asked.

I just looked down at my bare feet, raised my hands in a gesture of resignation, and said: "Not on me."

I then began to explain the intricacies—and defects—of the alarm system; how it went off when it chose to, how the Thurber House had just this day opened, and so forth. She walked into the dining room and pointed at its side door. It was, I could see through the gloom, ajar.

"There weren't any signs of forced entry outside, or any footprints," she said.

No footprints? I wondered. A hundred people had been milling around the house throughout the afternoon.

"Why isn't this door locked?" she asked, reproachfully.

Before the day's ceremonies had concluded, I had gone off to celebrate privately my imminent departure and had returned around midnight. I had let myself in, turned off the alarm within the thirty seconds or so one is allotted after entering, and, then, after securing the back door had turned the alarm back on.

Why was the dining room door slightly ajar? Burglars? Ghosts? Was this the night they both got in? The students? I turned to look towards the student housing, ready to point blame, but saw only, out of the various windows my gaze had gone by, two patrol cars parked obliquely, in the characteristic style of haste.

I shrugged.

"And this," the young officer said, her hand resting on a window that had resisted restoration to perfect plumb, "this needs to be completely shut." But it had not influenced the alarm. The ajar door had been the cause, I now had to presume. In the front room there was a device that reacted to disturbances in the air, that could detect ghosts if they happened just to leak through the walls.

The loud clomping of the other two officers' footsteps overhead had diminished. I followed the redheaded policeperson up the front stairway while she pointed out more misaligned windows and locks. Had someone actually pushed open the side door and been scared away by the ensuing ferocity of the noise?

The officer went into what had been Thurber's parents' bedroom, and I went ahead to the attic to get my wallet. I still thought my nightshirt should readily be seen as a proprietary outfit, but who knew what clever crooks this trio had encountered before?

I opened the attic stairway's door (it itself had a number of locks, which I had earlier unlatched) and stepped into the dark.

"Whew! You scared me," the other female officer said, emerging back into the darkness of the stairwell. She had just jumped out after stepping in.

"It's only me," I said. The officer continued down the stairs, and, as I reached the top, I heard the male officer's voice from within the apartment: "Wow! You should see this place. This is some bachelor pad. This ain't bad."

I was sure the donators to the Thurber House, especially the interior decorator and the stores that had furnished the apartment, would have been happy to hear his endorsement of their efforts.

Both women officers had come up the stairs after me. I turned on all the apartment's lights, and they began to look about. I did not get my wallet to show any identification. I was more or less forgotten, now that they had assured themselves that someone did live at the top of the old empty house. Police everywhere in the attic apartment. Grandpa Thurber couldn't have encountered more.

Finally, as if a late-night party had just broken up and they were the last three straggling guests, the officers gathered at the apartment's doorway, and I bid them good evening. Only when they were halfway down the steps did I realize I would have to follow them all the way to the first floor and lock the kitchen door behind them.

"How long did you say you're going to be here?" the male officer asked, interrupting his descent.

"I'm leaving in the morning," I said, and immediately regretted it, since the coincidence sounded suspicious even to me: *I'm out the door right after you leave, sucker.*

"You see," I went on, thinking further explanation was required, in order to allay suspicion, "I'm the first James Thurber writer-in-residence and my stay is over, as of today. I've been here over two months."

"You're a writer?" the officer asked. It was a rhetorical question. He wasn't looking for any elaboration. "Yes. I am."

"Thurber?" I heard a female voice say. I wasn't sure which of the two women officers' voices it was, coming from one of the second-floor rooms, "Thurber? Wasn't he some kind of writer?"

"Yes," I said loudly, "Yes, he was."

The three officers wandered through the rooms just as the afternoon's crowd had, looking at the memorabilia, inspecting the construction, admiring the new chandeliers, the pictures of Columbus and some of its citizens, circa 1914. They weren't ransacking the place like the Irish constables did in Thurber's stories, but police were everywhere. I waited till they were done, wondering what their usual forays into dark houses at four A.M. brought them. Something other than this, I supposed.

"Bye, now," I said as they departed. I thought they would file some sort of report, though they didn't tell me of their plans. I still couldn't get over the look of their new uniforms, which made them look like characters out of an operetta.

I glanced at the alarm's control panel. The last thing in the world I intended to do was turn the alarm system back on. I shut off the lights and went back upstairs, locking the apartment's door behind me. The student dormitory was still provocatively dark, with the exception of one room where a red light burned behind an old window shade.

Being half-awake means that you are also half-asleep, so I got into bed quickly after turning out the lights. The shaft of high-intensity streetlamp fell across me once again. I pulled the covers up to my chin and wondered: given the madcap method of their inspections, would the operetta officers have uncovered a burglar if he (or she, given the evening's example) had secreted her- or himself inside? I was too tired to care, even though I knew there were many cubbyholes in the large old house that they had not looked into.

The Night the Ghost Got In, indeed, I thought.

In the impaired darkness I heard the attic's former white-haired resident bark out? "Back, ye cowardly dogs!" and shut my eyes. Thurber? Wasn't he some kind of writer?

CATHOLICS COMING OF AGE*

D uring a benefit for the newly opened Thurber House in Columbus, Ohio, I was listening to Christopher Durang read excerpts from his hit play "Sister Mary Ignatius Explains It All for You"—a host of nun jokes that are perennial but not always popular. The audience was laughing appreciatively at Durang's witticisms, the antic dictas of Sister Mary, even though much of the humor had escaped from a time capsule. Durang reminded me of something, and I finally realized what: a yuppie Catholic version of the Jewish hipster Lenny Bruce. Durang was acerbic, but acceptable, pungent, yet polite. And certainly well received, without a doubt.

Durang is one of a number of writers whose coincidental popularity has given rise to a phenomena mirage: Catholics, as subject, are now à la mode in the general culture. The sales of books by Catholic novelists, most notably the Reverend Andrew M. Greeley's, rival those of Jacqueline Susann from an earlier decade. Though the number of writers involved is not large, it is sufficient to form a constellation—some recognizable animal in the commercial literary skies.

When I was a midwestern teenager, one with a Catholic background who aspired to be a writer, I never expected my first book to have the word "Catholic" in the title. It did: *The Harrisburg 7 and the New Catholic Left.* The book's appearance in late 1972 coincided with the departure of the so-called new Catholic left from the public's consciousness—or, at least, the decampment of the national media, who took with them their own brand of lights, camera, action.

Catholicism, as a topic in the popular press, quickly dropped from view in the early seventies. "Born-again" Christians received the lion's share of media attention. Jimmy Carter accounted for some of that, just as, ten years before the notoriety of Catholic antiwar radicals of the Harrisburg period, the

---

* First appeared in *New Catholic World*, vol. 228, no. 1366, July-Aug. 1985.

election of John F. Kennedy had brought Catholicism prominent coverage.

Such cycles are not confined to ten-year periods—nor are they necessarily cyclical. What is required is a rhythm of attention and neglect. The media and the popular consciousness work something like medieval farmers, with their system of rotating fallow and fertile fields. It is difficult, in any case, to pinpoint—since the causes are varied—who or what prompts this sort of fluctuating attention, the Cyclopian focus of the media, when all eyes, hence one eye, seem to be turned toward a single group. And, for the last couple of years, that group has been Roman Catholics. There is a bushel of contributing causes (or effects): an activist Pope, Solidarnosc, "Catholic" Central American countries in revolution, the ongoing abortion debate, the reinvigorated nuclear peace movement, the Bishops' letters, Geraldine Ferrarro's campaign for vice president, and so forth.

Amidst this broad global and national interest, there is a narrower vogue, a thin vein of literary riches. One reason for its emergence is demographic: the numbers are healthy. The population that constitutes the general book-buying public has been shifting over the last decade. Catholics now make up the highest percentage of first-time students in institutions of higher education (source: U.S. Department of Education, National Center for Education Statistics). Over the last decade, Roman Catholic students went from 30 percent to nearly 39 percent of the total, whereas Protestants peaked in 1973 at 45 percent and have now declined to 34 percent (fall, 1980 figures). This ripple in the population influences the currents of the literary marketplace. And the trend upwards of educated Catholic readers is matched by an opposite trend downwards: there are now fewer priests and nuns. And the percentage of grammar-and-high-school-aged children now being educated by priests and nuns has precipitously declined. Durang was taught by nuns. I was. And as one set of figures increases and the other decreases, where those vectors cross a hot spot of nostalgia is created, a need for remembrance.

Our post-1945 generation has produced not only writers but also a large audience, though one not yet particularly sophisticated. Put simply, the baby boomers are now reading about themselves, and a disproportionate share of that boom happened to be raised Catholic. (Which accounts for the recent publication of a preppie-handbook-styled paperback titled *Growing Up Catholic*, edited by late-fifties-born and nun-and-priest-educated Catholics kids—perhaps the last large group of children to so be.) And, tellingly, as the primary sources for this literature declines (the ubiquity of priests and nuns), the need for written folklore increases. The oral tradition starts to turn into the written by beginning to die out. Durang's nasty jokes in his most successful play are not so much arch as archival. They are being recorded, not merely regurgitated.

Andrew Greeley's literary career plots a graph of the process of social change that has taken place. I hesitate to make use of the beleaguered Father Greeley, but the price of success is that you become a commodity, and people do with you what they will (although it would become Father Greeley if he were more aware than he seems to be that you cannot make the lion of Mammon lie down with the lamb of Good Intentions without ending up with a few scratches). In my youth there used to be two kinds of Catholic writers: the first was a writer who grew up with a Catholic background but did not employ it directly or exclusively, one whose literary qualities were of sufficient excellence that his or her Catholic background did not immediately leap into the foreground. The second sort was a writer who wrote about "Catholics," principally priests and nuns. In the past, the better the writer the less likely he or she would slide into the second group. Most Catholic writers readily recalled would fall into the first group. A good many forgotten names make up the second. But today there is a third group: members, current and former, of religious orders, who write.

Of course, there was Thomas Merton. Wouldn't a third group always have existed? Wouldn't Merton have been a member of it? I don't think so. It was one of the quandaries of my youth—the question of how you could be a Trappist monk, bound by intricate vows of silence, and publish best-selling books, the first and most famous and autobiography that seemed as much of a fiction as many autobiographical first novels. Merton indeed was a harbinger of many things, a chink in the armor of orthodoxy that would soon be a rift, as the fifties turned into the sixties. The many changes, both in style and in substance, that took place during that period in religious orders, as well as in the general population, produced the third group.

In addition to the social upheavals of the recent past, there took place a subtle literary sea change that has added to the lure of the novels of Father Greeley (as well as those of the ex-priests James Carroll and Eugene Kennedy). In the late sixties and early seventies, the novel was certainly not the most fashionable literary form. The sixties kicked a lot of sand in the eyes of its novelists. The nonfiction narrative, the so-called New Journalism, was in ascendancy. Nonfiction thrived over fiction simply because it could boast it was "true." Early eighteenth-century fictions had to claim a nonfictional source, and by the late twentieth century that again had become expedient. And priests—or ex-priests—writing about priests conferred their own imprimaturs of "truth" to their fictions.

In articles and interviews (and in an afterword to his own *The Cardinal Sins*), Father Greeley speaks of his fictions as teaching aids, ways to bring profound issues before large audiences. He is right. One of the last great priest-popularizers, the Most Reverend Fulton J. Sheen, did the same thing and by means of the same forum that helped create an audience for the new form of romance Greeley writes: television.

During the seventies, publishers watched with interest the growth of what appeared to be a new audience for a new genre of novel: the romance, or "romantic" novel. Its forebears are not the Italian *romanzo* or Cervantes or Rabelais or any other precursors of the modern novel. Its traditions derive from television, from soap operas, not other literature. Its hallmark is a kind of crude reticence: realism shorn of reality, description without depth.

Father Greeley sums up, inadvertently, the ethos of this genre in his poem, "Visitor in a Bikini," found in a volume entitled *Women I've Met*, published by Andrews and McMeel in 1970: "Curled up in a chair / Small breasts / Soft white belly / Rounded haunches / Slender legs / All deviously deployed / . . . From a safe distance / To be savored / And enjoyed." "From a safe distance" is the key. And the sort of writing that fills these novels always provides that distance—bad writing always does. Father Greeley's own novels are written in a flat, pedestrian prose. Picked randomly from *The Cardinal Sins*: "I had been in Rome only a week. The sky behind St. Peter's was crystal blue. The dome itself shimmered almost white in the crisp morning sunlight." This is grammar-school-primer prose, one step up from Dick and Jane. Most novels of the romantic school are written with the presumption that the reader has read no other book ever written. Other literature does not necessarily come equipped with the safe distance from the deviously deployed.

The audience, largely female, came, via television, away from magazine fiction (which no longer serviced the demand) to paperback books. And as the audience grew larger and larger publishers accommodated it. The romance novel proliferated at the same time the "novelization"—where a TV or movie script is turned into a "novel," not the other way around as had been the case—was born. Soon bodice-rippers, the gothics, the "romance" novel advanced from paperback to hardback, from supermarket racks to book club selections.

The bulk of this readership never grows old, insofar as it hardly develops, rarely graduates to other "better" books. The audience doesn't mature, but it is certainly replicated. This readership has always existed. It is its tremendous growth that is new—and the shift away from magazines to paperback books. There is no need for the authors who service it to improve either, generation after generation. Is a Jacqueline Susann novel better than an Andrew Greeley? In prose style? Narrative technique? Hardly. That more that audience changes (replaced by younger members) the more it stays the same.

Father Greeley is in many ways a new print incarnation of Bishop Sheen, the way Christopher Durang is a new playwright version of Lenny Bruce. In the strange hierarchy of popular culture, print still has more status, but less effect, than television. Imagine a Bishop Sheen on prime time television today. Impossible. Yet, at the same time, everything is on television. There is even a "religious" cable network. Catholics, though, have seized the high ground: books, not TV. In the past, before Catholic parents sent a couple of generations of sons and daughters to college, Catholics were pleased to settle for TV. But the trashiest best-selling novel is still somehow more respectable in educated circles than the "PTL Club."

Book clubs function as arbiters between the low and middle cultures (as well as between the middle and high). Currently, it is the ex-priests Carroll and Kennedy who appeal (along with Greeley) to the book club audience, as well as the younger novelist, Mary Gordon, whose first two novels, *Final Payments* and *The Company of Women*, could not exist without their priests. Book clubs do the same thing *Playboy* magazine accomplished: they make the hitherto impolite genteel. *Playboy* packaged photos of naked women as just another product of the consumer culture, thereby removing them from criticism, at least by the millions of proponents of the consumer culture. Book clubs let the middle-culture audience dip down into the sudsy trough of the lower TV romance culture. And though better writers than Father Greeley, Carroll, Kennedy, Gordon, and others who use priests and nuns as characters, are availing themselves more directly of the new constituency of Catholic readers, along with capturing non-Catholic readers who come to such novels as anthropologists come to remote villages.

Characters who are priests and nuns resurrect the classical forms of hero and anti-hero. They possess qualities and attributes that can be tested against a standard. Today, no character in a novel can be assumed to be a paragon without the author demonstrating that he or she is one. Except for priests and nuns. Most readers will accept them on faith—if nothing else—alone. They will not at once assume their celibacy, pangs of conscience, impulses to self-sacrifice, and so on to be some consequence of pathology or trauma. With most characters (other than perhaps children or the purely allegorical), an author will have to earn goodness for them, not just state it. And so priests and, as always, alas, secondarily, nuns, become powerful characters in fiction because *they mean something*. Paradoxically, priests and nuns are among the few stereotypical characters who are always fresh. That is why a writer as good as Robert Stone, who avoided Catholic subjects in his earlier work, made one character a priest in his 1981 novel, *A Flag for Sunrise*, because he needed some benchmark for conduct unavailable otherwise and made another a nun, so her destruction would not seem to be totally masochistic, but, in some way, elevated.

What needs to be kept in mind is that the number of Catholic writers who are capturing large audiences is still small. (And, as in the past, some of the best contemporary Catholic writers are not quickly, if at all, thought of as Catholic, such as Paul Theroux.) Father Greeley, regardless of the factors I have been discussing and his novels' intrinsic attractions, would not have been propelled into best-sellerdom without the heavy initial investment of the publisher Bernard Geis, who promoted him, ah, religiously and well. And, in Eugene Kennedy's case, he, like Father Greeley, was already well-known for his well-received nonfiction when he turned to fiction relatively late (as did most of these priests and ex-priests); and it did not hinder him to have another well-known Catholic as his editor, Jacqueline Onassis.

It may be most appropriate to think of the current crop of Catholic writers as just another literary movement, people who share similar ideas, concerns, and topics, folk who enjoy the same sort of cultural forebears, rituals and rites—like, say, the Beat writers. But what we have is, not a ragged, eclectic group of like-minded personalities, but an extended Catholic family of writers—though a group made up, significantly, not of parents and children, but of teachers and their young pupils, who, in the early eighties, perhaps surprisingly, have all come of literary age at the same time.

ELLEN FRANKFORT'S *VOICE**

O ur time is full of irony and an "ironic age" does not necessarily sound corrupt, but you must remember that irony comes from a Greek word meaning ignorance purposely affected. So ironies abound, and not the first or last is how similar Time, Inc. and the Village Voice, Inc. (and that "Inc.," lest we forget, is more powerful than printer's ink) were in conception. Both were the offspring of two men (Henry Luce and Briton Hadden; Ed Fancher and Dan Wolf—Norman Mailer was more godfather than active parent); both were exactly what the historic moment called for (*Time* in 1923, the *Voice* in 1955); and both were a mixture of blatant opinion and less blatant fact. In both partnerships one was the "creative" mind (Hadden and Wolf) and one was the financial (Luce and Fancher). Hearst and Pulitzer may have brought us the Spanish-American War, Henry Luce the cold war, but from Ellen Frankfort's *The Voice: Life at the Village Voice* we learn that Dan Wolf (more so than Fancher, who in Frankfort's telling drops out of sight much the way Hadden politely died early in Luce's career) practiced a modern guerrilla war, an attrition of the spirit that mirrors so well most of the failed movements of the Sixties.

This tempest may have taken place in a teapot, but it is still all the more personally acidic for so doing. Dan Wolf was the magical editor who got the "best for less," and when he and Fancher sold the *Voice* in 1970 to Carter Burden and Bartle Bull for three million, that was part of the pitch: "They were told that Dan was the only person in New York who could get people to write for so little—people of talent and originality . . . it was the genius every financial wizard wished to possess. Any man who can exploit people and have them think he is wonderful is no mere conversation guru. He is a very shrewd businessman." Wolf, as he aged, turned out to be the Lear who escapes with the loot

* First appeared in *Commonweal*, vol. 104, no. 14, July 8, 1977. A review of *The Voice: Life at the Village Voice* by Ellen Frankfort.

and leaves his daughters (and sons) penniless. Nothing begats nothing is an axiom any capitalist would applaud.

Frankfort rightly casts Wolf as a father figure; Henry Luce was much more than that, the Lord of the Manor, rather than a mere householder. Wolf's balm was that he made his writers what they were, gave them the *Voice* as a showcase, turned them into Stars. (Can you name them? So much for Stars.) When they found their wings, they were expected to leave the nest. Writers succumbed, for as any beginner (or middler, or ender) knows, getting into print, nay, being read, is the coin sought after. The *Voice* had readers (thanks to the New York newspaper strike of 1962): "On Pearl Harbor Day, 1962, the New York Typographical Union Local No. 6 called the longest newspaper strike in the history of New York. Readership jumped from 17,000 to 135,000. Mostly from newsstand sales. The paper increased from twelve pages to seventy and advertising expanded from 20 percent to 65." All publications are fan magazines, and the *Voice* readers were literate fans. One delusion Frankfort does not dispel is that the *Voice* acted as a careerist platform. The truth is most *Voice* writers turned into *Voice* writers. They graduated from twelve-hundred-word articles to magazine journalism. Only a handful of exceptions come to mind. Wolf stunted his writers in ways never perceived. He never gave them enough space. (Indeed, the major criticism of Frankfort's book is that it reads [as does her earlier *Vaginal Politics*] like a series of articles. Other criticisms are: Disputed accuracy on a few minor points; a number of inconsistencies; no index; a general "Hell hath no fury like a journalist scorned" tone.)

Timestyle became a cliché and so did *Voicestyle*. The confessional journalism practiced in the *Voice* became self-parody. Individual voices could be given a free reign in the *Voice* as long as they fell within the frequency received.

Newspapers are elementary economic textbook cases. The consolidation of advertising destroys the multiplicity of publications. Advertisers deal in numbers, and advertising goes one place: whoever has the most readers. And if the demographics are too similar, competing publications are doomed. So-called specialized audience publications are said to be healthy. In television the bloodletting is more obvious; the smallest percentage differences in ratings are the straw that break a lot of backs.

With fewer read publications, there are more writers crying for space. The *Voice* literally has hundreds of freelance writers to tap; it was (and is) a buyer's market. A writer's narcissism (to see himself in print) will overwhelm his greed (or even permit the most miserable conditions—Frankfort tells separate victim tales of a number of women, including herself, who wrote for the *Voice*).

A writer's misgivings are often as large as his ego. And the *Voice*, being a liberal paper, "anti-establishment," had any number of other guilts to trouble. Rich young men and women writing about the poor, the oppressed: there was a deep well of neurosis to pump, and Wolf did not see it run dry.

The *Voice* was not just a bright mirror to the changes it saw during the sixties; it was mottled as well. The silver began to flake, and—in places—you could see through it. In book publishing, where once firms had unlimited supplies of young women from Seven Sisters schools looking for a temporary mooring in the city, they found they had women who intended to stay and who wanted to advance; they had unions knocking at their doors. *Voice* writers eventually became staff writers, the gyre slowed at the end of the sixties, old blood did not want to be spilled for new, and indeed as staff writers themselves aged, security beckoned. The staff lifted the rock and finally saw what lived beneath. They were being paid $150-200 a week; many who wrote regularly, but not on staff, were getting much less; Dan Wolf was making $72,000 a year.

The economics of the *Voice* startled and disturbed them. Idealists are by definition naive, and no one had turned investigative skills (nor even their common sense) on the *Voice*. Follow the money, as Deep Throat suggested to the equally naive Woodstein duo. Luce was never duplicitous about the editorializing (or free enterprising) in the news articles of *Time* (his prospectus spelled it out), and Wolf never had to be duplicitous about where the profits went because no one asked him. When it was sold in 1970 for $3 million, a few writers raised their eyebrows, but it took the unsteady course of the new owners (Burden and Bull) and the almost unconscious abandonment of the helm by Wolf to finally bring it all out.

Some of the participants acted better than others (READ ALL ABOUT IT!!!). Frankfort's book embarrasses most everyone.

Again, as a bellwether of our times, Clay Felker's purchase and renovation of the *Voice* in 1974 is as appropriate as its beginning: Wolf, the closet capitalist, exploiting his minions while seeming to espouse a more equitable world; and Felker, his motives quite upfront in the style of the liberated seventies, unhidden. The lack of hypocrisy (our decade now growing weary of irony) as Frankfort implies, might be a tonic. Her book is valuable on many levels: as ragged journalistic history of a ragged journal, and as another personal fable of our times.

DIFFICULT WOMEN AND MINOR CHARACTERS*

Both of these books, by writers in their forties, are mid-life memoirs, a form usually practiced only by celebrities and those who have rubbed shoulders with them. In David Plante's case the famous are Jean Rhys, Sonia Orwell (George Orwell's widow), and Germaine Greer; in Joyce Johnson's, Jack Kerouac and friends. These are all, of course, literary celebrities, and whatever flaws both books have, they will reward and fascinate any reader who takes an interest in the people in them. The literary memoir is a comfortable form, a hammock suspended between fiction and journalism, and it makes for pleasant reading. *Difficult Women* does not yield enough of Plante himself to succeed as memoir but does somewhat better if looked at as portraiture, in the manner—if not with the depth and brilliance—of Ford Madox Ford's remembrances of Crane and Conrad, and Gorki's of Tolstoy and Chekhov.

When the portion of this book devoted to the novelist Jean Rhys was published in the *Paris Review*, Plante was criticized in certain quarters for being "indiscreet." But what Plante is too discreet about in *Difficult Women*, is himself; one is made quite cross-eyed having to read between the lines, as this book is also, indirectly, a portrait of the young writer's progress, a highbrow version of "What Makes David Write?"

Plante met Rhys in 1975, just around the time that Rhys was being "rediscovered" (though it might be more correct, at least in America, to say "discovered," as there was never any earlier vogue for her work here). Her novels were being reissued; praise and interest began to gush everywhere. She was a personage, though one beset with the problems of old age and alcohol.

---

* First appeared in *Book World, Chicago Tribune*, Mar. 6, 1983. Review of *Difficult Women* by David Plante and *Minor Characters* by Joyce Johnson.

Plante has published eight novels; his trilogy of the Francoeur family has received generous attention and praise. There are similarities between Plante's and Rhys's prose styles, and it is clear that when they met, Plante already had something in common with Rhys's sensibility, her acute but oddly detached faculty of observation. But in *Difficult Women* Plante continually questions his motives for the attention he lavishes on her. "What am I doing here, listening to her?" And then a page later he answers himself: "It was as if she suddenly opened the door to the closed centre of her life, a cafe in Paris in the '20s . . . It was a cafe I had, since my adolescence, fantasized about . . . She was going to take me in and give me a seat by her in the cafe."

In any case, Plante's account of her last years is touching to anyone who admires her novels (as I do), though you need to bring some esteem with you to read Plante's portrait with sympathy, as it would not be obvious from it what there is to admire in the woman.

Elderly revered writers are quite often made dotty by their long lives, and whoever writes about them tends to show us the messy back of a tapestry instead of the appealing front. The front, of course, is the writer's work, which is to be justly admired. The back of the Jean Rhys tapestry is certainly one of blurred images, loose threads, and unattractive knots. I do not think Plante is being indiscreet in his portrait, just not probing or astute enough. His best remarks are the nasty ones; he has difficulty conveying his kindlier feelings toward her. Rhys yells out from the bathroom, "Oh my God!" and Plante thinks: "It occurred to me that she had seen her face in the mirror."

For a book dealing with writers, there is little said about writing in it. After a discussion with Sonia Orwell, one of Plante's sponsors in the literary world, Plante muses: "Well, it's true, I can't think. But I tried to tell her that I didn't trust thinking, that writing, I believed, didn't come from drawing conclusions." Doubtless he is being coy about that not-being-able-to-think business, but in *Difficult Women* he draws almost no conclusions. You may be able to write fiction taking that as a principle, but it is difficult to write nonfiction that way.

The pages devoted to Sonia Orwell are the least substantial; perhaps this is because she figures in Plante's life as a filter, through whom other people pass into his acquaintance. The most entertaining, though the most slapdash, portrait is that of the feminist author Germaine Greer. What's different is that Greer, in addition to being alive, is more nearly Plante's contemporary, and he does not have the fixed distance on her that age and death afford.

The Greer section, as do the others, raises many questions about Plante that he should have answered himself. One woman accuses him of being a "tease"; he complains when people discuss "queers," is affronted when referred to as a "fairy," but after watching Germaine Greer take a bath he falls peacefully to sleep. He does seem confused about his intentions and sexuality, and I am afraid he leaves his reader confused as well. His tale of their friendship—they take the most touristy of trips to Santa Fe—is, for the reader, one of "Will David finally bring himself to sleep with her?"; and the suspense, though not killing, is certainly deadening. *Difficult Women* will not do much for Plante's critical reputation, which is, albeit unintentionally, a mark in its favor. The book is honest in spite of itself.

Whereas Plante's experiences with difficult women would best be used for fiction (as they doubtless will), Joyce Johnson's memoir of her youth and of the emergence and disappearance of the Beat Generation benefits from the hardness of fact. She, unlike Plante, does draw a number of conclusions about writing and life, and she presents at least as well as he the texture and atmosphere of a time intensely lived. A novelist herself and a discerning editor, she seems to have a pretty good idea of who she is—neither too inflated nor too self-deprecatory. Plante, if he has a good idea of who he is, feels obliged to keep it to himself.

Johnson and Plante, though roughly contemporary, describe two different literary worlds, and it shows in the writers who made up the center of each of their lives. Jack Kerouac helped give America back to its writers, whereas Plante expatriated himself and went to live among the influential remnants of the age of Auden. Kerouac could not live without this country and made flamboyant use of its coarse and rich materials. Plante's style is so refined and spare that only the sated can draw nourishment from it. Kerouac made a feast for those who could not be presumed to have enjoyed many.

Johnson's memoir, though published as a sprig of Kerouaciana, is her own story as well, and the more affecting for that. The Beats were the last den of literary lions with no lionesses allowed; women played the role only of handmaidens in that circle. Thus Johnson's memoir is told from the point of view of both spectator and participant, but her eye is all the more judicious for that. Unlike Plante, she never needs to question the interest she takes in the people she writes about. There is more to be found in *Minor Characters* than the frustrating part Kerouac played in her life; in fact, it is one of the best memoirs of the period that I have read—for its lack of posturing, if nothing else.

She says at the end: "The '60s were never quite my time," and she is right. The Beat Generation was never really a generation, because its members were never allowed to grow old. It was a moment of cultural shift between the fifties and the sixties. It wasn't Jack Kerouac or the Beats who were being ignominiously packaged by the end of it; they were the first wave of what became the wholesale merchandising of youth, the beachhead of the baby boom. Johnson's book wonderfully captures the evanescence of that time, charting how Kerouac appeared as an unwitting avatar of the generation to come and ended as a throwback, a mother-ridden pensioner.

One danger arises when young writers choose to write about older, more accomplished ones; what is absent in the books at hand is bound to remind you of what is great about the authors they write about. Neither Johnson nor Plante escapes that peril. At the same time, both of their books intelligently and movingly explore the writers' lives and the problems and allure of fame; Johnson describes Kerouac as someone who was crushed by it when it fell his way, being totally unprepared for it. That is a far cry from the present generation of writers—Plante included—who seem to do nothing but prepare for success, even if it never comes.

ON BECOMING A NOVELIST AND PANIC AMONG THE PHILISTINES*

" P eople who live in glass houses shouldn't throw stones." But who lives in a glass house? Politicians, celebrities? Well, yes and no. But the indisputable tenants of the world's glassiest houses, those who live the most revealed lives, are writers. And, these days, the shattering of glass can be heard everywhere. There has been no shortage lately of articles by novelists and poets with a variety of grievances. Given the present social and political climate, there is a lot to complain about—I have a few complaints myself. But surprisingly, the trouble, according to most of the essays that I have seen, is, not the fickle public, the publishers, or the late twentieth century, but other writers!

Two long pieces of this sort by "someone named" Bryan F. Griffin (that is how Griffin introduces people of insufficient renown) ran in *Harper's* some time ago and have now been expanded and issued as a book. He throws quite a few stones, though what usually upsets him is that the writers most vulgarly known are the most vulgar, a tautology he seems not to notice. John Gardner, the author of fourteen books, many of them novels, takes a different tack in the posthumous *On Becoming a Novelist*, but he, too, heaves a handful of stones, though his principal aim is that of a buoyant real estate agent, showing off a few glass houses to eager buyers.

One complaint heard often today (and made a number of times by Griffin) is that there are already too many writers. But, of course, there wouldn't seem to be too many writers if there were more readers to go round. There are certainly more "creative" writers of ability today than there were fifty years ago, just as there are more talented golfers, tennis players, basketball players, too;

---

* First appeared in *Commonweal*, vol. 111, no. 1, Jan. 13, 1984. Review of *On Becoming a Novelist* by John Gardner and *Panic among the Philistines* by Bryan F. Griffin.

more engineers, lawyers, and so forth. But though the number of practitioners of literature is increasing, the audience for their work seems to be an endangered species. So, like white mice in an overpopulated cage, writers have begun to cannibalize each other; it is a disheartening display of literary anthropophagism. If you have readers, you feel you have enough space around you; if you are denied readers, or access to them, the claustrophobia becomes lethal.

John Gardner's book is aimed at aspirants, those foolish enough to want to join the fray. It is a how-to book, though Gardner, along the way, gives his views on how to separate the gems from the paste, the true artist from the phonies. The material in the first half of the book is the sort of thing you would hear if you attend a solid creative writing class, say, one taught by the likes of a John Gardner. These pages reveal an obviously warm and generous spirit.

It is instructive, though, to contrast his ideas with those found in Annie Dillard's *Living by Fiction*, published last year (1982), which has been recently reissued in paperback. There Dillard writes disapprovingly, "People still magically regard novelists as helpless, fascinating neurotics who compose in deliriums or trances . . . young writers may be misled into thinking that novelists are rich or even that they are active. But this is silly."

Silly or not, that is, more or less, how Gardner describes novelists. It is, he tells the novice, beneficial to have something wrong with you: "A psychological wound is helpful . . . some fatal childhood accident for which one feels responsible . . . embarrassment about one's own physical appearance: all these are promising signs." He is also very much of the "trance" school of fiction composition, even to go as far as suggesting methods of self-hypnosis. Gardner was also well-off and died actively in a motorcycle accident.

Annie Dillard, at least in her published work, has been thus far *living by nonfiction*; she may be a novelist-to-be. I do not know. But anyone who has written a novel will not entirely laugh off some aspects of Gardner's description—even if it is ridiculous as instruction.

One aspect of Gardner's book that needs noting: it is a success story. You do not want to learn how to get rich from someone who is poor. But Gardner's pages on how-to-get-published can be had from anyone; it's the same advice someone who has never been published but who has tried will give you. What Gardner would have needed to reveal to explain his own success—well deserved though it was—was how to be at the right place at the right moment, and in front of the right person, which, of course, is impossible to learn.

A seasoned author, therefore, will look in vain for some irony through the book, especially in a second half, which is, in many ways, embarrassing. There most of the straight advice is doled out: "Neatness counts," and so forth. Where is his tongue in cheek? one asks, when Gardner does a shill's soft shoe for

Bread Loaf-like writers conferences, complete with an adman's puffery: intense "love affairs" shaking the bushes! Raymond Carver's memoir of Gardner as professor and Carver as student, which serves as a foreword to the book, is more to the point of how to become a novelist.

The kindest and most sympathetic reading of Griffin's *Panic among the Philistines* (his first book) will turn up at least one point: there were more good books written in the last twenty-five centuries than in the last twenty-five years. I don't think the author most spat upon in Griffin's long diatribe would disagree with that notion entirely. But, on most other things, people will disagree. I looked forward to reading this material; I enjoy Davids attacking Goliaths. The hugely successful should be made to endure a few knocks on their well-padded reputations. Who has a heart so kind that he wouldn't enjoy Mr. Griffin's wielding his chain saw on the grotesquely overpraised? But, alas, he has set back the whole noble cause of the kamikaze attack. I fear his book will have the same effect on the literary celebrated he takes potshots at as did mad Hinckley's attack on Reagan—it will bring them only sympathy.

Though one may tolerate Jerzy Kosinski's getting kicked around yet again, this time for his pornography collection; and one may even think Griffin right, but for the wrong reasons, about D. M. Thomas's novel *The White Hotel*, it is discomforting to realize that even when one (here and there) agrees with him, his prose remains insufferable and so, too, the attitudes that infest it. Griffin has the sort of style That Gives One A Headache (to adopt his manner of enlivening every third sentence with the stuttering capital). His writing has, like a cheap appliance, three settings, low, medium, and high. Low is a sort of anti-fan magazine diction: no one "said" anything. Everyone he quotes either "giggles" or "sighs" or "sobs"; "giggled David Ansen of *Newsweek*," "sighed young David," "sobbed Mr. Ansen"—and that's just one paragraph. The medium speed is the tone of the uppercrust snob, a preppy dismissiveness; everyone who is not a household word is introduced by a demeaning label: "someone named Earl Ubell." If it happens to be a person of startling output, his name is prefaced with the most everyday of his accomplishments: "a fifty-year-old professor of creative writing named John Barth."

Griffin has a good deal of scorn for professors—he uses the label only as an insult—but his book would have had some mischievous value for future literary historians if it had been outfitted with some scholarly apparatus, including a citation of sources and an index.

Lord knows there is a lot wrong with the literary community these days, but Griffin is not the sort of charismatic fellow you'd pick to head your crusade, despite his rhetorical similarity to Rev. Jerry Falwell. What fills out the bulk of *Panic among the Philistines* is what Griffin calls, typically capitalized, "The Important Subject": sex and its depiction in various forms in print. Sex exercises him mightily. Griffin's arguments bring to mind the picture of the backwoods judge who views all the pornographic films three times before issuing an injunction against them. But, even after dwelling too long on the material that disgusts him, what he cries out for is not that it be banished but that an offender like Christopher Isherwood be "reprimanded" for "reminiscing in public about the dear dead days when he used to cavort with German prostitutes . . ." It's in the *public* that really seems to bother Griffin; what he desires is a return to gentility, to the world before 1917 (his date), to a world whose hypocritical but dignified surface is restored.

But when I hear it complained that sex and violence have increased in our visible culture, I wonder why it is not more generally observed that violence has carried the day. John Irving and his *Garp* come in for a lot of Griffin's raspberries, but if Griffin has actually read Irving's book he must know that violence overwhelms the sex in it—as is the usual case these days. A little sex, a lot of violence. The reasons for this would make an interesting subjects to pursue, but Griffin is not overly distressed about violence. Indeed, he barely stops short of calling out for lynch-mob justice against the lewd scribblers he sees hogging the arena of popular culture. That brings us to his third and last voice, the high, the hortatory: "In practical terms, it is the battle between those who would use the tools of civilization—education and knowledge and liberty and peace—to savage those values . . . It is the everlasting battle in which there are no truces, the battle between the smile and the leer, between innocence and sophistication, beauty and lust, truth and cynicism, love and pornography . . ." And on and on.

Again, even with a sympathetic ear for some of his complaints, one still must say that Griffin seems woefully ignorant of recent literary history. He does not seem to have grasped that the literature of earlier centuries appears purer than ours because time has already blown the chaff from the wheat (and along with it, alas, some of the best wheat). He does think his side, the "intellectually militant people," have been winning the battle. And so Griffin stands like a small boy in a duststorm, not knowing why his eyes smart, but standing there stubbornly, rubbing them all the same.

FAMOUS PEOPLE HE HAS KNOWN*

"You can't tell a book by its cover," we've all piously been told, but some books want to truly *announce* themselves by theirs. The R. Crumb drawing on the cover of Ed McClanahan's memoir, *Famous People I Have Known*, is nothing if not truth in advertising, since the book strikes the same chords throughout as R. Crumb's well-known drawings: cartoony, droll, playful, positively no hard feelings, counterculture to the max, laid-back.

Most memoirs are by definition success stories, and McClanahan's is no exception. "In 1963, *Esquire* magazine devoted an entire issue to 'The Literary Situation,' the centerpiece of which was a massive list of all the Noted Authurs [*sic*] in the land, and sure enough, there it was, my very own personal name, prominently displayed smack in the middle of something *Esquire* called . . . 'The Red Hot Center.'" McClanahan became "The Most Famous Unpublished Author in America," and in 1963, if not today, that bit of attention could fuel a career "working the Visiting Lecturer in Creative Writing circuit." He had yet to publish a book, and so it remained for twenty years thereafter.

Then in 1983, his first novel, *The Natural Man*, appeared and had deserved success. It was greeted with (in jacket-copy phraseology) a "chorus of praise," though some of the cheering was the hearty sort that accompanies the last runner who crosses a marathon's finish line.

There is but a handful of unflattering portraits in "Famous People I Have Known," rare for a writer's memoir. McClanahan's pen gets dipped in vitriol only when he describes "the celebrated French pederast cutpurse incendiarist Marxist-Leninist writer and all-around fruitcake, Jean Genet, fresh out of prison for who-knows-what heinous offenses against whatever passes for human decency in France," during the time Genet was barnstorming California for

---

* First appeared in *Book World, Chicago Tribune,* Nov. 17, 1985. Review of *Famous People I Have Known* by Ed McClanahan.

the Black Panthers. But, overall, McClanahan's recollections are bathed in the mellow shades of R. Crumb, where every scene, no matter how lurid, is rendered slightly soft and pudgy. McClanahan's famous folk are the likes of Jimmy Sacca, Little Enis, Beast, and Wheatgerm, and the memoir spends most of its time with these vivid but transient personalities who never found themselves a seat in the limelight, though they may have drunkenly stumbled through it once in their lives.

It is difficult to criticize a book too sharply that has made you laugh out loud more than once, but after those high points a certain impatience sets in when McClanahan *refuses to get serious*, though such abstinence on his part may well be the wisest strategy, given his material. The literary world is always darting in and out of his story, and McClanahan picks up where most recent memoirists of the Beat Generation leave off: in California during the late fifties and early sixties, where the vestiges and inheritors of the short-lived Beat period went after life in New York City became just too hard.

In a memoir not given over to much introspection, McClanahan writes, "Like everyone else who lived in California during the 1960s, I Went Through a Phase." That is an accurate assessment. Because the man who stands revealed seems not to be very different from the raw youth he was way back in 1952, when he was a freshman at Washington & Lee University, a brash young man who became, in a very typical American way, a mixture of cracker and connoisseur, a good ole boy saddled with advanced degrees.

Despite all the social history that occurred during his twenty years of famous obscurity, McClanahan steadfastly remained a true child of his age, an Eisenhower-era product, more redneck than egghead, now happy and contented with his no-longer-hollow fame, his new wife and young kids, glad to be back home in Kentucky, a living testament to the American Dream, fifties-style, which, in truth, may well be the style of the eighties.

THE POST-MODERN AURA*

One of the most appealing aspects of Charles Newman's "The Post-Modern Aura" is how it functions as a somewhat disguised apologia for Newman's own writing; or, rather it is his investigation into the role economics and society at large plays in the reception of his own work. He is explaining something to himself. When young writers-to-be are growing up, they actually imagine that their literary lives will take the shape of the generation of writers before them; whereas, in most cases (save those where wealth will purchase any fantasy), their literary lives are formed by contemporary forces they haven't yet been able to identify.

Newman is obviously quite correct to point out that "serious literature disappears from the mass market," though there is always the question of whether, and in what guise, it existed in the so-called mass market. Clearly, in sheer numbers, the audience for the pulpiest of pulp fiction has grown, while the audience for literary fiction, always a minority, has become an even smaller minority, a percentage that does not now gather—or warrant—much attention from the marketplace. But, what is surprising is not how few literary novels are published but how many, considering the demand, or lack of it.

One difficulty writers have when considering the matter of audience is the example of their own experience. Newman voices a commonly held opinion when he states: "I think it's fair to say that no serious fiction writer in America today can tell you whom he is writing *for*." (Though, perhaps, the *shes* could.) Today's writers are, in most cases, passionate readers—and were such before they became writers. They are conflicted missionaries who, though they bring to their listeners the glory of the word, are in the paradoxical position of desiring no converts; they want readers, not more colleagues, competitors.

Yet, one of the "victories" of the postmodern period was to make the

* First appeared in *Salmagundi*, no. 67, Summer 1985. A response to Charles Newman's, "The Post-Modern Aura."

transition from spectator to participant, from reader to writer, easier. One of the things most completely devalued during the age of "inflation" was the amateur state. The sixties was a participatory time, and doing it was more than a mere motto. The arena may now be full of writers, but the stands are empty of fans. In universities across the land, graduate writing programs have prospered during the last decade-and-a-half, while the number of English majors has everywhere declined. There was an often heard cliché of the fifties: "Everyone has one book in him." The last two decades have proven that to be true; moreover, practically anyone who has a book in him or her has published it. And it is the universities (as Newman acknowledges) who are subsidizing the surplus population of writers—as they should.

Newman's central point is unassailable; the writing of books has been devalued in post-industrialized countries. Without a doubt, the economic forces that govern production and distribution are a leading cause, but the result is also shaped by the perceptions and actions of the literary community. Even Newman's argument is prompted, not because the books don't exist, but because they have become so weirdly superfluous. It is sobering, and appalling, to authors to see how many worthy novels are published each year and how few are paid any attention whatsoever. It takes four reviews from a list of more than seventy periodicals to be included in the venerable reference source *Book Review Digest*. I know of quite a few novels by important writers of my generation that did not even gather four reviews and, subsequently, do not even exist as a reference. And those that are reviewed receive only a handful of notices, except for a baker's dozen each year that receive as much attention as there is to get.

To any complaint raised about the lack of audience for serious fiction there is trotted out the example of the one or two literary novels that have achieved a spot on the best-seller list that year; but this is only proof we have a particularly disturbing and precarious kind of Noah's ark culture; we only need one or two examples of the species to believe that all is well in the kingdom.

The typical literary critic doesn't know much more about contemporary fiction (who is writing it) than the folks who read *People* magazine. And, even when you ask novelists who they read, and are aware of, all that most can name are their friends and acquaintances. However little or much contemporary fiction is published, it is still more than the critical establishment can read and comment upon. Newman's own book-to-be appears in a journal that (upon consulting the two-year index found in the same issue) does not review contemporary fiction at all.

And there is an additional irony that Newman might appreciate himself: "The Post-Modern Aura"'s publication in a quarterly has, more than likely, brought it a larger audience than it would have achieved if it had appeared solely as a mere *book*.

PROTESTING N.E.A.*

T here are a number of reasons that I, unlike Joe Papp, am not refusing my National Endowment for the Arts grant this year to protest the new Jesse Helms-inspired obscenity "restriction" attached to the award. The first and foremost: Returning the money is just what Senator Helms and his supporters would want me to do.

The other reasons flow from that, but given the tenor of the discussion surrounding the N.E.A. controversy, they need to be stated. As a writer who came of age during the late sixties, I find it curious to contemplate the nineties definition of protest that has been articulated and promoted: Writers are supposed to "protest" the N.E.A.'s new "restriction"—which reads like some high school student's scrambled paraphrase of the obscenity standard—by refusing their grants.

In the late sixties and early seventies, protest had an element of jeopardy to it, and bodily harm and jail time were often what was being risked. I believe the best method of protesting the new "restriction" is this: You accept the grant, do what you wish with it, and risk prosecution, jail, or whatever by the authorities. That is how you protest a "restriction"—not by refusing something until the government gives you immunity.

The new standard, refusing a grant because some risk is involved, is a Bush-era kinder, gentler form of protest. It is protest with a celebrity face. A sixties sort of protest would entail collective action, some sense of solidarity, and would require artists not to apply for grants, which would cause a speedy demise of the N.E.A., which, of course, is just what some wish. Celebrity protest plays into the hands of those who would like to privatize the funding of the arts, turn it over completely to philanthropists, foundations, and any other thousand points of low-watt light that happen to blink on.

Take Papp's situation. There is a difference between individual artists and arts administrators/impresarios—and, indeed, Joseph Papp is a consummate

---

* First appeared in *Nation*, vol. 250, no. 25, June 25, 1990.

impresario. First he protested the restriction, gaining some attention; a bit later he wrote a letter saying he was contemplating refusing the grant, which brought him further notice; then, after that had had time to percolate, he refused the grant, to a crescendo of publicity. He is not a theatrical producer for nothing.

Let me contribute some information I haven't seen discussed elsewhere. A month before I learned I'd won a creative writing fellowship, the N.E.A. sent me a form to sign—lest my application be considered "incomplete"—that declared I would not "engage in the unlawful manufacture, distribution, dispensation, possession or use of a controlled substance in conducting any activity with the grant." This restriction hasn't seemed to surface as a bone of contention, though its ramifications are more ominous than the restating of the current obscenity standard—because it concerns the artist's behavior, not the content of his or her work. That needs some protesting, too. Will homes and studios and theaters be visited by drug-sniffing German shepherds? Protesting that in the Just-Say-No period lacks the glamour that imbues free-speech issues. I protest.

The N.E.A. practices its own form of Catch-22ing when it gives out literary fellowships. The obscenity restriction sent to the fellowship recipients reads, in its entirety (the ellipses are the endowment's), "None of the funds authorized to be appropriated for the National Endowment for the Arts . . . may be used to promote, disseminate, or produce materials which in the judgment of the National Endowment for the Arts . . . may be considered obscene, including but not limited to, depictions of sadomasochism, homoeroticism, the sexual exploitation of children, or individuals engaged in sex acts and which, when taken as a whole, do not have serious literary, artistic, political, or scientific value."

Those who call that a "loyalty oath" are distorting language. The artists who have accepted their grants are not engaged in McCarthy-era betrayals of principles—or people. The "restriction" requires no denunciations of past associations (individuals or groups), it elicits no testimony, asks no one to name names. The so-called restriction, at least where individual artists are concerned, is as meaningless in fact as it is offensive in nature.

When the N.E.A. awards a grant directly to a writer, painter, or other artist, it is certifying the work of that artist as having, at the very least, artistic value. Such a restriction has no chilling effect on me. All my depictions of sadomasochism and homoeroticism have literary value, always have and always will. Any writer who doesn't happen to be thoroughly genteel always writes under the threat of, one, not being published and, two, being taken to court if he or she is.

Much has been made of the chilling effect of the restriction. But the government—in the form of the judicial system, including the Supreme Court—not the N.E.A., has been attempting its own refrigeration of writers throughout the Reagan and Bush years by means of various decisions involving libel and fair use, including but not limited to scholars making use of unpublished letters of "famous" authors. Writers and artists, if they are worth much, are always at risk. And as the cold war thaws, the porn and drug wars heat up.

But arts bureaucrats and impresarios, because they are in the business of attracting the public, are a bit more sensitive to these frost forecasts. They are doing public relations, whereas the artists are doing art. As Papp has indicated, the N.E.A. accounted for only 3.6 percent of his organization's entire budget in 1989. And it took him only a day to raise from private donors more than the $50,000 he turned down for a special project, the Festival Latino.

It ought to be further noted that most of the brouhaha has been over various gallery and museum board decisions, and the uproar has been directed largely at photographs, always the easiest prey of the virtue vultures. Jesse Helms and the porn posse have highlighted a family feud within the G.O.P. between mainstream Republicans and the party's right wing. Who sits on the board of Washington's Corcoran Gallery of Art? Not a lot of liberal working stiffs or writers. The current controversy doesn't entirely displease me, because a lot of it pits conservative fundamentalists against conservative connoisseurs. Let the feathers fly.

There are other reasons I haven't refused the grant in protest. But I find it annoying to have the ninety-seven winners of N.E.A. Creative Writing Fellowships being indirectly slandered by so many different commentators, supposedly sympathetic protectors of the arts. The *New Republic* called us all "lap dogs"; the press generally has taken this view.

Doubtless there are circumstances under which a grant should be refused. These aren't those. I have never written any of my novels to win a grant. I have applied for grants, as mountain climbers are in the habit of saying, because they are there. I happen to think peer review (the method the N.E.A. uses to judge who gets literary fellowships) a good thing—it is one of the few acts of approval and applause in the art world that is out of the market loop, beyond the reach of the gatekeepers and tastemakers, those who are involved directly in the commercialization of art.

If an arts administrator feels restricted by a grant, perhaps he or she should refuse it. Artists wouldn't and artists shouldn't. The N.E.A. needs to be defended and protected; it is the Helms-inspired congressional conduct that needs protest. Papp's is one kind of protest. But we creative writing fellows should accept the money and protest by writing what we will. If that places us at risk, so be it.

ARTISTS SHOULD ACCEPT GRANTS FROM THE ARTS ENDOWMENT*

I t's been an odd time to be one of the ninety-seven winners of this year's National Endowment for the Arts Creative Writing Fellowships. What used to be considered a prize has now become a stigma. Liberal publications, supposed defenders of the arts, have called us names for not refusing the grants, for not throwing them back in Jesse Helm's face, in protest of the Helms-inspired obscenity "restriction" appended to the grant. But, in all the commotion, there are a few things about the National Endowment for the Arts that are being overlooked and need to be addressed.

For one, the controversy surrounding the N.E.A. has its ironic side. The N.E.A. has always been controversial within its own constituency. Most of the battles have been sororal and fraternal, small and sour civil wars, especially when they involved the Literature Program, one of the smallest components of the N.E.A., and its Creative Writing Fellowships.

Often, mainly during the 1970s, after the yearly list of winners was announced, there would be a lot of gossip (and a few articles in small-press literary journals) consisting of finger pointing, scandal announcing, blame apportioning, allegations of back scratching, and subsequent back stabbings. A bit of which was warranted, most not. Michael M. Mooney's 1980 book, *The Ministry of Culture*, catalogues most of the abuses of the 1970s: friends' giving grants to friends, other sorts of intellectually nepotistic practices. Ninety percent of this involved poets and poetry presses: the least remunerative of the arts engendered the most palace intrigue. However, the amount of collusion and corruption in the Literature Program's peer-review panels is—was—infinitesimal, especially compared with other federal agencies' procurement practices.

---

* First appeared in the *Chronicle of Higher Education*, vol. 36, no. 40, June 20, 1990.

Be that as it may, those in Congress and elsewhere who wish to dismantle the N.E.A. have some artistic company. There has always been a segment of
the literary community that considers federal money "blood" money, regards all
grants quiche-fodder for wimps, and scorns those who apply for any of it. See
the *Wall Street Journal* (May 14, 1990), "Real Artists Don't Take Handouts,"
by Bill Kauffman, for a current version of that view. Mr. Kauffman asks: "Can
anyone name one major piece of American fiction that would not have been
written without the N.E.A.'s beneficence? How about a significant minor
work?"

Well, if Mr. Kauffman would look over the list of N.E.A. recipients,
even he might find a few authors of major and minor work: Cynthia Ozick,
Grace Paley, Alice Walker, William Gaddis, John Gardner, Richard Yates—
there are lots to choose from.

Mr. Kauffman, at his essay's end, berates today's "comforted, coddled,
cosseted artists," declaring, "If . . . Melville can produce *Moby Dick* without
Uncle Sam's patronage, then surely Robert Mapplethorpe's claque can express
themselves without a government handout." I don't think many writers contend
that a particular novel, story, or poem would have gone unwritten without the
winning of a grant; but a grant, at times, can make a difference in a writer's life.
Many things can make a difference like, say, having a rich relative, something
readers of the *Wall Street Journal* can sympathize with.

I don't know if Mr. Kauffman knows anything about Melville's career,
but, after the economic debacles of *Moby Dick* and *The Confidence Man*,
Melville had to go off to work for twenty years at a government agency, the
Custom Office. Perhaps if there had been direct government grants back then,
Melville would have had the wherewithal to publish another masterpiece in his
lifetime (it would have been *Billy Budd*), the sort of work Mr. Kauffman, in
vain, searches for these days.

Since 1966, roughly sixteen hundred Creative Writing Fellowships have
been given out: poets and fiction writers dividing the lion's share, a small portion doled out to "creative non-fiction" writers. I received my first N.E.A. Creative Writing Fellowship in 1981, after six years of applying for one.

It isn't easy to get two, so I was surprised to receive a second grant. I was
additionally surprised by a line in the letter referring to a packet of enclosed
instructions, stating: "Note that at paragraph two this information includes a
restriction on the use of Arts Endowment grant funds newly enacted by
Congress for Fiscal Year 1990. Please read this information carefully." Paragraph two of the packet read: "None of the funds authorized to be appropriated
for the National Endowment for the Arts . . . may be used to promote, disseminate, or produce materials which in the judgment of the National Endowment
for the Arts . . . may be considered obscene, including, but not limited to,

depictions of sadomasochism, homoeroticism, the sexual exploitation of children, or individuals engaged in sex acts and which, when taken as a whole, do not have serious literary, artistic, political or scientific value." (Their ellipses.)

At the time, I didn't give this "restriction" a great deal of thought. I was certainly aware of Jesse Helms and the growing controversy caused by the Mapplethorpe photographs. It just so happened that the Creative Writing Fellowship winners were the first grantees to fall under the new congressional restrictions. But it should be obvious that this "restriction" is no restriction at all. If the N.E.A. awards you a grant, it is certifying that your work has artistic value. The "restriction" has put a lot of smoke in people's eyes, but there's no fire. Funds appropriated for the N.E.A. can be given out by the N.E.A. only to projects that have artistic value, regardless of content. The controversy that swirls around the N.E.A. is a legacy of the cash aesthetics of the Reagan years: it is a question of not truth and beauty but what's it worth and who decides, a contest over value and control. Helms and company lust for control; the idea of censorship is merely foreplay.

At this moment, the N.E.A. does not need the artists who have been awarded grants to refuse them. Joseph Papp, the New York City theatrical producer who refused his grant, may have done the right thing for an arts administrator, but individual artists who have received direct grants need to help fend off the piratical attacks of the Helms crew, not jump ship.

And it should be noted, amidst all the clamor for privatization the current onslaught entails, that commercial publishers are being subsidized by the N.E.A. (as well as by universities) almost as much as are the smaller, more literary presses the N.E.A. funds directly. It took me more than four years to write my 1987 novel, *Criminal Tendencies*. I had a job—teaching—and I wrote when I didn't have to teach. Part time.

A fifty-page portion of *Criminal Tendencies* won me my second fellowship. In addition to settling past debts, the grant will help me buy the time to complete the novel I'm presently working on, *Notts*. The N.E.A. is subsidizing whichever publisher eventually buys it.

But the least obvious, although perhaps the most motivating, reason I applied to the N.E.A. was the expectation that a part of my novel, if not the whole, would get read by a desirable segment of its potential audience. Other writers. Writers are, by and large, quite busy and will read only what they have to or need to or the writing of friends—reading writer friends alone takes up a lot of time.

Many books are published each year (including more than three hundred first novels alone). One would have to read a novel a day to keep up. And, if one wants to find collusion, corruption, and so forth, one need only examine the process that decides which books get the most attention from the national review media—and what a pitifully small number of books of fiction and poetry that is, ultimately.

But, if a novel becomes fashionable enough, fashion alone will coerce readers, even writers, to take a look at it. There is a threshold of critical attention that you need to reach before you enter the fashion orbit. *Criminal Tendencies*, alas, had not quite attained it and the novel plummeted back to earth. The N.E.A. served me as a captured audience, provided a momentary ride in the fashion orbit.

For literary writers such as myself, the N.E.A. fellowship sweepstakes serves that important function. The judges, usually fellow writers of some accomplishment and standing, are an attentive audience that will read anonymously what you send them, thereby bypassing the style police, the corporate capos, the fashion gendarmes, the institutional gatekeepers who exist to gauge and set taste. The tastemaking media's reaction to the N.E.A. and its judgments, except when the present sort of controversy descends, is to overlook and ignore them.

The N.E.A. Literature Program does act as a microcosm of the literary community; the paradox is that this community is so hard to reach.

It is pathetic to apply for a grant to reach an audience even after being published by a commercial press, but that is what I did. And, even with all the controversy, no general-interest publication has even printed the list of this year's winners—or last year's, or those of the year before. However, since the N.E.A. became news, pundits from these same publications are engaged in the flip side of ignoring; they are attacking. And that is why the criticism of writers who have accepted their fellowships is so galling—and suspect. The *New Republic*, in an unsigned editorial, has labeled me (not by name, but collectively) a "lap dog" of the government for not refusing the N.E.A. grant.

I am aware of the melancholy fact that turning down the grant this year would have done me more good, in terms of publicity and good will, than accepting it.

Our federal government and its agencies do a lot of objectionable things, which should be protested—through writing, not by turning back money. Thinking that the N.E.A. can be purer than the government around it is a bit naive. But taking something never gains you the high ground, whereas refusing something often does. So the ninety-seven winners of the Creative Writing Fellowships have been put in the peculiar position of having to defend themselves from attacks—on all sides—for accepting grants they've been awarded through the accolades of their peers. The N.E.A. should be defended; it is the actions of a skittish Congress that should be protested.

But, without Jesse Helm's complaining and the porn posse's hitting the trail, most of the country would not even be aware that the N.E.A. exists, much less ever encounter the eccentric notion that its Literature Program acts in a very humble role: that of a hired and discerning audience for large numbers of writers who, for reasons both good and bad, fair and unfair, are unknown to their potential audience and, therefore, unlikely to be read, however much literary value their sadomasochism and homeroticism possess. Thanks, in part, to the testy gatekeepers of our culture, and to various forms of economic censorship, these writers are not known to most taxpayers, who, as our postliterate president so often points out, are forced to limit any serious reading to the reading of lips.

LETTERS TO EDITORS: THE N.E.A. AND THE LOYALTY OAFS*

The first thing I wrote about the 1990 N.E.A. controversy went unpublished. It was a letter to the *New Republic*; its April 9, 1990 issue contained a long editorial headlined "Indecent Request," one of the first pieces to set out at some length the issues that would be aired throughout the coming months.

Since I had received an N.E.A. literary fellowship in January, I took special interest in the magazine's remarks, which began: "Not long ago the National Endowment for the Arts notified ninety-seven writers that they had won grants to support their work." Then the unsigned editorialist made a connection that was quickly becoming the conventional wisdom: "The congressionally mandated anti-obscenity agreement hearkens back to the anti-Communist loyalty oaths demanded of government employees during the late 1940s and 1950s." Oh, it does does it? I thought, reading along. *Like hell it does*. I had signed the "agreement," the paperwork that comes with the grant, back in January. I had read through it, and since I can read it was clear to me what I was signing, and it was no kind of "loyalty oath." Congress was telling the N.E.A. what *it* could do, not what artists could do. The N.E.A. was informing the artists of the "restriction." You agree to "comply" with "terms and conditions." Is it possible to "comply" with a "restriction" that is aimed not at you but at the N.E.A.? And, uppermost, the "restriction" is self-canceling as written, since the N.E.A. is awarding you a grant for artistic merit, thereby anointing your present work, an endorsement it would find functionally impossible to retract. Near the end of the *New Republic*'s editorial was the line "It would be nice to see at least one writer reject the offer to become a lap dog, and return his [!] fellowship check."

---

* First appeared in *Another Chicago Magazine*, no. 24, Fall 1992.

Well, I certainly took that insult personally. I quickly dashed off a letter. I expected it to be published. How many of the ninety-seven writers responded, I didn't, still don't, know. But the *New Republic* didn't acknowledge my letter or publish anything from any of the smeared ninety-seven.

Here, in part, is the letter I sent:

11 April 1990

To the editors:

Lap dog of the government! Give me—us, all the Literary Fellowship winners, collectively—a break. I decided not to return my NEA grant this year, because giving the money back is just what Jesse Helms and crew would want. I would rather the NEA award grants to writers like myself. If you want to know why, read any or all of my books . . .

Why does peer recognition so bother gatekeepers and tastemakers?

By the time it was clear the *New Republic* wasn't going to run my letter, I had written another to the *Wall Street Journal*, which had published an op-ed article by Bill Kauffman on May 14, headlined "Real Artists Don't Take Handouts." His piece trotted out the older, pre-Helms art world objections to any participation by writers in the government grant sweepstakes competition. Toward the article's end, after puffing Hawthorne, Emerson, and Thoreau, Kauffman wrote, "If . . . Melville can produce *Moby Dick* without Uncle Sam's patronage, then surely Robert Mapplethorpe's claque can express themselves without a government handout." Now the ninety-seven writers had become part of "Mapplethorpe's claque"! The *Wall Street Journal* published most of my letter on June 6:

I always find it either naive or stupid (or both) when the Brahmins of American literature, Thoreau, Hawthorne and Emerson, are trotted out to bash those who accept grants. Working stiffs they weren't. Emerson (as quoted by Mr. Kauffman) advising writers to learn writing in the streets, not college, may make a figurative point, but such counsel coming from the well-off and well-educated is a bit much. And to bring in poor Melville! After the economic debacles of "Moby Dick" and "The Confidence Man," Melville had to work for 20 years at a government agency, the Custom Office (a political patronage job). Perhaps if there had been a direct government grant to get back then, he would have had the wherewithal to publish another masterpiece in his lifetime (it would have been "Billy Budd"), the sort of work Mr. Kauffman, poor fellow, searches for in vain.

In between those two letters to the editors (Kauffman, after my letter to the *Journal* appeared, wrote me a note assuring me I was a "kept man" of the Bush administration) I watched Joseph Papp take center stage. There had been protests in Washington. On March 20, as Erika Munk reported in the *Village Voice*, there was "a many-sided counterattack against the right wing's attempt to dismantle the National Endowment for the Arts. From nine until noon, 500 arts administrators, most of them from small places on neither coast, sat in the gloss of Washington's Mayflower Hotel listening to inspirational speeches from pols and artists." But, at the end of her April 6 article, Munk writes, "I was surprised I hadn't heard of any cases in which people who received NEA grants refused money rather than sign the required sexual loyalty oath . . ." The choreographer Ferne Ackerman's gesture in March hadn't gotten much press (she was the first to turn down a grant), but Joe Papp, after skillfully orchestrating the New York media, especially the *New York Times*, for maximum impact, had the country (or, the small part that reads the *New York Times*) paying attention when he refused on April 26 the first of many grants the New York Shakespeare Festival was slated to receive in 1990.

But, here, I should pause in the chronology to bring up some earlier facts. The so-called Helms amendment resulted from the stink Helms and various right-wing mail-order cash Christian PAC groups made about the Mapplethorpe pictures and Serrano's photo "Piss Christ." One doesn't need to point to any other examples but the N.E.A. controversy to illustrate what a postliterate age we live in. The Literature Program is one of the N.E.A.'s smaller components, though it wasn't always that, and direct grants to writers are an even smaller part of the Literature Program itself. Why there were five hundred arts administrators down in Washington was because the N.E.A. funds organizations first and individuals last. It might be necessary to review the entire history of the controversy, but let my following short version suffice: Serrano/Mapplethorpe/Corcoran Gallery/Helms Amendment/"loyalty oath"/Karen Finley. There. The absence of writing in all this was painful, but our culture is not about writing, it's about seeing. (I was on a censorship panel in early 1991 when an Indiana state legislator complained about *Playboy* magazine and "boys' reading habits." "Seeing habits," I corrected.)

But it was ninety-seven writers whom the *New Republic* libeled as "lap dog[s]" and who were being compared by it, Papp, and others to McCarthy-era loyalty-oath dupes. The robber baron Jay Gould once said that you could pay one half of the working class to murder the other half, and it took no pay at all to get artists of one kind or another to denounce their various brothers and sisters. So I wrote a long article in April laying out what I thought was going on. Now, there have been a number of cries the past few years for "public intellectuals," and a lot of crocodile tears shed for their supposed absence, but it isn't exactly easy to be a "public" intellectual. It is not a supply-side problem, it is a demand problem. One needs to find an organization that has enough agreement or respect for your views to print them. You can be a public intellectual if you can locate a soap box and a park, but you require a private publishing concern behind you (or more correctly, a television network) if you want to become what society considers a public intellectual. Getting the article (which eventually turned into two articles) published was a humbling lesson in being a private intellectual.

Eventually, the *Nation* and the *Chronicle of Higher Education* ran pieces, two articles made from one, both in late June. But by then it was clear to me that being right had nothing to do with what was going on. In our society only cash aesthetics count. Refusing money is the only thing that gives you standing, as lawyers say, in the court of public opinion, even if refusing the money is the wrong thing to do. After the N.E.A. refused at the beginning of July to award grants to the four peer-review approved performance artists, a paradox began to become clear, which did alter, or slightly mute, the arguments about the loyalty oath, so-called. How could one complain about Karen Finley not getting her grant if she was to refuse the grant the moment she got it?

Here is what I wrote in the *Nation*'s June 25 issue: (*See pages 66-68 in this volume.*)

Soon after that appeared, the *Nation* sent me a long letter it was going to run, written by Mary MacArthur, a former N.E.A. Literature Program employee. One pertinent issue that was in her letter (and referred to in my reply) was edited out by the magazine. In her first paragraph MacArthur wrote, "I'm surprised that *The Nation* would give space—and, hence, credibility—to a piece so lacking in political perspective."

Quite unselfconsciously, MacArthur displayed one of the most pervasive forms of censorship in our culture. That of the gatekeeper. What I had to say shouldn't even have been printed! This sort of censorship, by and large, is more powerful and ubiquitous than the sort Helms has in mind. Overt censorship does not always hurt an artist. There is a long tradition of that sort of thing. Covert censorship most often does injury. I still find it difficult to believe that Karen Finley was "hurt" by her run-in with the N.E.A.—except, perhaps, by the unpleasant frisson caused when one is turned from a personality into a celebrity. But censoring is the first thing on former gatekeeper MacArthur's mind.

There is a labor/management split in the controversy that people did not, do not, want to face. Management, in the form of arts administrators—all who turned down grants, until performance artist Rachel Rosenthal turned down hers in July, were management—telling labor (various artists) what to do. As I wrote to the *New York Times* on July 10 (this letter too, not surprisingly, went unpublished):

All along, arts administrators', Joseph Papp-style protest of the
NEA has been misdirected and ill-advised, especially where individ-
ual artists are concerned. ("Some US Arts Grants Turned Down in
Protest," July 9, 1990.)

The peer panel review process needed to be defended. It was the
device that kept government out of the arts—at least out of the deci-
sion-making end. Far from being state sanctioned art, grants that have
been awarded by the NEA, thanks to the peer review process, have
been worker/artist sanctioned.

The so-called obscenity restriction attached to the current round
of grants is an unactionable mishmash, but those organizations and
their administrators (including choreographers) that have refused their
grants have elevated the "restriction"—by describing it not for what it
actually is, but what they fear it to be, or become—into just what
Sen. Helms and company wanted it to be. By turning down the grants
they have thumbed their nose, not at Helms and the Congress, but at
the NEA's peer review process.

Rachel Rosenthal, instead of refusing her grant (though I know
at this point in the controversy it was very tempting to be the first
individual artist to do so), should have organized the fourteen performance artists who received fellowships to pool their grants and
fund themselves the four whom John E. Frohnmayer turned down
for political reasons. *[And, two years later, something similar was
done by playwright Jon Robin Baitz, a 1992 winner of a $15,000
N.E.A. grant, who announced he would make two $7,500 donations
to two institutions denied 1992 endowment grants by the agency's
current acting director, Dr. Anne-Imelda Radice.]* That would have
demonstrated to Frohnmayer the necessary artists' solidarity and
productive collective action that has so far been missing from NEA
protests. Individual artists need to remember just whose slogan "Just
Say No" is.

The N.E.A. spends more of its budget funding institutions than individuals. (Given the N.E.A.'s present funding mechanisms, that is not strange.)
The institutions and their administrators have one view, individual artists have
another. Administrators worry more, rightly, about legal entanglements. Papp
personified one perspective: here was one hen with a lot of eggs in her basket.
Can they always keep track of what their chicks are up to? The way a manager
views such a "restriction" is different from the way one who is managed does.
Papp's management point of view was so consuming, he never even spoke to
one of the ninety-seven writers to see what any of them might think.

MacArthur wrote in her letter to the *Nation*: "He [me] implies that, by taking the money and continuing to write as he always has, he will be engaging in some clever form of civil disobedience that will counteract right-wing pressures. But civil disobedience has a tradition of overt action. A covert, veiled challenge—a 'we'll see what happens if they notice me'—stance is worse than meaningless."

I wasn't implying that—most of MacArthur's letter is a case of stupendous misreading, a depressing fact in itself. Two things I couldn't elaborate on in my brief printed reply (August 13-20, 1990): one, it is clear she doesn't even know I wrote *The Harrisburg 7 and the New Catholic Left*, as she lectures me on the subject of civil disobedience; and, two, that she considers writing fiction and nonfiction to be *covert* actions (including, but not limited to, it seems, articles published in so-called journals of opinion). Alas, in our postliterate age, perhaps print on paper *is* covert. Mapplethorpe and Serrano's pictures, Karen Finley performing—we are a long way from words on the page. I thought that writers, individual artists, could fight this battle better in the courts than organizations could against Congress, especially since they were using the N.E.A. itself as their weapon. (A Cincinnati jury refused to convict its museum director and a San Francisco grand jury refused to indict the nude child art photographer, Jock Sturges.)

But, the public face of protest against the N.E.A. had become, as I pointed out in my *Nation* piece, a celebrity face. Anyone who differed from the institutional line was to be tarred as a new McCarthyite.

Papp and MacArthur and others toeing that line walked right into a trap set for them by the new cash Christian right wing. Talk about "lacking in political perspective"! If one believes the country has, since Reagan's election in 1980, moved to the right, one might notice how Helms's moves on the N.E.A. were actually late in coming. The N.E.A. was a Johnsonian Great Society program (think back to those days!) and the right has long wanted to dismantle it as it has dismantled the other programs of that era: civil rights, affirmative action, and so on. Giving artists some money after passing the landmark Civil Rights Act back in 1964 was no big deal; it was small potatoes. And the evolved institutional structure of the N.E.A., chiefly the peer panel system, had left it for decades pretty well shielded. The N.E.A. was in place; the only way to move it, change it, was to create enough furor so that the structure itself could be breached. You needed its supporters, not its detractors, to do that. Joining Helms in his attack on the N.E.A. by refusing grants was asking for it. Institutions couldn't resist the bait, though it was obvious individual artists could. None of the ninety-seven writers took the bait, but writers received their grants early in the yearly dispensation. Institutions began receiving theirs later; they ironically stood alongside Helms and let his Trojan Horse strategy begin to work.

The Helms amendment, as stupid as it was, put the onus on the individual artist with the N.E.A. standing in between—remember, all along Congress was telling the N.E.A. what to do, not telling artists what to do: then the N.E.A. talked to the artists out of both sides of its mouth. And the "amendment," since it contained the Supreme Court's *Miller* language—"taken as a whole," "serious artistic value"—was no more than an impotent restating of the current obscenity law of the land. (Indeed, so formulated, even Helms himself voted against the "Helms" amendment.) Indeed, the other restrictions, the drug vow, no lobbying, no foreign travel, could be more of a potential problem.

But the power of metaphor, of false analogy, began to take over; it is difficult to track down when it was first used. But once the "restriction" was branded a "loyalty oath," institutional cold feet found themselves on self-righteous warm earth. For writers, such an interpretation was an affront to language, but once used, in our soundbite culture, the phrase became the received wisdom, and few supporters or detractors feared using it. One should be a bit wary if one's detractors are as comfortable with a characterization as are one's so-called supporters.

Refusing to take Helms's bait would be considered—by the same sort of false analogy—an appeasement effort, Chamberlainism, even though it was nothing of the sort. One has to have some notion of how government functions to see how misguided Papp's and his supporters' tactics were. Conservatives for some time have had more control over the N.E.H. (Mr. Cheney being the secretary of defence, Mrs. Cheney, head of N.E.H., being the secretary of the humanities) than the N.E.A., because of the timing of appointment cycles and so forth. (The right made an unsuccessful run at the N.E.A. in 1981.) When Frohnmayer was appointed, it was necessary to have some upheaval in order to seize more direct control of an agency that was, in the view of the Bush administration, going far too much its own way. Enter Helms and the religious right. One only needed the cooperation of the arts community. One reason it is difficult to track down the first utterance of "loyalty oath" is that it is my suspicion that it was an instance of "disinformation" put out by the Bush/Helms forces and swallowed all too willingly by a certain segment of the arts community. Once the N.E.A. was separated from the artists it had so generously supported (Papp's theater has received millions over the years), the strategy was unstoppable. Frohnmayer could take control, the peer panel system could be weakened, and the N.E.A. generally discredited among its most natural constituents.

On July 9, 1990, I was interviewed on WBAI in New York while I was teaching at the Bennington College summer writing workshops. I pointed out a number of things, one being that regardless of the blame Helms was receiving, it was George Bush who was behind the present effort. In his presidential campaign, Bush called for more "social controls" to stem the slide into moral decadence (Joan Didion records this in her *New York Review of Books* essay on the 1988 Bush campaign). I also pointed out the labor/management aspects of the protest, and, though I can't confirm this, I presume someone working for Papp was listening to WBAI and told Papp about some of what I said, because a week later, traveling back to the Midwest, I heard Papp being interviewed on NPR, saying perhaps individual artists should take the money, but that institutions should make "symbolic" protest by refusing it. That certainly was closer to my position, and Papp was finally articulating it. For some time, by then, he had had to deal with the paradox of protesting the peer panel approved grants being rejected by Frohnmayer and the usual rubber stamp council, while, at the same time, wanting to reject the grants themselves.

But, by the middle of July, it was too late. "Loyalty oath" was here to stay. In MacArthur's letter, she writes, "He [me] is wrong when he tries to convince us that the language in question does not constitute some sort of loyalty oath. What else could a vow not to violate 'community standards' be?"

That line was mysterious to me since the phrase "community standards" wasn't in the materials sent to me to sign. Later, in September, 1990 there was issued "A Report to Congress on The National Endowment for the Arts," and in an appendix it printed the entire text of Public Law 101-121—Oct. 23, 1989, which, under "(b) It is the sense of the Congress: . . . (D) That a commission be established to review the National Endowment for the Arts grant making procedures, including those of its panel system, to determine whether there should be standards for grant making other than 'substantial artistic and cultural significance, giving emphasis to American creativity and cultural diversity and the maintenance and encouragement of professional excellence,' (20 U.S.C. 954(c)(1)) and if so, then what other standards. The criteria to be considered by the commission shall include but not be limited to possible standards where (a) applying contemporary community standards would find that the work taken as a whole appeals to a prurient interest . . ."

MacArthur, as she pointed out in her letter to the *Nation*, was a member of "the recently-formed COWO (Coalition of Writers' Organizations)," and when the group first met "only three of those of us attending believed that it would be better were the Arts Endowment not to exist than to exist with restrictive language . . ." Perhaps the COWO early on got a copy of the complete law; but MacArthur appears to have misread even that. The phrase "community standards" refers to what a commission is to look into, not what a writer "vows." And even that is qualified: "shall include, but not be limited to possible standards . . ." Reading the finished report confirms my initial analysis of what Helms/Bush were up to. That this commission was authorized *at the same time* as the so-called Helms amendment (quoted earlier) should have been the story, not the bogus "loyalty oath." As I wrote in the *Chronicle of*

Higher Education, "Helms and company lust for control; the idea of censorship is merely foreplay."

Again, it is how one feels about grants and what one's opinion is on whether the N.E.A. should exist. MacArthur and others (Kauffman et al.) would like to see it go. They would rather leave it to the secret and anonymous philanthropies—Guggenheims and MacArthurs, those ruling-class organizations and the aggressive right-wing foundations who know how to keep secrets, that are practically leak free. (Right-wing foundations have been bankrolling the rise of the right wing intellectual [Allan Bloom, Dinesh D'Souza, et al.] throughout the Reagan and Bush years.) Or whether a more open, generally more democratic process of conferring money and honor (small honor these days and not so much money) is preferable. Imagine, all these years, artists have been giving other artists money. But, it is also the "honor" involved that bothers gatekeepers. When they don't have control over dispensing it, they denigrate it; that was what the *New Republic* was doing. Attacking *is* the flipside of ignoring.

One of the lessons of the 1972 Harrisburg 7 case is ironically apt. When that prosecution was launched, the Nixon administration may have hoped to win it. It didn't; there were only convictions on two minor contraband counts. The jury was hung on the major conspiracy counts, of planning to kidnap Henry Kissinger and to blow up heating tunnels and so forth. But the government's principal object was achieved. The Catholic Left, which had gained the moral highground in the late sixties and early seventies, lost that costly perch. Their moral capital was squandered at the trial. By the time it was over, they were just another footnote to history. Helms and Bush have won the N.E.A. battle with the help of the "defendants," a segment of the arts community that took the bait and waded in, self-righteously proclaiming that they weren't going to sign any "loyalty oaths," attacking the N.E.A. as much as they attacked—what, Helms?—Congress. Eventually, some court cases were won. The publisher of Four Walls Eight Windows press told me last summer (1991) at Bennington that, because of court decisions, the press was going to get the money it had turned down—the "restriction" being officially judged the gobbledygook it always was. Performance artists Tim Miller and Holly Hughes received grants in 1992, though in May, current acting chairwoman of the N.E.A., Anne-Imelda Radice, as mentioned earlier, vetoed two grants for two college art projects. Miller and Hughes's suit for their denied grants (along with Karen Finley and John Fleck) in 1990 goes forward. One result of the suit is that on June 9, 1992 a Federal judge in Los Angeles declared that the new "decency" standard employed as a legislative compromise violated the First Amendment by being vague and broadly worded. The denied four's actual trial is less certain to be successful. They, thanks to Frohnmayer, never got the grants. An individual's creative work (not his or her right to be awarded grants) has more protection than does an individual or an organization seeking grants. That is why the so-called Helms amendment was not to be feared as a loyalty oath; its language had not stripped any rights from anybody. What of course is most worrisome, but for everyone, not just artists, is how the conservatively packed Supreme Court is whittling away at the rights of all—the recent *Barnes* decision (1991), the nude-dancing case (which didn't attract any of the attention the N.E.A. controversy did), was decided in favor of Indiana's notions of public decency over the reach of First Amendment freedoms. And the Supreme Court in *Rust* (1991) has declared that the federal government can restrict through regulation what physicians can say to patients in clinics that have taken federal money. And Bush administration prosecutors want to use *Rust* in the N.E.A. litigation.

The N.E.A. successfully has been altered, become another agency now firmly under the president's control, as the special commission urged it to be: more power given to the political appointees, more messing around with internal structures, including diluting the peer panels' powers. The new N.E.A. acting chair boasts of her willingness to employ her veto power. And, just as the Catholic Left was smeared, the N.E.A. is now tarred and feathered in the arts community, thereby fulfilling the wishes of the private sector's gatekeepers. For the Right it is win/win; for artists it is lose/lose.

A lot of this involves personal insults. In the macrosphere Helms insulted the art world. In the microsphere the *New Republic* insulted me and the rest of the writers who got grants, then Papp insulted me and them, and then Mary MacArthur (and others) insulted me with their nitwit interpretations of what was going on.

When all this is remembered, if at all, years from now, "loyalty oath" is what will be recalled. That will be history's verdict. "Loyalty oath," like "test-tube baby," will be the catchphrase—though egg and sperm meet in a petri dish, but the phrase isn't "petri-dish baby." Rhetoric triumphs over reality. The far Right claims it hasn't gotten *all* that it wants, but the more sophisticated Right, George Bush's sort, is not too disturbed at how things are working out. John Frohnmayer was an early 1992 election year sacrificial lamb offered to the far-right-wing presidential candidacy of Patrick Buchanan. Frohnmayer, always demonstrating ambivalence, had become something of a born-again supporter of artistic expression late in his ill-begotten tenure. But his acting replacement, Anne-Imelda Radice, has no qualms about her mission and no need of direct instructions from the White House. "It wouldn't be necessary," she told the *New York Times*, "because those people know me and my work."

A curious thing is that I used to work for Joe Papp, back when I was a graduate student at Columbia University and for a while thereafter, but before I published any of the work that won me two N.E.A. grants. Being a low-level employee (props, carpentry, stage hand) Papp likely wouldn't have had many or any memories of me. But I have a lot of memories of him. (Regrettably, Joe Papp died on October 31, 1991, after a draft of this article was completed.) I was a working stiff; Papp hung out with the "artists."

In December 1990, The National Emergency Civil Liberties Committee (N.E.C.L.C.), on whose national council I sit, honored Joseph Papp with its annual Tom Paine award for Papp's untiring work on behalf of the First Amendment. I was a no show at the ceremonial banquet. And the evening of the N.E.C.L.C. dinner in New York City, when I happened to read the following in my local paper, the *South Bend Tribune*, after most of the N.E.A. controversy had died down, I had to smile—ruefully, that is:

> December 5, 1990. Almost one-third of the Public Theater's full time employees will be dismissed as of Dec. 31 to save money, Joseph Papp, the producer of the New York Shakespeare Festival said Tuesday. All 30 of the employees to be let go work in the theater's in-house shops—electric, scenery, sound, props. Papp said he decided to close the shops rather than pay a 5 percent increase in their rent, effective Dec. 31. Although the theater will send its work to outside shops, Papp said the closings would result in net savings of about $750,000 a year in operating costs.
>
> Papp has turned down grants totalling $748,000 from the National Endowment for the Arts this year because of what he called the "restrictive measures in NEA legislation."

To paraphrase Calvin Coolidge, the business of the arts is, more often than not, business.

III

FICTIONAL TIMES:
AMERICA, ENGLAND,
IRELAND

CRAIG NOVA

Craig Nova, 1*

T*urkey Hash*, the title of Craig Nova's first novel (the winner of the Harper-Saxton Award) is not a drug term. It is a bilious recipe of F. Scott Fitzgerald's found in *The Crack-Up*: "This is the delight of all connoisseurs of the holiday beast, but few understand how really to prepare it . . . it must be plunged alive into boiling water . . . placed quickly in a washing machine and allowed to stew in its own gore . . . To hash . . . a bayonet will serve the purpose . . . Hash it well! Bind the remains with dental floss and serve." It is a definition beyond any in Ambrose Bierce's *Devil's Dictionary*, and it is from this black lexicon that *Turkey Hash* finds its language.

Turkey Hash is a novel of growing-up that makes clear why so many young men are exceptionally well-prepared to fight a war in the jungles of Indochina. It does not treat the seductive milieu of most precocious novels of adolescence: in *Turkey Hash* there are no quiet New England hamlets, insular prep schools, ritual trips to the Sodom-Gomorrah of New York City; nor are there the village squares and rural bucolics of the Midwest, nor the turgid antiquities of the deep South. It is the bondage of childhood to be a slave to your geography and *Turkey Hash*'s is the blasted terrain of southern California. Nova uncovers it beneath the accumulated layers of pop cliches that have been heaped upon it; it is one thing to have lived there, it is another to have been born there.

The childhood he describes is a Parris Island of the heart ("We've got half a family, I think, all of the hate, none of the love"), though it will be recognized as definitive by thousands who have experienced it. L.A. for them is not a symbol but an actuality. All traditions are American: relics are the remains

---

* First appeared in *Mulch* 8-9, vol. 3, no. 4/vol. 4, no. 1, Spring-Summer 1976. Review of *Turkey Hash* by Craig Nova.

of advertising; sacred books, mail-order catalogues. A theology of objects has grown there; mythology has saturated daily life, but all the gods have been popularized. The world of *Turkey Hash* is a diminutive epic; the allusions are as thick as Milton's, but the grandeur is inverted.

Southern California is populated with senile children, and amidst them the young are left to act out a terrible burlesque of adulthood. All Mr. Nova's characters have Spenserian trait names, for his book is fable. The mother, Burned, is an epileptic, and the novel opens with an account of her seizure, and afterwards, "In the morning, shockwarm she stands in the hall. 'What are you doing in my house?' says Burned . . . 'It's Niles. Niles,' I say, 'your son.'"

Here is a family tableau, the mother experiencing another fit, the father, Hawkeye, "kneels over her, exposing the soles of his shoes, the bits of metal stuck in them from the floor of the airplane factory where he works. They look like bits of shrapnel. Sis lights incense in her room and begins to chant. Hari, hari, hari . . . I bite my tongue until it bleeds, pleased with the salty taste."

The narrator, Niles, is fourteen; he becomes a sneak-thief breaking into homes in the Hollywood hills. He is interested only in discovering a past, obsessed with history in a land that denies the existence of any: "I look for birth certificates, documents, secret plans, run across a pile of checks written over the last twenty years."

His father, Hawkeye (literary descendant of James Fenimore Cooper's, the alien who "conquers" a threatening environment), after these nocturnal excursions, awakens him by clicking a Halloween Cricket, unable to say his son's name. The lineage has stopped; a generation of strangers inhabit their homes:

> "There's a detective here to see you," he says.
> A man with a suicide-ledge expression, a shiny suit, and greasy hair sits on the couch, smoking a cigarette, avoiding my eyes. He fiddles with his tieclip, one that's about as wide as a carving knife.
> "You haven't got a thing on me," I say.
> "What?" says Tieclip.
> "I'm clean," I say. "You're wasting your time."
> A looney, thinks Tieclip. I get 'em all on this route.
> He ignores me and takes from his briefcase his samples of soap, perfume, brushes, depilatory, the Fuller Brush man's burden.

Niles rummages through junkyards: "I walk around rusting metal, washing machines, a slaughtered bus, think of a war cry, the scream of jets, Indians howling at the airport. I search through open engines, look for hints, clues, a residual patrimony."

Nova's prose deals with objects the way a sightless man learns shapes. Each scene in the book is raised by the dignity of its observations. The characters in *Turkey Hash* cling to each other with the pragmatic desperation of the random survivors of a holocaust. The casual brutalities endured by the narrator, Niles, are acts of affirmation. Pain is another part of the landscape and it is described as such: "I know there are dark bruises on my face, as though there were soot beneath the skin." Leaving his parents' home at seventeen he is initiated into a club. The rite, exactly described, could be lodged in the pages of Frazer's *Golden Bough*: "The rest of them, The Guests, run toward us, as though they'd been given a signal, swinging their branches . . . The leaves sting like vipers' mouths, bite into the skin, draw blood. The air is filled with moving clubs." It is the discovery not that two things are similar but that they are the same. Their lives are not challenged by the past, since they have none.

The book is filled with the startling poetry of the obvious. Niles, while working at an all-night gas station, notes: "The city wakes by color; dark sky, dark faces, garbage men sitting high up in the cabs of their trucks; yellow sky, yellow faces, Orientals in their pickups, buying gas for the lawn mower; white faces appear at dawn."

All of *Turkey Hash* is raised by its elevation of accuracy, things described so well that their absented humanity is restored. A whore's third customer, "walks now with a slow and careful gait, as though lingering sensation were a tub full of water." A misspent ejaculation: "It's like breathing. Molten pearl clings to her breasts, coalesces into shiny drops."

If *Turkey Hash* is flawed, it is by the weight of its own imagination which leaves it with an apocalyptical ending that strains the heightened realism of the prose. It is a flaw in steel though, and such structural falterings when they occur are referred to as examples of "metal fatigue," a wise understatement that holds true for this powerful first novel.

Craig Nova, 2*

The Geek, Craig Nova's second novel, is an amazing feat, an action novel that is entirely introspective. Set on the Greek island of Samos, *The Geek* deals with elemental relationships: The island is not only the setting but is also the novel's motif—a geography harshly limited, where only people can be driven to excess, since their boundaries are so foreshortened. "I understand now," Boot, the novel's protagonist, says, "money isn't simply stuff that changes hands, bits

---

* First appeared in the *Village Voice*, vol. 20, no. 44, Nov. 3, 1975. Review of *The Geek* by Craig Nova.

of paper and metal," but is something that leaves each "bill and coin charged by the agony of getting and keeping it." The island reduces life, brings the novel's action and characters into sharp focus like the measured reductions of a powerful microscope. It is a Camus landscape, but Nova's own.

Countering John Donne's famous cliché, Nova shows that every man might be an island, separated by perilous straits dangerous to cross. Boot, a displaced Californian, settles on Samos for a year, becomes an irritant the villagers accept. Then he finds the body of a mysteriously murdered girl and brings it into the village strapped to a jackass. This act of affrontery and trespass by a foreigner releases all the hidden treacheries of the island. Boot becomes the object of the islanders' revenge, and they, in turn, of his.

Each respective move is as significant as a chess game's; *The Geek* is not so much tightly plotted as it is committed to the outcome of its events. There are opium smugglers, bizarre carnival performers; the bearded geek, chief celebrant in this religiously ritualized novel, is a man "so far beyond self" that when he performed his debased communion, biting off chicken heads, "the men and women who watched him [did] so in silence, struck dumb by the spectacle, as though the geek were the animated remains of a saint, something more holy than abasement."

Had this novel been set in America, it could have taken place only in the rawest backwoods town overlooked by modern civilization. (Overlooked in both senses: on the island of Samos, Nova's only nod to the twentieth century is the radar dish turning on a mountain top.) Boot, while obsessed by his part in the ancient drama of fated revenge, becomes involved with Mara, another American, recently arrived. They discover each other as two creatures of the same species find one another in the dark. Mara has indeed been marred, like all of Nova's characters, yet "there was a used quality about her, but it enhanced rather than diminished her beauty, since it made her features appear faintly roughened, or diffused, or anyway changed as though her body had absorbed not only injury, but the kernel of vitality in abuse." And it is just this "kernel of vitality in abuse" that Nova gives (or finds) in all he sees.

The Geek resembles Jerzy Kosinski's *Steps* and recent *Cockpit*, in that the protagonist occupies a diseased world where he can be immune only by being entirely disconnected, turned into an amoebic island without linkage to any of the corrupt larger systems around him. Nova, however, lacks the relish for this experience that Kosinski displays. Nova's writing is so clear and precise that there is no distance between description and what is being described. An old woman farmer gestures: "Her hand had spent so much time in the soil it looked more like a root than flesh."

Nova's novel has the strange allure of sunsets colored weirdly by being screened through pollution. And the eighteen illustrative drawings by Brad

Holland make it one of the handsomest volumes published this year or any. Nova is one of the finest writers of his generation (post-World War II) and, more importantly, one of the few in possession of an entirely unique voice.

Craig Nova, 3*

Though Craig Nova is not a writer who has lacked critical attention, he is not a household word, and if you have yet to be introduced to his work, *Trombone*, his new novel, his seventh, is not a bad place to start.

Nova's middle novels, *The Good Son* (1982) and *The Congressman's Daughter* (1986), especially *The Good Son*, extravagantly praised by John Irving as "the richest and most expert novel in my recent reading," somewhat enlarged Nova's audience and reputation, and were departures in subject and tone from his first three novels, which, truth to tell, I more generally favor. His sixth, *Tornado Alley* (1989), was a transitional work, a slight defection from the upper-middle-class milieus of the preceding two.

But with *Trombone*, Craig Nova has come home again, and not just to southern California. His first novel, *Turkey Hash* (1972), was set there; the second, *The Geek* (1975), on a Greek island; the third, *Incandescence* (1979), in New York City; then the novels packed up and moved to rural New England, putting down roots on rocky, though expensive, soil salted through with deep veins of Faulkner and Sherwood Anderson. *Tornado Alley* was a restless novel, moving about the country, full of car romance (Nova is the poet laureate of American males' love affair with the automobile), which tugged him westward.

Trombone is Nova's homeboy novel, set in and around Bakersfield and Los Angeles, with two side trips, one to Las Vegas (that town being merely a gaudy appendage of L.A., linked by a highway umbilical cord.) And, in this novel, his characters, like a lot of people nowadays, have become downwardly mobile. But home is not merely individuals and landscape in *Trombone*; it is a return to the literary soil of southern California, too, the books and authors that supplied the texts for Hollywood's forties' *film noir*, the hard-boiled novels of Raymond Chandler and Dashiell Hammett; but instead of a mature gumshoe, in *Trombone* we have a young son doing detective work on his father, an arsonist named Dean Gollancz, who has the personality of the title's instrument, mournful, yet boisterous, hard and simple; trombones are just this side of bad taste, as is Dean Gollancz. His son, Ray, has a very private eye and

---

* First appeared in the *South Bend Tribune*, Aug. 23, 1992. Review of *Trombone* by Craig Nova.

follows his father into arson (and into an affair with his high school sweetheart, Iris), and displays a sensibility that is quite different indeed, more tremulous, very much in the string family.

The plot of *Trombone* is about as straightforward as, well, a trombone's slide; it is a tubular race track, and what goes around does come around. Dean, Ray's father, has been dealing with what used to be called a "sinister Chinaman," Mr. Mei, who doles out keys to soon-to-be-incinerated real estate. Everyone is trouble in this world. Nova's trick is to ice-skate on this desert of old movie cliches, and, for the most part, he manages not to crack the novel apart and fall in. *Trombone* is not so much a derivative work as it is homage; its originality is more a matter of consciousness than materials.

There are a few minor lapses that would subtly undermine a more realistic novel, but realism isn't what draws you to Nova's work (though *Trombone* is set around 1970, it's hard to tell). Nova is not, or not as yet, a social novelist. He's frying other fish. In all his novels there is a purposefully incantatory voice, with the deliberate intensity of a man with a tale to tell, usually the story of a bad accident, some witnessed calamity. That sort of hypnotic focus isn't always conveyed in brief excerpts; but here is Ray on a short detour as a freshman at an eastern college:

> Ray went to the river at seven o'clock each morning, when the water looked like a mirror from which a mist was rising. He rowed, keeping the pressure on the balls of his feet, the entire sense of the shell moving through the water coming almost as an oiled, fleshy push, the surface behind him marked by the roiling of the puddles where the blades had been. The puddles went two by two, and as they spread, with the pattern of water where someone has thrown a stone, the concentric rings interfered with one another. The leaves were reflected in the water: it seemed as though the river were on fire, the soldering-iron orange of the maples mixing with the yellows of the poplars. Ray passed over what seemed to be a chaos of flames.

There is an otherworldliness here, but it is Nova's own, not ours. And it attracts, pulls you in. All six of Nova's earlier novels are currently in print, in paperback, a rare feat for a serious writer of his generation. After reading *Trombone*, give them a try.

JOHN UPDIKE*

E ach writer sets his own pace, and when one has run a four-minute mile, what can be said when he jogs? Usually, that he is doing it for his own pleasure or purposes; record-breaking requires pain.

John Updike's seventh novel, *A Month of Sundays*, shows the author outfitted in a sweatsuit, loping around his block, waving to friends mowing their lawns. Updike keeps in training by writing ceaselessly and, tempted perhaps by contemporaries who publish whatever they write before it perishes, presents us with a book of thirty-one days, a preacher's sermonizing. The tale is simple if familiar: a satyric cleric banished from his flock to a rest home-cum-resort keeps a diary detailing his carnal transgressions. The *persona* of the Reverend Tom Marshfield is Humbert Humbertian. He's a cultivated flasher of language, though the jacket copy warns us that his style is "wonderfully overwrought." Since Updike's own distinction is his style, this caveat is puzzling. Updike has long skirted the possibility of becoming the Andrew Wyeth of prose, gathering the same large audience for the same reasons. He is undoubtedly our finest American writer when it comes to describing someone walking across a room. But to exaggerate his own rarefied voice is to babble, to produce a parody of himself wherein his best writing rears its head only occasionally, as when real faces pop up among a midway's painted grotesqueries.

Updike evidently wishes to be as prolific as Trollope, whom he obviously admires (and from whose Palliser novels he filched the *Redux* for the return of *Rabbit*). It was Trollope's remark that a novel should give "a picture of common life enlivened by humor and sweetened by pathos" that, unfortunately, gives a fair estimation of *A Month of Sundays*. When the first space colony is established, its population will doubtless resemble Updike's suburbia—so Episcopalian!

---

* First appeared in the *Boston Pheonix*, Mar. 5, 1975. Review of *A Month of Sundays* by John Updike.

This is an occasional novel, rooted in the mulch of yesterday's newsprint. The Reverend Marshfield is an odious creature, a *Bartlett's* of recent religious quotations, and at times Updike seems to share our scorn. *A Month of Sundays*'s principal text is SEX and "the adultery of the hopelessly married," but it doesn't reach the glandeur (the Reverend's addiction to puns is catching) of his earlier *Couples*. The cleric defaults on his wife with his church's organ player (Updike's language too coyly becomes a briar patch of wordplay—note the hay he makes with golf). The organist has found lost chords elsewhere, betrays him to his wife and, after he moves on to other stormy ports, betrays him to the Church hierarchy, which results in his forced march West, the desert, the rest/resort, golf, poker (poke her?), all overseen by a Ms. Prynne (patron saint of American women) to whom he addresses his jottings, expecting—correctly—her snooping. In the end his prose seduces her, though readers may not be as moved, perhaps because they finger the cold printed page and not the warm Ms.

The conventions of fiction fit so loosely that one suspects *Sundays* to be a poorly disguised essay on the present-day manners and mores of the "poor Wasp stung by the new work-ethic of sufficient sex . . ." Updike writes about his own prisoner of sex (though in this case more MIA than POW) and cannot—by habit or choice—desert a mode of fiction that provides so little because little is asked of it. The prose of the reverend betrays glimpses of Updike's true self only now and then:

> "I'm kissing my own cunt!" she signed unforgettably once when I fetched my mouth fresh from below and pressed it wet upon her own. The lover as viaduct. The lover as sky-god, cycling moisture from earth to cloud to earth.

And later:

> There is this to be said for cold women; they stick. So beneath our raptures I heard the tearing silk of infidelity, and she heard the ticking clock that would lift me, from whatever height of self-forget-fulness, on to the next appointment, and home, to check the patch of invisible mending on my absence.

The novel begins with the words "Forgive me" and one is tempted to overlook the overwrought goblet that provides so many cooling draughts. Updike's writing has always given me pleasure, but even if *A Month of Sundays* is more winces than winsome, read it. Updike is one of the four-minute-milers, and they are rare—though this novel, considering Updike's entire performance, is only an *entr'acte*.

NICHOLAS DELBANCO, DONALD MARCH, KATHERINE DUNN, ROSALYN DREXLER, KENNETH PATCHEN, HARRY CREWS, ROBERT HEMENWAY*

NEWS. By Nicholas Delbanco.
William Morrow & Co. 243 pp.

Nicholas Delbanco's fourth novel in about as many years follows the postgraduate lives of four preciously educated young men and their marriages, either to women or a cause. One takes to the Deep South to do research on an arcane historic episode when a black separatist state was created (which in Delbanco's rendering still remains remote in history). Another goes to California and sets up a revolutionary cell; he is a white leader who holds his authority over his black troops by superior karate techniques. Another, his trust fund in some precarious state, puts his knapsack in his Thunderbird and lives simply in Mexico, where he finds an illiterate beauty who dies tragically from painting the floor of their shed and expiring from the fumes. Another lives in Vermont and is referred to as a "poet and therefore unemployed."

Delbanco has one strong character in *News*, but he has drawn and quartered him to produce four: they do different things, but all have the same way of thinking. Delbanco creates this hydra, with short, well-done expository introductions to each chapter, over and over again until he establishes a barbershop mirror effect. He has retinal accuracy. The surfaces of these men's lives are completely there, like the small print of a medicine's harmful side effects. The last few paragraphs of each chapter begin to loosen up, a jar lid finally

---

* First appeared in the *Nation*, vol. 210, no. 16, Apr. 27, 1970; vol. 211, no. 5, Aug. 31, 1970.

coming unstuck, but then another chapter begins, and because there are several stories winding around one another, you never get to dip into what you've just opened.

Gifford, the white leader of the black cadre, lists (the skeleton of this book would be a list) at one time debits and credits: "Debits: too much education." It goes for the novel as well; this is an overeducated book: it knows too much, but gives back little insight. *News* starts everywhere and ends nowhere; open to any page and this is what you'll encounter:

> Harrison learned vanity at Wesleyan, the way to braid a rope as belt and paint his leather knee-boots blue. He hung a Sebring poster and a hunting horn above his bed, used a sea chest with an inlaid whale for shoes. . . . He blended Jasmine and Darjeeling and then Orange Pekoe tea, and barely passed physics and French. He drove one day to Plymouth Rock, with a girl called Corliss, looking for lineage in rain. They shared a Whammyburger and a double Shook-Shake, fondled slickers, did not leave the car.

It is the six o'clock news forever. News. The gram weights of objects and information decide a man's character. We know the elegant minutiae of the characters' lives, but when one commits suicide, another murdered, we are not moved. None of the men get beyond the age of twenty-nine in *News* and Delbanco himself is not yet twenty-nine; instead of turning out a book every year, he might, if he took enough time, finally write a good one.

THE STONE HUMPERS. By Donald Marsh. Delacorte Press. 242 pp.

The Stone Humpers appears to be a book by a self-educated man, and at times the vocabulary suffers from this, not by lack of words, but by the inept pairing of them, "frenetic homosexuality," "convenient persiflage," and by such writing as: "Mid-Manhattan. Streets and activity impossible to believe, easy to imagine, dull to describe." That is really a sinful omission, or admission.

The stone humpers exist in New York's damp Hudson Street area; they are the men who arrive for day work as movers, at 6:00 A.M., "beginning a new day. The fortunate, the old good hands, will work, the unlucky will sit bored, reading, talking, sit in a shoulder shrugging desuetude and wait." Into Danny's moving company, an illegal, nonunion limbo they come, the men who are heroes only in books; the dead who win posthumous medals.

People drop out of this book as they do in life; after a few chapters you vaguely recall (and with some regret) that someone is missing. Poverty shrouds each particular barbarity that these day-help Hectors and Achilles are involved in. A fighter who was never good enough to take a fall; con men so petty even police don't respect them. The men who get "'No raise. No promotions. Man you can't even get near that kind of scene. Just wages.' A pause. Seeming to taste something brassy in the mouth. 'What a word. Men get their noses rubbed in shit daily for wages.'" Marsh makes you feel that hard fact of life *hard*.

Danny, the prime mover, revenges the murder of one of his men by another, a Homeric killing where the victim is dragged behind the moving van-chariot along Eighth Avenue. Though they be the crassest of gods (revenge, eye-for-an-eye, hard-hat fatalism), Marsh believes in them and he brings a crude butcher's thumb to press on his scales of justice. Most of the book is written in telegram prose. No articles. And it is this primitiveness that matches the story pound for pound that gives *The Stone Humpers*, a book about shiftless movers, a moving quality. This is Donald Marsh's first novel. He is forty-two.

ATTIC. By Katherine Dunn.
Harper & Row. 134 pp.

Attic, also a first novel, presents a case of precocity that you can detect by its interesting spots. Miss Dunn uses her own name for her narrator, which manufactures that oxymoron, the fictional memoir. A young girl college dropout ("Don't you see I'm gifted! . . . I mean I write poetry and things . . . This magazine selling is just a joke because I ran away from college") is lost in a "dank and Independence November," locked in the Jackson County, Missouri, jail for many months for passing a bad check. Miss Dunn is slumming. She has a knack for withholding and implying, the stuff of dreams. Though *Attic* is written in the first person, it reads like third, so little do we get of herself.

"Miss Dunn" is given the chance to call a lawyer, and she calls the time instead. A recorded voice. Hers seems less alive. Very spaced out. While she is selling magazines to indigents in the Ozarks (with a detached heartlessness similar to a member of the Spahn Movie Ranch family), she sees in a hovel a "heart-shaped satin pillow from the greatest show on earth." Advertisement euphemisms replace nouns. A spare-parts imagination. Her scatological musings are as primitive as her cell's plumbing. "I never thought of other people wiping different." In the novel's penultimate sentence she is still worried about flushing a toilet and what for a few pages was interesting observation has long before revealed itself as complete obsession. The only thing she tries to come to grips with is her own carnality. After a dream of "pretending," it "makes me sick to remember in the daylight—shuddering hungry all through me and I lean my face against the cold steel and close my eyes until it goes away." Some of the description has a lewd eagerness to it, but it is pin-up girl forthrightness, eyes staring dumbly into the camera; behind the deadpan there is boastfulness. "I feel trapped in my own history—memory is such an aggressive thing—I have two lives—this still one in the cell where nothing changes and that eats at me—not what happened but what I can remember—there should be somewhere it turns off —" There sure should be: *Attic* is definitely a one-night stand.

ONE OR ANOTHER. By Rosalyn Drexler.
E. P. Dutton & Co. 168 pp.

As much as Miss Dunn's novel, Rosalyn Drexler's *One or Another* is perfected in its limitations. Like a café entertainer who needs only interest a certain group, she turns on a set piece, novel interruptus. Again it is the wavering first person, a strange radio station discovered in the early A.M. A teacher's wife is having an affair with a young boy. In New York. The time is the present (and how quickly it is going to become the past). The book entertains in the same way as do Miss Drexler's plays: chic, spiny attitudes that can't be touched, a porcupine's defense, since even the author won't embrace them, though she will espouse them. She satirizes a black high school militant (at her best at this), science, pornographic films, modish causes in a hide-and-seek fashion, since she's there amid them. For Miss Drexler it is not the banality of evil any longer but the banality of madness. "But then I can always live in my head. What I dream is infinitely better than what I do . . . the hazards far less." "Infinitely" in Miss Drexler's mind is the distance between channels 5 and 7. There are some people you would prefer being bored by than others, a just criterion for her fans.

AFLAME AND AFUN OF WALKING FACES:
Fables and Drawings. By Kenneth Patchen.
New Directions, 87 pp.

A short book that is even shorter than its eighty-seven pages. Patchen's rearrangements of old chestnuts provide a chest of nuts, but: "Better to be threatened with a bad rule than measured with a good rope." For admirers $1.50 in paper is cheap for a smile or two. The puns in the fables are largely visual, producing a "What Is Wrong with This Picture?" feeling. The drawings are put in a critical realm only because they are preserved: fossils of animals still alive. Patchen is a heckler of literature. This volume, nonce-essential, slyght, is in many ways a diminutive coffee-table book.

THIS THING DON'T LEAD TO HEAVEN. By Harry Crews. William Morrow & Co. 186 pp.

Harry Crews can write a simple sentence without revealing it to be a cliché. Since Gothic has come to read like New Realism, Crews's dwarfs, grave salesmen and Haitian mombos existing in Cumseh, Georgia, seem every-day in their dealings with Axel's Senior Club, where an attendant named Utopia can be "an expert on the mechanics of death. She loved the little smile that appeared on the face of the dead, loved it so much that she had gone to the trouble to ask about it and found its Latin name: *risus sardonicus.*" Not often does an author explain the expression that is on the face of his reader. Crews should spring himself from writing light reading: he wastes good lead on clay birds.

THE GIRL WHO SANG WITH THE BEATLES: And Other Stories. By Robert Hemenway. Alfred A. Knopf. 209 pp.

Collected, these stories undo one another. Mr. Hemenway's characters are brand-name mutants, dwellers in the East Side singles ghetto, whether mar-ried or not (usually it's the second marriage), are tolerably good-looking, and say such things as: "Enivrez-vous! Always be drunken, if you are not to be the martyred slave of Time! That's Baudelaire. Of course, he didn't mean only booze." Hemenway often glosses as helpfully. He notes symptoms, but can't diagnose. In the title story (which won the 1970 O. Henry Prize) the girl is observed: "sitting on the sofa for hours," watching TV, "wearing one of the at-home hostessy things from Jax or Robert Leader . . . Looking so pretty, and with those audio operator's black headphones on her ears. The sight made Larry melancholy and he continued to work lying on his bed . . ." Larry is translating Camus. Hemenway neither escapes nor inhabits his creations; the prose does not elevate or get under them. Most of these stories appeared in the *New Yorker*; at best they have the oblique veracity of that magazine's ads.

DAVID BLACK*

D avid Black's richly evocative first novel calls to mind one of those gymnastic feats performed by different generations of a family of daredevils, each member suspended on poles by another, all responsible for their collective safety. Individually they are the picture of seriousness; together (usually garbed in spangled costumes) they look ridiculous. But family solidarity is just that: absurd and grim. Black's lyric novel depicts such a picturesque tribe, though the high wire they walk is found in no circus.

The narrator, Dennis, a young man newly married and freshly matriculating in the counterculture's late 1960s back-to-the-land experiment, finds his hopes for the future rudely punctured by the past when his father arrives unexpectedly, having just "run away from home."

Their confrontation on the farm was an award-winning story when it appeared in the *Atlantic*, and, opening the novel, it has lost none of its power. Even more extraordinary and compelling than Dennis's father is his grandfather. Dennis is emotionally suspended between his two male progenitors, each demanding his love and respect. There is no Solomon here to settle the quarrel, except Dennis's own understanding and the aid of the women in his life. If Oedipus must kill his father, what is he to do about his grandfather?

It was probably impossible to balance the larger-than life portraits of the fathers with equally grand women. It is the women's sage counsel that provides ballast for the wild flights of the men (the women, ironically, are the strong, but not entirely silent, types).

The dilemmas of family are the most universal, and Black juggles these traditional themes nimbly. Like Turgenev's *Fathers and Sons* (which the novel echoes in both content and style), the social conflicts of our day are limned; Black reveals most accurately that the back-to-the-land impulse, was, of course

---

* First appeared in *Bookreview*, vol. 1, no. 3, Sept. 24, 1979. Review of *Like Father* by David Black.

deeper than soil. He, in fact, roundly chastises his own sixties generation by creating these venerable examples of fierce individualism, boisterous self-determination, and rebellious nay-saying, who have come, quite touchingly, to lead Dennis out of his own wilderness.

The prose of *Like Father* is sure, melodious and chaste. If anyone is looking for moral fiction, here it is.

JAMES CARROLL*

F or novelists there has always been the Ripley's-Believe-It-or-Not problem: truth has shown itself over and over to be stranger than fiction:
more vivid, alas, more imaginative. In consequence, writers have often cleaved
to historical sources; redoing dramatic public events has long been a staple of
popular fiction. Readers get, they hope, a ringside seat on *how it was*. Usually,
the events depicted are at least a generation old, principals dead and buried.
When recent history is used, the fictional device employed is the *roman à clef*,
where foolhardy authors dare libel laws and serve up "thinly veiled" characters
lifted from life. In some cases, *romans à clef*, key novels, are attempts at serious literature; the ringside seat books are potboilers, generational sagas, Leon
Uris-like fare. James Carroll's new novel, his fifth, *Prince of Peace*, falls somewhere in between the two types, half historical soap opera, half *roman à clef*.

The narrative method Carroll has chosen may have been the easiest, but
it leaves the novel with a plodding structure and a repetitive way of telling the
story, which is, roughly, the tale of the 1960s Catholic antiwar resistance, as
lived by the war hero, priest, and movement celebrity, Michael Maguire, told,
with some mixed emotions, by his adoring boyhood chum, Frank Durkin. The
novel reads as an informal biography composed by a friend, but a friend, unfortunately, who is not a likable chronicler. Durkin accurately describes himself as
"a two-bit professor at a second-rate college, a sometime contributor to small-
circulation journals," a fellow who hopes to write a novel one of these days, and
who is, apparently, something of an unexamined sexist, a classic homophobe,
a licentious prude, and, most injurious to the book, not a very good writer.

Carroll may have wanted to portray just such a person, but he certainly
risks censure (and a flawed book) when he makes such a creature his novel's
narrator. We are treated throughout to such gems of reflection and dead stick

---

* First appeared in *Commonweal*, vol. 111, no. 22, Dec. 14, 1984. Review of *Prince
of Peace* by James Carroll.

prose from Durkin as, "I was filled with regret, but also stern acknowledgement that opaque hardening is the only law that heartbreak knows"; and "Jesus was the ultimate Mister Goodbar."

The hybrid mentioned earlier, part soap opera history, part *roman à clef*, though a taxing form, can be handled dexterously. E. L. Doctorow's *The Book of Daniel*, which uses the Rosenberg case, is an example; but Doctorow keeps the central figures of his story intact and distorts the peripheral figures, while Carroll does just the opposite. His peripheral characters are true to life, but the central figures are distorted. His priest-resister, Michael Maguire (whose last name may be a dig at Cardinal Spellman's chancellor, Archbishop Maguire, who had a hand in giving Daniel Berrigan the bum's rush out of the country in 1965) is a Frankenstein creature: the torso of Philip Berrigan; the head of Dan; arms and legs, ecumenically, of William Sloane Coffin and Daniel Ellsberg; and the fingers of anyone's guess. For those familiar with the actual history and personalities of that period of Catholic resistance, *Prince of Peace* is an affront. Carroll can rightly claim that few know that history intimately anyway—and that his book is a novel and should be judged as such. But it is as a novel that *Prince of Peace* falters most: what is verified history is at least informatively retold; what Carroll invents is hackneyed and too easy.

The soap opera gravity of Carroll's reimagining of events and participants pulls all action and characters into the most predictable of orbits, rather than the weird and eccentric orbits of actual life. Popular fiction demands rather simple conflicts, but Carroll's model seems to be more an episode of *Dallas* than, say, *Gone with the Wind*. Father Maguire and the narrator form a not-so-classic triangle: they are in love with (and both eventually marry) the same woman, an ex-nun from a wealthy family. Maguire performs the original marriage cere-mony in some sort of sacred and profane version of a *ménage à trois* (overall, the sex in the novel is written in a romantic style where breasts seem always to be described as "flaring"). The FBI eventually makes use of the goings on between Father Maguire and the narrator's wife as blackmail against the hapless Durkin, who becomes, first an Iscariot, then a Benedictine monk.

Here is a sample of the dialogue between Durkin and his wife, Carolyn, the ex-nun, that takes place during their period of antiwar work. Durkin tells Carolyn:

> "You're an artist. That's the longing you feel, the unhappiness. You're not *working*. You must work. Your paintings are the opposite of war. That's how you resist. That's how you keep faith. You are an artist, Caro!"
>
> She leaned against me, and I felt the tension drain out of her. "You mean I can?" she asked, "I really can?"

"What, go back to painting?"

She nodded.

"Darling, you must."

Her arms went around me. "Oh, Durk, you know me, don't you? You take care of me. No one takes care of like you do."

"That my job, love. I'm your husband."

"You're my best friend."

"Same thing."

The novel doesn't improve much when we're away from domestic wars and onto the battlefield. Maguire's heroics in Korea, as depicted, are right out of a *G. I. Joe* comic book: "Why didn't the man in the chopper jump down and help him save Pace? But that was impossible. Still he started pleadingly up at him. Don't leave us here! He focused on the soldier's breast insignia off which light glanced. The silver cross. The man who'd been firing from the doorway was Father O'Shea."

There is a serious and important subject buried in the center of Carroll's novel; and, because of it, *Prince of Peace* is more disheartening than bad. At the novel's core is the history of the Vietnam war, told from a Catholic perspective, though one quite chauvinist; "given its peculiarly Catholic origins we should have" felt responsible for Vietnam, the narrator keeps reiterating. Where Vietnam is concerned, though, there is plenty of blame to go around. Most of this is done through you-are-there conventions, since Carroll makes young Father Maguire, newly ordained, the right-hand man of the aforementioned Father O'Shea, who is the right-hand man of Spellman while the Cardinal tours and wheels and deals in Vietnam. That material is the most affecting, since it reads, more or less, like straight history, not the chopped-up and rearranged story of the Berrigans and the East Coast Conspiracy to Save Lives.

Prince of Peace is slated to become a best seller (it is a Book-of-the-Month selection, has a "major" paperback sale), but I'd be surprised if it actually becomes one. Perhaps publishers feel, given the evidence of Father Greeley, that there is a large audience out there for romantic fiction about current and former priests and nuns, if there is enough sex and guilt in it. But it will not be the many narrative flaws, wooden characters, and lack of eloquence that may prevent *Prince of Peace* from becoming a best seller; more likely, it will be its one principal virtue: too much depressing and painful history about the Vietnam war, served up too plainly—and, in that case alone, all too true.

MARY GORDON*

T he late Jean Stafford told a friend the following story about her first husband, Robert Lowell. Lowell had converted to Catholicism at the time he married Stafford, and his romance with the Church was of sufficient fervor that it led him to excessive attentions to ritual: attendance at novenas, benedictions, early morning daily mass, and so on. After a while, all of these displays of devotion and dawn departures became a bit much for the feisty young bride, and she began to pack her bags, fed up with the new convert's enthusiasms. She was filling a valise, Stafford recounted, and Lowell rushed into the bedroom and exclaimed, "Don't go, Jean, don't leave. I'll stop it now. I've got the vocabulary."

Well, Mary Gordon certainly has the vocabulary, too—the language, signs and symbols of the Roman Catholic Church (though Gordon's father was Jewish, he—like Lowell—was an enthusiastic convert). Every writer needs a subject, and Gordon has laid claim to Catholic terrain. Her second novel, *The Company of Women*, repeats the narrative formula of her successful first novel, *Final Payments*. Both employ the Rip-Van-Winkle, Time-Machine, Wild-Child-of-Borneo principle: a character emerges from a grossly sheltered existence into a "new" world, appearing to be a primitive faced with outlandish customs, similar to the Japanese soldier found in the jungle decades after World War II who is then whisked off to modern Tokyo.

As one of the characters says late in *The Company of Women*, "Clare thought once more of the extreme parochialism of her friends," and so, once again, does the reader. *Final Payments* gave us a young woman who cared selflessly for her dying, devout, demonic father, and thereby missed the second half of the twentieth century. After her father went to his reward, she went out into the world, found it wanting, retreated into the care of a crazy old woman

---

* First appeared in *Nation*, vol. 232, no. 6, Feb. 28, 1981. Review of *The Company of Women* by Mary Gordon.

105

and, in the last pages, was, with the help of friends, about to give the world one more try. She seemed to be suffering from some chronic form of spiritual agoraphobia.

In *The Company of Women*, another young woman, Felicitas, grows up surrounded by women bereft of men ("All her life she had lived among virgins and widows. She knew nothing about life"). But these women do have a man at the center of their lives: a tall, handsome priest, Father Cyprian. Cyprian, for those who lack the vocabulary, was the first Christian bishop to suffer martyrdom—he, too, was a convert to Christianity. But Father Cyprian's effect on the women seems to have more to do with that other Cyprian, Aphrodite, the goddess of erotic love and marriage, since he is the surrogate romantic interest for the women of the novel's title. Father Cyprian rules their imaginations and something of their lives. He is their standard, the embodiment of what Gordon wants to demonstrate with this novel: how difficult it is for women to have an inner life that is not controlled by men; how hard it is for women not to listen to men who think they know more about women than women know about themselves. Her novel certainly demonstrates this dreary difficulty—if, indeed, it is central to women's experience.

Father Cyprian is seductive and tyrannical. A Father father figure. One of the company of women is briefly married to a madman and Father "Cyp" has him permanently committed, but when the woman, Mary Rose, later asks if she might marry someone else she has fallen in love with, Cyprian informs her that "her marriage to Burt had been a lawful one; Burt had not been insane at the time of their marriage"—something the reader knows is false—and "whatever God hath joined together, let no man put asunder." Mary Rose gets angry; Cyprian says nothing, whereupon Mary Rose falls to her knees and asks his forgiveness. Women spend a lot of time at Cyprian's feet in this novel. Felicitas, early on, thinks, "She wanted always to be there kneeling, looking at his black shoes below the black cuffs of his trousers and the long white alb."

It is hard, I suppose, to escape a working-class Catholic upbringing without nurturing the desire to be crucified sooner or later, but Gordon's women seem to have appetites whetted only for mortification. Of the women, only Felicitas has a fleeting experience of sexual pleasure, and she later thinks of it as "an odd disease, her adoption of sexual interest, but it was over now." For all the interest Felicitas showed in such matters, it was less a disease than a common cold.

Mary Gordon's characters are such a strange tribe that readers may be attracted to them for the same reasons the typical nineteenth-century reader neglected the best of Melville but sought out his early seafaring books: the lure of exotics, the freakish. In Gordon's case, she didn't have to travel to discover her curious primitives. If there were some Catholic version of an anti-defamation league, it might find something to object to here. The most becrazed antipapist would delight in either of her novels, though I don't believe that was what Gordon had in mind. It does take quite a leap of faith to swallow her characters whole.

The Company of Women is partitioned (it often seems some rough carpentry was employed to put this book together) into three sections, each section locked in a specific time: 1963, 1969, 1977. In the 1969 section, Felicitas, now a student at Columbia, takes a political science class and discovers that her professor is "the handsomest man she had ever seen." With soap opera predictability, an affair ensues. He is a bastard who mistreats her in a cartoon version of late 1960s born-again piggishness, asserting: "I didn't know what women wanted because I was completely out of touch with the feminine side of myself. Now I wish I had been born a woman. A black woman." He lives in a commune of four: three women and himself. (The parallelism with Cyprian is so crude you want to ignore it.) The professor is the kind of teacher who seems to know no more than his students, which might be the author's fault.

Though Catholic vapors are redolent throughout the novel, Gordon's Catholic women resemble not so much Mary McCarthy's intellectual coreligionists as James T. Farrell's 1930s men and women who were dominated by the Church—figures to be condescended to, helplessly entrapped by harsh, unrelenting dogma and grammar school theology. Gordon writes a leaner prose than Farrell (there are two or three bright patches in the book), though she doesn't often risk a figure of speech, which is good, since when she does we get something as ill advised as: "Felicitas said goodbye to Gidget with the vengeful edge of a lord who has sold his patrimony to a manufacturer of artificial limbs." Or something strained: "Like a homesteader pacing his land, she rolled down the car window." Or something commonplace: "Felicitas slipped in behind her mother like a spoon." Felicitas is supposed to be brilliant (she studies Greek and Latin), but she seems to be the quintessential "good student"—a mirror reflecting exactly what it has been shown. If Felicitas has an original thought in the novel, I missed it. It has been pointed out that the one character novelists can't create is someone who is smarter than themselves, but why do some novelists, Gordon for one, insist on giving us principal characters who are so much less intelligent than their creators?

There is a melodramatic scene in an abortionist's waiting room (Felicitas would get an F in contraception), and Felicitas flees, deciding to have the child "out of wedlock." She and her mother and her mother's circle of friends—those virgins and widows—retire to Cyprian's property (which the wealthiest of the women has provided for him), and the novel's third section commences in 1977, when Felicitas's child, Linda, is seven. Linda's thoughts occupy the last pages of the novel, and though she is but seven she has a prose style similar to

Gordon's. Nevertheless, those pages aside, the last section is the novel's strongest—at least some of the naiveté has departed.

Buried here and there throughout the book are traces of an interesting subject: Felicitas wonders: "Why should any man love her, having the face she had? She had no beauty, and she knew what beauty bought, had always known, although abstractly, for never in her life had anyone suggested that beauty would be her portion. Even as a child she had been valued for her sense." And later: "It must be that, like many plain women, I am overly impressed by beauty." If Felicitas has any claim on our sympathies, it stems from this largely unexplored, but nonetheless acknowledged, injustice—far from those conferred by church, state, and society: that women suffer more than men from the benefits so easily accrued by their more beautiful sisters (an issue largely undiscussed in feminist novels).

We leave Felicitas at around age twenty-eight, when she has become desperately resigned, full of bitter wisdom (think, all this because of one semester's worth of experience with men!). Felicitas doesn't practice what she may like to preach, though. The only men worth her regard are the beautiful. At the novel's conclusion, she is about to marry one, "the most desirable man in our area."

The Company of Women is not an advance—as I hoped it would be—over *Final Payments*: it stands alongside it. And though I am all for (relatively) young writers being encouraged, in this case, bad notices will not affect the novel's fate, since it is already a success (Literary Guild dual main selection, condensed in *Redbook*, paperback sold to Ballantine), and it will not be denied an audience. A certain kind of success makes you immune in this country, immune even from criticism, because once that kind of success has been attained, you are provided with a moat sweetly filled with the juice from sour grapes and no one can wade across it unstained.

Nonetheless, *The Company of Women* is a disappointing piece of work that inexperienced readers may enjoy (not knowing the same ground has been covered so much better so many times before). Mary Gordon once said within my hearing that she couldn't create a relatively normal, heterosexual male character, one who didn't seem twisted, misshapen. With the evidence of her new novel, it seems she neglected to add that she has the same difficulty with her female characters as well.

CLARK BLAISE AND MADISON JONES*

E ven something as neutral as placement side by side will invite compar-
isons, and, in this case, the two novels under consideration share much
more than mere proximity. Both have strong southern settings, both revolve
around teenage males suffering varying degrees of emotional aphasia, both
dwell on the cusp of violence (and finally wade knee deep in it), and both take
their protagonists no further than the exit of adolescence and leave them at the
entrance of what used to be known as adulthood. The similarities do not end
there. The strangest bond they share is that, even though both novels are written in a rather conventional—though at times quite lyrical—style, they raise
more questions about the nature of fiction than do novels written in experi-
mental prose. Usually the last thing I wonder about when I read a novel is
"Why has this book been written?" but both *Passage through Gehenna* and, to
a lesser degree, *Lunar Attractions*, bring up the question.

Perhaps one reason for the question is that the one thing literature suffers
no shortage of is novels about young white males growing up. And, in addition,
even though the novels each contain a modern element (*Lunar Attractions*:
transvestitism; *Passage through Gehenna*: legal abortion) the major portion
of their concerns and events could be taking place in any decade of the twentieth century. But even identical twins want to be treated as individuals, and it is
time to separate them. *Lunar Attractions* is more rooted in history, and time and
place are more particular and necessary to its story. *Passage through Gehenna*
has all the timeless aspects of parable and fable that its title might lead you to
expect. Its young man, Jud, is a sensitive nitwit, but a nitwit nonetheless, and it
is difficult to moor a long narrative to such a free-floating and empty-headed
boy. Why he does something is no more clear than why he doesn't, and the only
control you are sure of is Madison Jones's (who has written a half-dozen other

---

* First appeared in *American Book Review*, vol. 2, no. 2, Oct. 1979. Review of
Lunar Attractions by Clark Blaise and *Passage through Gehenna* by Madison Jones.

novels), and it is the logic of the storyteller that we follow rather than any logic the characters possess.

Jud is steeped in a hot southern brew of fundamental Christianity, odd zealots, witches and saints, the whole Gothic congregation. Jud gets involved with a group of pot smokers; this association leads, *Reefer Madness*-like, to ruin and perdition, and Jud is saved from a long jail sentence by a reverend and his young daughter, who befriend him and thereby set in motion more tragic missteps. The daughter, Hannah, for reasons unclear (except that Jud appeals to all women in the novel), becomes involved with Jud in episodes of amateur carnality, is made pregnant, which leads to her obtaining a legal abortion. To realize at that point that it must be the early seventies in the rest of the world comes as such a shock that it lays the author open to the charge of anti-southernism (affirming all northern prejudices about backwardness) the way some Jewish writers are accused of the most virulent anti-Semitism. Hannah dies. Jud ends up back in jail, but not before indirectly causing, in all, three deaths. The novel is told in the voice of a preacher who has gained Jud's confidence and heard his tale, though this device often strains credulity, even while advancing the Old Testament tone.

Hannah dies, not because of the abortion (which is quite successful), but because she is run over by a truck. She seemed to be a pleasant young woman—except where religion made her daffy—and the memory of her goodness finally causes Jud's eventual redemption. But, for the last seventy-five pages, as Mr. Jones sorts out the twists and turns of his neatly dovetailed plot, Jud is in a swoon state and doesn't know whether things actually occur or are dreamed up by him—and neither does even an attentive reader. The prose overall is skillful and, at times, evocative in the way it is meant to be, but it really is Jones's fault that when I finished his book I felt like I had acquired a knickknack, a weird curio with little purpose, at a Tennessee tourist stand. Which is probably why the novel was published by a University press and not a trade house.

Lunar Attractions has far more power and use, though I still puzzle over its genesis, though more because of regret at its missed opportunities than concern over its ultimate impact. It is told in a pseudo-memoir style and drifts from first to third person as it suits the narrative. There is one major annoyance caused by the voice: you get the early precocious years, plus the wisdom of reflection, but you have no clue as to what has become of the narrator beyond the years portrayed. The method trivializes *Lunar Attractions*, leaving its various episodes the charms dangling from a bracelet on a wrist attached to an arm to a body we never get to see. It makes the novel less than it could have been, and leaves it a series of scenes rather than a single sustained performance. And it is a shame, because the acts are all interesting. David, the young man, is the outcast genius who longs for normality while falling under the same powerful sexual spells of puberty that afflict Jud (though without the stifling simpleminded religious dualisms); David lives in a recognizable America (whereas it is Jud who is lunar and could be living on the moon), and David meets the vagaries of growing up with wonderful displays of attention and analysis. All childhoods are exaggerated by the simple fact of proportion, if nothing else, since when we are children everything is truly larger. And Clark Blaise has caught all this and more in his first novel. Blaise's prose is often a delightful mixture of clarity and precociousness: "Those perfect American lives terrorized me. I felt I had no right to them. They nagged at me like the nutrition charts that hung in classrooms, honored like dictators' portraits. Wholesomeness eluded me."

David's encounter with the high school tart (here is the transvestitism) is so well done that it doesn't defy belief until it occurs. *Lunar Attractions* contains dozens of remarkable scenes, and I would urge anyone interested in good writing to read it; I would have liked to have been able to recommend it unreservedly as a good novel, but it isn't. *Lunar Attractions*, in that regard, is as frustrating as finding the only copy of a beautiful book and discovering it has had its last hundred pages ripped out.

HUGH NISSENSON*

T he highly praised short story writer and chronicler of contemporary Jewish life (in the collections *A Pile of Stones* and *In the Reign of Peace*), Hugh Nissenson, departs in both form and content from his earlier work and has fashioned in his second novel, *The Tree of Life*, a mock document, a journal kept by one Thomas Keene during the years 1811-12 and presented to his son, Ezra, thirty-three years later "unexpurgated, as promised," to show Ezra "how your Ma and I come to wed." Keene then adds, "She [Ezra's Ma] has long since read it and forgiven me." There are a few activities in *The Tree of Life* that require forgiveness.

Today's literary writer is always faced with a dilemma: how to tell a story "realistically" while avoiding the nagging problems of conventional narrative, conventions that have been debunked and lampooned throughout the postmodern period by one's serious contemporaries but are still employed with impunity by lesser writers to brew up one steamy potboiler after another.

Writers of Nissenson's quality, those who value the illusions and effects of verisimilitude, have hit upon, in the main, two solutions: write in the first person (as Nissenson did in his first novel, *My Own Ground*), or travel back along fiction's evolutionary chain and do what Daniel Defoe did in the eighteenth-century—create the pseudoartifact, the journal of Robinson Crusoe. In this case, Nissenson has created the journal of Thomas Keene, a forty-year-old widower, former pastor, educated at Harvard College, who "denied [his] faith," became a "common laborer" and worked his way West.

The Tree of Life, as artifact, achieves a gritty, compelling authenticity by exploiting the pared-down nature of journal jottings, leading to the effective use of detail, such as found in the following description of the body of a man killed by snake bite: "Young Cooper, dead since 8:20 PM, was laid out in his ruffled

---

* First appeared in *Book World, Chicago Tribune*, Oct. 27, 1985. Review of *The Tree of Life* by Hugh Nissenson.

shirt, gingham trowsers, no shoes. His right foot and ankle were black and swelled; the skin was split between the first two toes." The last detail is the one that convinces us.

The "West" in 1811-12 was barely the middle of Ohio, and Nissenson's portrait of life on the frontier, as transcribed (as well as illustrated with primitive drawings) by the pen of Keene, is a long way from Louis L'Amour's—and more credible, though such a judgment depends on which author's vision of the old "West" a reader considers the more revisionist. Nissenson's world, Thomas Keene's world, is contemporary in any number of ways, even beyond the novel's stoic ironies, hard-edged prose style, and carefully rendered scenes of horror.

An up-to-date element is Nissenson's use of the truly famous as supporting characters: "Johnny Appleseed" is portrayed as a charming loon, smitten by Swedenborg, who is the confidant of the indigenous Delaware Indians. John Chapman (Appleseed's actual name) plays a pivotal role in the lives of the handful of settlers that Keene's journal records; Shawnee Chief Tecumseh and skirmishes of the War of 1812 also enliven their existence. Nissenson, through Keene, gives us the stink of the coarse, everydayness of these people: their food, shelter, business transactions, sicknesses ("the bloody flux"), and deaths.

Another modern element is the frankness (and their very inclusion) of Keene's entries on sexual subjects: *masturbatus sum* appears almost every other page, with noted time ("10:30 PM"). But the Latin is not a gesture of modesty, since Keene depicts in a manner more matter-of-fact than bawdy his encounters with Lettiece, a black slave, as well as his fantasies involving Fanny, his wife-to-be, recently impregnated by (though also the new widow of) the aforementioned Cooper: "Fanny will still be nursing after we're married. Her stained bodice, its smell excites & disgusts me."

Though all the sexual contract is described sparingly, the horror in the journal is more fully depicted: "The Injuns dig a pit deep enough for Jethro Stone to stand upright. Then they put him into it, hands tied behind his back, and rammed earth all round his naked body, up to his neck. His head was above ground. Immediately, the new moon rose—about 7:30—Tommy Lyons [a Delaware Indian] scalped him and there let him remain for three hours." What then follows is grisly business, indeed. Like many a contemporary novel, the violence in *The Tree of Life* is lavished with more close attention than any of the sex.

The Tree of Life succeeds in most everything it attempts, however limited and circumscribed its author's aims. Nissenson has produced a document as truly eccentric and provocative as a genuine one would be, if such a journal had been discovered in an old metal box buried deep in some damp Ohio cellar.

JOHN BARTH*

I f your heart doesn't skip a beat upon hearing the news that a new seven hundred-page John Barth novel has appeared, you may need some persuading to dip into *The Tidewater Tales*, his latest.

In a self-interview supplied by his novel's publisher, Barth asks Barth, Why another long novel, with "modernism gone the way of industrialism? U.S. literacy gone the way of U.S. numeracy? SATs down, VCRs up? Books out, cassettes in? Minimalist realism *si*, maximalist fantasy *no*?"

Though I assume Barth knows better, in the novel his narrator and alter ego, Peter Sagamore—*more saga*—keeps equating maximalism/minimalism with matters of length, whereas the debate actually has little if anything to do with length (there could be, though it is unlikely, a minimalist novel of seven hundred pages); it has to do with prose style and what the prose says. In minimalist fictions, ignorance is bliss: the less the characters know the better, and that goes double for the author. Maximalist prose tends to be richly constructed, high in vocabulary, full of allusions, redolent with metaphor, and dandy to read. Not just long as is, alas, *Tidewater Tales*.

Barth, whose work, from *The Sot-Weed Factor* (1960) on, was deservedly taken up by academic scholars, as well as the tonier popular critics, since the bulk of his writing reminded professors and high-minded literateurs of what they taught and studied—if that happened to be the early English novel.

But, unlike *The Sot-Weed Factor* or *Giles Goat-Boy*, this novel deals not with the late seventeenth century or the ivory tower world of universities (subjects that allowed those superior novels' form to somehow fit their content) but with the very contemporary 1980s, and the result is far too precious.

With great leisure Barth tells his droll, whimsical tale, every few pages stopping for lunch—"Chilled artichokes vinaigrette, salmon salad, Perrier" is

---

* First appeared in *Book World, Chicago Tribune*, June 7, 1987. Review of *The Tidewater Tales* by John Barth.

the typical menu—and if you accept "droll" and "whimsical" as complimentary attributes, you may well be amused.

The social concerns of the novel involve the CIA and industrial polluters; these pages are interesting, though they are but a fuller version of what Barth has already sailed through in his last sailing novel, *Sabbatical*. If you desire a shorter cruise through the same waters, look to it.

Tidewater Tales, above all, is a version of Barth's ongoing literary autobiography, clothed in the author's too reliable mixture of modernism and parody of eighteenth-century novels. Sagamore, a "famous" but blocked writer of minimalist (i.e., short, very short) stories is vacationing from his work as "an okay instructor in the art of literature from its manufacturing point of view and a first-rate coach and critic of apprentice writers."

But such employment doesn't always buy the sort of vessels this novel floats around in, though it's the younger wife's money (and family) that provides the wind for the story's sails. I am ready to believe that the denizens of Maryland's Gold Coast, the well-to-do of many generations who line the shore and sail the Choptank, are also the same families who run the CIA and the State Department as a family business rather than a government agency, but I am a little less ready to feel exercised by the skullduggery the narrator uncovers.

What does one get worked up over is four stories that intertwine, three of literary parentage, the fourth of spook novel incest. For the overread we get a reworking of the *Odyssey*, which will hold some pleasures for anyone familiar with one's Homer, and some interesting analysis of *Don Quixote*—characters from these works appear, or I should say, are "imagined," by our narrator and do double duty in his tale—and some captivating explication of the mathematics of reproductive cycles in *The Arabian Nights*, along with a rehash of CIA corporate toxic waste diabolicism.

Given the variety of the stories told, they are all *written* in a rather undistinguished prose. Barth has no ear, it seems, for any rhythms other than the regular uninterrupted cadences of waves lapping on the shore. And because a great deal of this novel has the plot of a country weekend estate novel populated by eccentric gentry— except that it is set in boats on the water, sailing being some eastern shore version of Going to the Hounds—it at times reads as if it had been written by J. P. Donleavy on lots of downers.

In *The Tidewater Tales* Barth doesn't convey experience, he just tells us about it. Sagamore remarks, in a Don Quixote phase—"he is able to enjoy the passing scenery and the bright sunshine—if that is the word for a clean light that seems to come from everywhere and nowhere like the glow of lucid prose." A glow that one longs to observe in these pages. There is lucid prose, but no glow.

The result is maddening; stories told second, third, fourth hand, in the stodgiest of narrative styles by a congenial host aboard a splendid sailboat. But if the reader is in a chair at home and not under the spell of such lavish hospitality, such glorious scenery, such wonderful weather, the stories can be easily pronounced tedious. Whereas, if we were shipboard guests, enjoying all of the good cheer, we might well find each long tale charming indeed. Pass the chilled artichokes vinaigrette, please. What? This is just a story and not life? What a disappointment.

GORDON LISH*

O ne of the commonplaces of late twentieth-century fiction is that the horrors of real life outstrip the imaginations of writers, and, as a consequence, those who write about *real life* are often fascinated by the horror they see, since they are unable to top it, invent better, be *that* imaginative. It is not puzzling that any number of sophisticated writers dote on murder and mayhem, summoning their descriptive powers to show just how macabre violence is.

Writers' pens are turned into the tools of microsurgery, and readers get to see it all, enlarged, examined with care. Not just a film clip of savagery, but a dissection, where the process of fiction becomes autopsy, not on the pitiful corpse, but on just how the wounds are inflicted. It's a literary version of if-you-can't-beat-them-join-them. If you can't leave the war to the generals, then you can't leave the crime to the criminals, murder to the merely vicious.

Gordon Lish's second novel, *Peru*, is similar to his first, *Dear Mr. Capote*, in that it uses the voice of a cracked persona throughout to tell its tale. But if you don't feel comfortable reading the monologues of psychotic characters, especially ones who are not particularly articulate, you will not find *Peru* an entirely rewarding experience.

There is much less opportunity for satire in this novel than in *Dear Mr. Capote*, since, in *Peru*, Lish tells the story of a six-year-old boy who kills a six-year-old playmate in a sandbox with a toy hoe. (The novel is dedicated to, among others, a boy who died at the same age and shares the same name as the character killed in the novel.) Child murder by children doesn't lend itself to black humor as easily as adults murdering adults may.

The novel begins with a confused (and confusing) telephone call to a television station by the narrator, who is trying to discover where a news clip of violence originated (Peru, it turns out). The novel then becomes a rambling,

* First appeared in *Book World, Chicago Tribune,* Feb. 2, 1986. Review of *Peru* by Gordon Lish.

pedestrian account of that same night when the fiftyish protagonist is packing for his young son's trip to camp, interlaced with his remembrances of the 1940s, when he killed the boy in the sandbox.

Those recollections are bathed in the consciousness of the protagonist's six-year-old self and do, at times, capture a child's nostalgia for the period: big Buicks, dotty nannies, "colored" men, early sexual humiliations, the rich and not-so-rich: "I tell you, when you live next door to someone richer, there is no end to what will enter your thoughts."

Gordon Lish, as his publisher's publicity correctly says, "has been a force on the contemporary writing scene" for quite some time, as fiction editor at *Esquire* during the late sixties and early seventies and now as an editor at Alfred A. Knopf. He has played a role in making a number of writers fashionable, as well as in shaping the tastes of a generation of readers. One may conclude that when such an editor turns to writing novels well along in his career, the fiction he writes is likely to reflect what he thinks of the present state of the art. If so, Gordon Lish thinks it's in a bleak and sorry state, indeed.

Peru is not a pleasure to read. The fascination of writers with the truly horrible has, at best, the same moral implications and purposes of, say, Goya's series of etchings on war: his depictions of impaled and rotting men, women, and children are drawn so wonderfully that the eye can't resist them. In the late twentieth century, though, the eye tries to resist all it can. As the book's narrator states, "Nothing is not seen, nothing is not heard." He goes on to say, "I believe that there is no one who does not know everything—even the dumbest person."

And many writers have taken it upon themselves to enliven the imaginations of the dumbest as well as the smartest by attempting to imagine the worst things for them, such as what you get to see when you kill a child with a toy hoe: "You have to imagine dents—like a trench—in his hair, in his head. Whereas with his face, it was more like a peach pit with some of the peach still left on it."

Given Lish's demonstrated acumen as an editor, it would be difficult to imagine that he would have selected this particular novel to publish himself. *Peru* is desiccated, airless, joyless—though that is probably just what the author intends. We are all child murderers is its text. As his narrator remarks, "It doesn't pay to keep thinking about a thing like this."

THOMAS MCMAHON*

Thomas McMahon's new novel, *Loving Little Egypt* (coming after the highly acclaimed *Principles of American Nuclear Chemistry: A Novel* and *McKay's Bees*), is a delightful tale, full of charm—of the sort we all recognize as enchantment and as the kind of attraction physicists felt for quarks when they termed some of them "charmed." That this novel has both types of charm is not strange, considering that its author has a Ph.D. in fluid mechanics from MIT.

Loving Little Egypt is set in the 1920s, and McMahon makes use of imaginative characters, ones real and made up, people whose lives are part of American folklore: Alexander Graham Bell, Henry Ford, Thomas Edison, William Randolph Hearst, and lesser-known figures who, though they are cast in the shadows of the brighter names they are associated with, are responsible for much of our modern world. All these actual lives are, each in their own way, fantastical, but McMahon manages to do two amazing things with them: he makes the individuals more human while he makes their goings-on even more bizarre.

The novel's protagonist, the character with charm, is Mourly Vold, a nearly sightless prodigy, a student at a school for the blind, who possesses something of the genius of a present-day whiz-kid computer hacker.

Mourly also has a gift for mimicking sounds, and he discovers a way to patch into and manipulate the nation's young telephone company; there he creates his own world, a plane of voices, wherein live the denizens of other schools for the blind and impaired—youngsters with names like the Syracuse Stallion, Beetlejuice, and Billy the Boozer.

But it is principally the author's own charm that holds sway over the novel. His story makes ample use of the social history of the jazz age, and *Lov-*

* First appeared in Tribune *Books*, *Chicago Tribune*, Feb. 22, 1987. Review of *Loving Little Egypt* by Thomas McMahon.

ing Little Egypt turns into a slam-bang adventure tale (complete with *Ghost Busters*-like death rays), as Mourly and his friends are pitted against Ford, Edison, and Hearst for control of the telephone company and preservation of the American way of life. It is amazing to see how much mayhem and confusion can be wrought by Mourly and his improbable gang; he uses the hardware and technology of the phone company as a single device, and it becomes a terrible one.

Along the way Mourly himself becomes a notorious figure, wins the love of a wonderful woman, gains as allies and friends Alexander Graham Bell and his deaf wife Mable in his attempt to outwit the robber barons who want to ignore Mourly's warnings and predictions.

For a novel full of ideas, it is at the same time set in a very palpable world. Here is Mourly, atop a telephone pole, set to do mischief: "He discovered himself helpless. The moon vanished behind a cloud and with so little light he could see next to nothing. He found the wires by listening to them—the wind made them reveal themselves. They struggled when he touched them. Terrible forces pulled on them. It was as if every human being in the world were on the other end of the wires, pulling them out of his hands. The wind set mechanical shocks flying up and down their length. Then the sky cleared for a moment, and with the moonlight so strong he could see well enough to complete his splices."

McMahon's novel has its own mechanical shocks flying up and down its length; it is, beneath the colorful crustation of eccentricities and melodramatic spectacle, an allegory of responsibility, a treatise on scientific and inventive duty. The telephone company stands as an unspoken parody of less seemingly benign inventions, nuclear power plants and bombs.

Mourly is Little Egypt, a nickname he takes after he looks through an Edison Kinetoscope and sees one of Edison's hired dancers. By "clipping his homemade double-lens system to his spectacles and pushing it down into the eyepiece of the Kinetoscope, a queer and happy optical accident allowed him to see the scene. The image flickering in front of his eye appeared to him clearer than anything he had ever seen in real life." But Little Egypt is also symbolic: it is, like the dancer Mourly sees, what is intrinsically lovely when viewed clearly. For Mourly, and many scientists, it is often ideas, pretty ones, that they especially love. And this novel's world of handicapped premature "phone phreaks" reminds us that we all do not see clearly, especially when we look at history, except by queer and happy accident.

Henry Ford and Edison, especially Edison, are the chief villains in McMahon's Kinetoscope: businessmen who distort what others may know but are too handicapped (by ideals, a sense of charity, a lack of ruthlessness) to employ. Separating what is actually historical fact in this novel from what is invented is beside the point, it all seems too true.

"Loving Little Egypt" has a happy ending, of sorts; for as the novel delights in its own power to make the grim amusing and the dour delightful, it leaks its own positiveness onto the reader, lighting the air around him like the "electric wind" that fascinates Mourly.

JAMES T. FARRELL*

F rom a detached and rather cool third-person point of view, the reader observes Joseph "Dopey" Carberry shamble into the dining room of his Uncle Mike's and Aunt Anna's home and sit down to eat, only to begin yet another Saturday night of bickering and blathering with his relatives. Dopey and his two sisters have been living with their aunt and her brother since their father remarried. He is harangued by all assembled for his shiftlessness. His Aunt Anna directs the abuse: "We've helped him, fed him, clothed him, waited on him, coddled him, tried to point the right way out to him, but it's just not in his bones." Dopey hardly listens; he silently laments his lack of "two bucks to lay on Red Pepper after Len had come around the corner with that hot tip," earlier in the day. He eventually offers some excuses and evasions for his lack of energy, and his aunt retorts: "Yes, I know what you want. A banker's job from twelve to one, with an hour for lunch." Given the brevity of the scene, there is more satire displayed than bathos, and the bigotry and corruption of their milieu are deftly sketched.

In the second scene (there are ten in all, matching the straightforward chronology of the evening), Uncle Mike counsels young Joe (who, since quitting high school has had a number of jobs—one of which he describes as "a slave factory for dopes"—and a period of vagabondism) to change his ways, and Dopey tells him, "I'd like to go back to sea or else be a bookie." Through a ruse, Dopey then manages to borrow five dollars from his uncle.

Phil Garrity arrives in the fourth scene, looking like a "Big Shot," as Dopey's sister Kate tells him. "Why, Phil, you're all togged out like Joe College." Phil has just made a large amount of money "legit," playing the stock market with money from his La Salle Street job, and has just purchased a new used car, a Lincoln. He is attracted to Kate but has not gone out with her for six

* First appeared in *Masterplots II: The Short Story*, edited by F. Magill, Salem Press 1986. An "analysis" of James T. Farrell's short story "Saturday Night."

months. He and Kate banter about dating, but Phil is not able to extract a commitment from her. He and Dopey go out for a night on the town, and, through scenes five and six, the third-person point of view severs its attachment from Dopey and secures itself to Phil, who thenceforth assumes the position of protagonist. Farrell manages this switch rather smoothly, since it coincides with a change of location, from inside to outside.

Phil and Dopey drive to the corner of Sixty-third and Stony Island, where it is "bustling with Saturday-night activity, crowded with people, noisy with the traffic of automobiles and streetcars." They join a crowd outside a drugstore, and Phil muses on his lack of success with women, his hopes for marriage to Kate, her lack of interest in him, wishing all the while that he could be "wild, carefree, dashing, romantic, brave, a guy who didn't care two hoots in hell for anything in the world."

After picking up some speakeasy gin, as well as another friend, Marty, they "put their liquor in their pockets and left to see Jack Kennedy." Kennedy's apartment, where "most of the space is taken up by a wide in-a-door bed, which was unmade," is full of the din of single young men recounting old times and former glories, their unsatisfying work and lack of money. The dialogue is brisk and fresh throughout. Phil yearns for Kate and is sent out to buy more liquor.

After his return, Phil, Dopey, and Jack set off for the whorehouses of Twenty-second Street and Red Murphy, another acquaintance of their big-city—yet excruciatingly tiny and parochial—world, staggers up to them as they are getting into Phil's new car. As Phil drives badly down the Midway, the essential realism of Farrell's style keeps this foreshadowing from being too heavy-handed when the remains of an earlier wreck catches their eyes and they stop and survey the debris. "There's a lot of blood in one person. This blood might mean just one poor sonofabitch killed," Red comments.

The drunken men arrive at the "Sour Apple" on the near North Side, a tearoom and dance hall with a bohemian reputation. Phil hesitantly asks a young woman for a dance, and she "acted as if she had not heard him. He repeated it, humiliation eating inside of him." Rejected, he retreats into further reveries of Kate and unintentionally insults a husky lad by telling him that he "can't dance to the Notre Dame *Victory March*." A brawl commences. When the club's proprietor asks what started the fight, a denizen of the Sour Apple explains, "Four drunken Irishmen with liquor, four sober Irishmen with girls."

Unable to secure pickups at the Sour Apple, the four friends depart and find the brothels on Twenty-second Street closed by an unexpected police raid. They do manage to pick up four older women who are leaving a nearby dance hall. With Phil at the wheel, they drive out to the country fields. "Large shadows raked the road, and the car whipped on." After a few miles it smashes head-on into a Cadillac "going as swiftly as Phil's Lincoln."

Phil and one of the women disentangle themselves from the wreckage, and Phil drags her, dazed and drunk, into the fields, where they are found later by the police with their britches down—an effective, if moralistic, yoking of sex and death. "You ought to swing for this, you sonofabitch," the cop tells Phil. The bodies of Jack and Dopey are pulled out of the car. Phil is left delirious and uncomprehending.

"Saturday Night" repeats many of Farrell's central concerns and subjects. His fictional world, the cosmology it describes, echoes, in many ways, the teaching that was instilled in him as a boy growing up in a Roman Catholic family and attending parochial schools on the South Side of Chicago in the early twentieth century. There is a sense of predestination and original sin with which all his characters come equipped, though Farrell's own attitude seems to be one of alternating cynicism toward and respectful anger at this worldview. Dopey does not elicit much sympathy in Farrell's depiction; his death, though, is a consequence of his closest friendship, albeit a friendship of convenience and exploitation on Dopey's part. Phil is trapped in his own unrequited longings and sexual inexperience and ambivalence, the perpetual boyishness visited upon most of Farrell's male characters, and he becomes the agent of destruction. Farrell has retained a good bit of the Catholic puritanism of his youth. Phil's sexual initiation is only accomplished at dire cost. Both society and Farrell disapprove of the boys' behavior.

Farrell reveals his own ambivalence as a left-wing social critic in "Saturday Night." The most amusing lines are given to Aunt Anna, a conservative scold, and to the habitué of the Sour Apple, Wolcroft, a self-proclaimed poet. In addition, Danny O'Neill, Farrell's closest counterpart in the O'Neill pentalogy of novels, is spoken of at Kennedy's apartment as a "cracked socialist" who "was trying to write books," and the terrible fate of the young friends is presented not in the language of Marxist determinism (these young men all being sacrifices to alienated labor and the inexorable march of capitalism) but according to Farrell's own personal determinism, which he is exercising over the blockheads of his youth who did not appreciate the special young man whom they had in their midst. The Sour Apple, indeed: "Saturday Night" could be described as a mixture of sour grapes and bad apples.

James T. Farrell has never been praised as a stylist; in fact, he is often described as an undistinguished writer of prose. His power comes, as it does with many American writers, from sheer force and accumulation, the command and sweep of factual material that does not need or solicit strenuous interpretation (though the car crash could be viewed as an allegory for the stock market crash to come). Farrell overwhelms the reader with the visceral, with what he describes, somewhat mockingly in "Saturday Night," through the words of poet Wolcroft, as not just "realism. That's old-fashioned. My poetry, now it's superrealist." Farrell's early naturalistic writing was in the mainstream and remained fashionable until that stream was thoroughly diverted and rechanneled after World War II.

Farrell, though he wrote many short stories, was not so much a master of the form as its earnest supplicant. The stories he wrote that were short enough became short stories instead of novels. Farrell had a novelist's skill at synthesizing but also the novelist's appetite for size, for the repetitive scene; the short story form does not profit from that sort of segmentation. Farrell's stories are often novels in miniature, rather than short stories in full bloom—although "Saturday Night" is one of his most effective, rich with humor, energy, and life, not simply scenes from a novel writ small.

JOSEPH CALDWELL AND JAMES REID*

The two novels at hand deal with murder and death, corruption and innocence, love and lust. Priests are central characters in both, and whenever
there is a priest in fiction there is the possibility of a great fall (for he is a figure
elevated with lofty assumptions.) There are fewer resemblances than differences in the novels, and though neither is very good (*The Offering* is dreadful)
they do illustrate a curious fact.

The Offering is a potboiler of the worst sort; unbelievable people are
drawn in dead-stick prose, but the plot they till is thick with important issues
and events: contemporary Irish and American politics, terrorism and the IRA,
the complicities of church and state, splashed on the grand canvas, where the
world's a stage. As *The Offering* is profligate, *In Such Dark Places* is chaste: its
prose is careful and clean; the characters depicted are marked individuals, lives
judiciously examined. But what occurs, the activity itself, is the cliché. Joseph
Caldwell, a playwright whose first novel this is, has constructed a delicate
machine that ticks; James Reid, in *The Offering*, a tall, ugly edifice that collapses. The curious fact these books illustrate is this: the hack writer will more
often appropriate large, powerful events to fuel his crude machine, whereas the
careful, deliberate craftsman, such as Caldwell, will seem to be limited by his
prudence and be left with the smaller bite of experience his own life has provided.

In Such Dark Places is set in a section of New York City's lower East
Side, the part which for a brief period was christened the "East Village." It is
still unredeemed by the middle class; there the poor are always. Eugene, the
novel's elliptical protagonist (we rather sketchily, but never satisfactorily, get
his history) is an aspiring photographer, a just uncloseted homosexual, and—
more puzzling—a *recent* fallen-away Catholic. In one of the novel's least ele-

---

* First appeared in *Commonweal*, vol. 105, no. 14, July 21, 1978. Review of *In
Such Dark Places* by Joseph Caldwell and *The Offering* by James Reid.

gant patches of prose we learn (after a homosexual encounter in a Bowery shelter): "Somewhere around this time, Eugene stopped going to Mass and to the Sacraments, not as a conscious decision, but out of perplexity. He no longer had any sense of where he stood among men and God, and the placement bureau within him seemed to have shut down without notice."

The novel begins with a Good Friday procession, which Eugene photographs, that erupts into a melee, ending with a murder and a theft (the murder of a teenage boy Eugene had developed an interest in, and the theft of his camera with the pictures of the parade and perhaps of the killing). The plot turns into a detective story (Will the camera be recovered? Will the killer be identified?); but it pales, or rather, falls into the shadows cast by Caldwell's fastidious rendering of the quotidian. The novel is told in practically unlapsed time, which provides needed momentum. Along the way Eugene's sexuality is confronted, and he grapples with the loss of faith and the gains of carnality. They both traffic in a good deal of religious symbolism, if not content. "Murder, thought Eugene, jealousy, revenge, all aroused by sex. But was there even more to it than that? As he had lain there in the nighttime dark, there came to him as well his wish from the Saturday procession, that Johnny thrust all his strength, not at the cross, but at him, so that after his orgasm of fury the youth would lie conquered and spent, helpless and defeated. A kind of castration, a kind of death." Actually, Eugene seems more in the need of a therapist than a priest.

The boundaries of the novel are small (the lower East Side is not left); and what climatical acts occur are committed upon sundry bodies, since they are the novel's true territory. The most compelling character is the priest, Father Carusone, only because he, at least, is always saying the unexpected. He, unfortunately, is not the main character; it is Eugene, who carries the unhappy flaw of a protagonist who is not as intelligent as his author.

The Offering's priest is Tom O'Neill, tall and handsome, though we learn late in the novel that he has never kissed a girl, until he meets the IRA tootsie Mara MacRaimond (modeled in a wacky way after Maria McGuire, author of *To Take Arms: My Year with the IRA Provisionals*).

Father Tom (who is something of an Uncle Tom) collects money in America for the IRA—and as portrayed, a murderous lot of shanty Irish are they—and then is shocked that a million dollar contribution (arranged most nefariously by the State Department) he has received is a gangster's tainted money, so he righteously intends to return it, setting off a domino theory of murder and mayhem. It is part of Father Tom's irking innocence that he never considers that *anybody's* million dollar contribution would be tainted money— behind every fortune there is a crime and so forth. But that, and a great many other things, are beyond Father Tom. But the blame should fall, not on his broad shoulders, but on author Reid, London-born, late a serving officer in the British Rhine Army, an advertising account executive, an art dealer who recently has moved to the south of France and, according to his publisher's jacket copy, is spending all his time (not, alas, *all* his time) reconverting an old farmhouse. One cannot take too seriously Father Tom, who protests, after a series of disastrous missteps, "Look I'm a priest. At least I was a couple of days ago. I don't know what I am now." Why novels of this sort are filled with air travel, exotic locations, gobs of violence, is self-evident. No one would read Harold Robbins if he wrote about the poor. Only glittery voyeurism will do, and Mr. Reid follows suit, except he does what no writer of violence should do: his descriptive powers fail him in the middle of a gory murder, and, even though I reread it several times, I could not figure out how the physical feat was accomplished.

    The Offering caused me to laugh out loud a few times when it rose to heights of self-parody, though the parody is not deliberate, and, in the end, *The Offering* is not funny at all.

JOHN CHEEVER*

T hese days, kiss-and-tell books are in the news. But they are accounts of politicians' lives and deeds, not artists'; for some time now, artists have had to take a back seat to the more respectable and powerful when it comes to generating scandal and prompting bizarre behavior.

But this first full biography (there are likely to be others; and a memoir, *Home Before Dark*, by Cheever's daughter, Susan, has already preceded it) of the novelist and short story writer, John Cheever, who died in 1982 at age seventy, will gain notoriety because of its kiss-and-tell aspects, though that genteel phrase doesn't capture the nature of what gets told.

Scott Donaldson, a professor at the College of William and Mary, entitled the first biography he wrote *Poet in America*; its subject is Winfield Townley Scott, a man who shared many things with Cheever, except the form in which he wrote. Donaldson's present biography of Cheever could be titled "Short Story Writer in America," for his method is the same.

Biographies are deceptive: you learn in the best of them as much about the time and the place of the subject as the subject himself. Biography is social history, and Cheever is an illuminating beacon, shedding light on a great deal of literary history along the New England/New York City axis.

There are two major conflicts described by Donaldson in Cheever's life—and there is much more simple description than intricate analysis, good for a writer of fiction, but not necessarily for a biographer. The first was Cheever's excellence as a natural short story writer during a period when the novel was king; and the second was his bisexuality in a period when such a topic would be deemed unsuitable for a mainstream "family" magazine like the *New Yorker*, Cheever's principal outlet.

* First appeared in *South Bend Tribune*, July 17, 1988. Review of *John Cheever: A Biography*.

Today, both conflicts have been resolved by time. The short story is the most fashionable literary art form and the *New Yorker* magazine's fiction is decidedly not closed to overtly gay subjects.

As often is the case, the life of a man who warrants a biography is revealed to be more interesting in the years before he became famous than during his time of celebrity. Cheever is another example of the often-over-looked fact that for his generation World War II was its primary experience. And Donaldson does well recounting those times, the stateside wartime life of Cheever, married and a new father laboring in Astoria, Queens, "as part of the propaganda war that Frank Capra—deputized by President Roosevelt—was leading against the sophisticated techniques of Joseph Goebbels and the Nazis."

Cheever, who was kicked out of a prep school (and almost immediately published a short story about it in the *New Republic*), was swept along in the postwar boom, contributing babies, existing on the ample surpluses of a number of his rich friends, all the while writing and publishing. As is often necessary for a successful literary career in this country, Cheever started at the top. What he wrote he published, and in the paradoxical condition of the period, even though the novel was the most esteemed form, there existed a large, well-paying market for the then critically less regarded short story.

Cheever's early life—domineering mother, ineffectual father—provided him with a sufficient number of lifelong psychological difficulties (alcoholism among them); and though he saw psychiatrists, he had little regard for them since he was much more articulate than they were.

But that he could see his own problems didn't mean he could do much about them. As was the typical case during the fifties and sixties, Cheever's homosexuality was kept from public view—and not just by him—because it created discordant notes that the society very much didn't want to hear. But, as Donaldson points out, it was in his fiction, though closeted even there.

Cheever's great and uncontested success, when it finally came late in his career, as he rode the wave of the short story's own ascendancy, was due to his dual role of chronicler and prophet. He saw and well documented the cracks in the expensive surface of the glittering respectability of the Big City exur-banite he so knowingly wrote of, in such stories as "The Swimmer," "The Sorrows of Gin," "The Five-Forty-Eight."

Anyone who would want to read this biography should be familiar with them. (And it would be advisable to have the fresh taste of Cheever's prose in one's mouth before biting down into the staler Donaldson's.) Then you can read about the life and see what kind of kindling, what dross and suffering and dry trash, goes into making such wonderful fires.

NORMAN KOTKER*

Norman Kotker's second novel, *Miss Rhode Island*, published ten years ago, was an unlikely triumph. It turned the story of a Miss America contest into a sweet fable, an affectionate portrait of our national foibles, a satire simultaneously cutting and cauterizing. His third novel, *Learning about God*, has the same paradoxical mission: it heals as it wounds. But Kotker has put aside the pop icon of a beauty-pageant hopeful for a much more troubling icon of the twentieth century, a concentration camp survivor, and the result is both excoriating and forgiving.

Chaim Fogel is the survivor in *Learning about God*; we first encounter him at the annual Bergen-Belsen survivor's banquet taking place at the Plaza Hotel. There is something both ludicrous and appropriate about a "survivor's banquet," and Kotker is able to locate that quality in almost every aspect of life. He continuously mixes the morbid and the humorous, the ordinary and the significant.

Fogel is beset with headaches, physical and spiritual, prompted by his past and his present. He is a professor of history in both senses: he teaches it and he believes in it and its lessons are stark. But it is Kotker's wonderful ability to take material that can overwhelm the senses and fashion a novel out of it that is affecting, entertaining, and reasonable.

Fogel goes into group therapy in hopes of curing his crushing headaches, and one of the younger patients asks innocently (getting the name wrong), "What's Bergman-Belsen?" after Fogel mentions the concentration camp. "Tell them," the doctor instructs and the narration continues: "As Fogel had dragged bodies to the burial pits at Belsen to earn food, so Dr. Wax, also to earn food, was attempting to drag Fogel to talking. Did talking stop headaches? Not yet. Fogel sat squarely on his chair, his legs inflexible. Now let the chair break.

---

* First appeared in *South Bend Tribune*, Nov. 27, 1988. Review of *Learning about God* by Norman Kotker.

Maybe its years were over. 'They should already know. Let them read history books.' History was carrying them, fast as a subway train. Last stop. All out."

Or, let them read *Learning about God*. Fogel's life is battered by the monolithic oppression of his past, the dense insanity created by the Nazi state, and the lack of tradition and focus late twentieth-century America provides. We watch Fogel wrestling with those two worlds. He is that rare thing in fiction, a totally believable yet symbolic figure. Fogel stands for something and he stands. He is a character whom you learn to know, come to like, and admire. He has a wife and two children, all of whom are real but representational. Son Steven is an aspiring filmmaker living in Los Angeles. Fogel is on the phone with him: "'Make a movie out of me.' A film spectacular: 'Inside Fogel' . . . 'Be a good boy. You enjoy.' As if a father had to remind a son such as Steven to enjoy, a son who insisted on going to film school in California, even though there was an outstanding film-studies program at New York University, where his father was a respected professor and where tuition therefore cost almost nothing."

Fogel's daughter, Marlene, is newly married to a black professor of urban studies at a Boston university, and their union provides Fogel with the last crisis he needs to endure, as well as the novel's climatic forlorn tragedy.

Learning about God takes on the big questions, justice, evil, the nature of God, but never does so ponderously. It comes at those questions the way people do in daily life, even though the life of Chaim Fogel is far from ordinary. Kotker's novel is not heavy, despite its subject—he somehow manages to levitate despair—and his prose is light, but it has the swift delicacy and strength of a scalpel. *Learning about God* is a compelling book, certainly one of the most remarkable novels of the year.

RICHARD ELMAN AND ROBIN HEMLEY*

D isco Frito, novelist and journalist Richard Elman's twenty-first book, is a collection of tales that take place in Nicaragua, that strangely American place, insofar as it is known by most of us through the eyes of the American media.

Elman himself wrote a trenchant nonfiction account of events in revolutionary Nicaragua, *Cocktails at Somoza's*, published in 1981. That book was cast into a literary no-man's-land, since it was simultaneously judged hostile to American involvement with the Somoza regime and insufficiently sympathetic to the leading Sandinista ruling families. It was something close to the truth, not a quality that gathers much support from either side of warring factions.

Disco Frito—the name applied to a Somoza-era nightspot burned by insurgents—appears to be suffering the same fate. Since its setting and subject is Nicaragua, a topic of interest chiefly limited to partisans, Elman's writing remains an irritation; and in our literary culture, if something is an irritant, it is not scratched but ignored. So, this quite important book is being generally afforded the most typical kind of American censorship, neglect.

Its interconnected sketches—portions of which have appeared in the *Boston Review*, *Antaeus*, and the *Michigan Quarterly*—give us a fractured vision of life in Nicaragua's postrevolutionary world. The country, in this telling, becomes something of a dangerous zoo, one visited by a host of foreign freelancers of various quixotic stripe—reporters, mercenaries, businessmen, functionaries of many different governments, the usual cast of adventure novel supernumeraries.

Elman is more than aware of that aspect of exploitation. *Disco Frito's* repeating characters—two journalists: one, Prudhomme, a Frenchman; and the other, Rik, an American who serves as the principal narrator—briefly visit

---

* First appeared in *South Bend Tribune*, Jan. 1, 1989. Review of *Disco Frito* by Richard Elman and *All You Can Eat* by Robin Hemley.

Paradise, Honduras, two days after encountering Nicaragua's chief of state at a battle site near the Nicaraguan border; they listen to a speech by Contra leader Aldolfo Colero:

> He's a heavy-set man with a saturnine smile, and I could not say his speech was any less affecting than Ortega's. Well fed himself, he fed all those puny kids, sweating inside heavy green fatigues, words; that the time was coming when Nicaragua was going to be liberated and freedom was going to be restored. Later they were served beans and G.I. rations.
>
> Again Prudhomme took notes and before I could ask why, he told me. "In order to put some distance between myself and pathos," he said. "One side or the other. It's always like that when people are dying."

And Prudhomme's remark—"to put some distance between myself and pathos"—explains what *Disco Frito* accomplishes. It will show you what you'll never see on the nightly news or read in most magazines.

It is an outsider's stance, and since the Nicaraguan revolution is not over (the way the Vietnam war is now "over"), books written about it get held at arm's length by partisans of either side. Vietnam war novels were not conspicuously popular until after that war had ended—and even for a few years beyond that. For all the colorful detail, the sharp smell and tang of how it is that Elman captures in *Disco Frito*, Nicaragua remains for most a black-and-white conflict. But reading Elman's stories will expose you to the splash of ambiguous gray on the tropical palette, all the startling juxtapositions, the vividly ordinary, in a country both besieged and beset. It's an extraordinary book.

Robin Hemley's collection of stories—a first book, if one doesn't count his small-press publication, *The Mouse Town*—treats a different sort of warfare, domestic warfare, as its subject.

All You Can Eat has had a wide reception and has been greeted with sustained, deserved praise. Hemley hails from a literary family; his mother, Elaine Gottlieb, is a novelist, and Hemley's father was the founder of Noonday Press.

Like Elman's collection, *All You Can Eat* comprises separate stories (though of a more traditional shape), but they too weave their own unified kaleidoscopic tapestry. Hemley, like Elman, is both amazed and appalled by what he finds at large in contemporary life.

Hemley's stories are up to date, not because the sensibility is current, but because of the manner of telling. They are often told in the first person, whether or not the narrator bears any relationship to the author.

One of the collection's best, "Installations," is told to us by a Chicago Transit Authority conductor. Making the nonliterary literary is one of the stickier modern conventions. We will avoid noticing the ventriloquist holding the dummy and listen attentively, if the dummy is well done.

As might be expected from a young author, a lot of childhood is covered in *All You Can Eat*. "The Mouse Town," "Riding the Whip," "What's That in Your Ear?" are among the best—there are quite a few "best" in the collection. The beginning of "What's That in Your Ear?" is illustrative of Hemley's methods: "On the Brewer side of my family, I'm related to two famous people; Houdini and, according to legend, Attila the Hun. From these two strains have emerged a fine blend, personified in the lives and characters of my great-uncles Tony and Maury and my great-aunt Rose. It's like a nice coffee mixture; a little bit of Houdini, a pinch of Attila, and a bunch of beans of undetermined variety."

Hemley, like Elman, is able to capture a number of things at once: history, humor, sociology, detail, whimsy, as well as the odor of the times (e.g., the coffee analogy).

Families make up the subject of quite a bit of contemporary fiction these days. The family is undergoing so many rapid changes that writers are busily chronicling that which might be about to disappear.

But sooner or later, even in fiction, we must leave our families. *All You Can Eat*'s last story, "Installations," takes on the country outside the living room. It is infused with the wonder of—and wonder at—the world at large.

"Did you see that?" its narrator yells at the story's conclusion. "Did you see that?" Happily, Hemley has seen it and is letting us see it, too.

NETTIE JONES*

Nettie Jones's first novel, *Fish Tales*, published in 1984, was both highly praised and rudely damned. *Fish Tales* was an episodic novel in the manner of Renata Adler's *Speedboat*, comprising short scenes, the hearts of vignettes, and was a story of one woman's contradictory oppression and satisfaction through sex, drugs, and alcohol, rendered in graphic, uncompromising prose. It was a cathartic book, scalding in its honesty, marred only by a slightly obscure ending. *Mischief Makers*, her second novel, is a large step beyond and away from *Fish Tales* in both content and narrative form.

Mischief Makers is in many ways a minimalist saga novel. Its brief 163 pages cover three generations, span the 1920s to the 1950s, and depict a slice of black history not much covered by contemporary writers. If one compares Nettie Jones to other living black women writers, one notices that, in *Fish Tales*, she exchanges long sexual description for extended depictions of violence and, in *Mischief Makers*, she often deals with subjects that are not in current political fashion, such as the slippery issues of blacks "passing" as whites and assimilation.

The family tree in her novel holds people of both colors and the experience of diaspora as southern blacks go north, some floating out of their pasts on the ether of light skin. As pernicious as the laws of the old (and not-so-old) South were in specifying exactly who was "a Negro" by calculating the smallest fractions of black "blood," the laws' existence did at least demonstrate how commonplace such mixed racial heritage is in America.

The matriarchal protagonist of *Mischief Makers* is Raphael de Baptiste, the daughter of light-skinned professional parents. She leaves Detroit for upper Michigan to work as a nurse and passes for white.

Raphael meets and married Mishe Masaube, a Chippewa Indian who has land and a commanding manner. Three daughters result: Blossom Rose,

---

* First appeared in *Chicago Tribune*, May 15, 1989. Review of *Mischief Makers* by Nettie Jones.

Lilly, and Puma. Their lives and fates become the novel's subject. (Raphael dies giving birth to a fourth child, a stillborn male.) Each daughter learns, in her own way and time, of her forebears. But what they chiefly are—and it would seem to be Jones's point—is very American.

Though lip service is still paid to the old melting-pot aspect of the American dream, more energy of late has been spent reinforcing narrower, tribal "ethnic" identities, leading various national and racial groups to separate themselves from the mainstream while asserting that they are the "true" Americans. Jones's novel offers another history.

Lilly is killed in Detroit's race riot of the summer of 1943. Blossom Rose is blinded by a bullet meant for her aunt. Puma flourishes. There is melodrama here, but the prose of *Mischief Makers* is serene. It has the feel of old stories being told, turned smooth and handsomely polished by being handed down from one generation to another.

Fish Tales was a disturbing novel, and so is *Mischief Makers*, though for entirely different reasons. Jones has managed to tell a very complicated story with calculated simplicity, and the characters, though broadly sketched, are never stereotypes. They are all tangible, flesh and blood.

As daring as *Fish Tales* was in matters of sex, *Mischief Makers* is even more daring in its portrait of color and class in America. Jones is a mischief-maker indeed.

C. E. POVERMAN*

Anovel in the form of an autobiography is often many novels at once. C. E. Poverman's long and challenging third novel, *My Father in Dreams*, is, or could be, three separate novels—the first, one of growing up: prep school, championship diving, an elite college, life with father, young infatuations; the middle part could be a novel of adventure and exotica: a young man teaching in India, his transformation into a well digger during a period of the most bitter famine; the last part could be a gripping novel of contemporary erotic relations, with crime-thriller overtones.

The most contemporaneous story, the one which acts as a net thrown over all the parts of *My Father in Dreams*, concerns Jed Hartwick, the narrator, and his last (of a long line) girlfriend, Gracie, who is expecting his child. Chapters of the book in this time frame are labeled "Baby." The other chapters detail the chronological story of Jed's entire life, about three decades worth.

Gracie, "self-possessed, with an easy athletic grace—tall, blond—and comfortable with people," is but one of a number of remarkable women Jed has encountered; and he is leaving her, at the novel's start, after she has announced her pregnancy. One begins to guess early on that at the novel's end he might be returning.

Another link connecting the narrative is Jed's relationship with his father, Dr. Hartwick. He is an accomplished surgeon, adored by his patients, revered by his friends. Jed is an only child, and his predicament isn't unusual: how to please or gain the respect of a dominating, successful, attractive man.

But there is a question beyond his childhood here: What is Jed to do with his life? He is smart, good-looking, sensitive, athletic, but does not want to join the fraternity of men who, in Jed's father's eyes, run the world—doctors,

---

* First appeared in *South Bend Tribune*, June 25, 1989. Review of *My Father in Dreams* by C. E. Poverman.

lawyers, military men and financiers. Jed trying to solve the questions of his father's contempt and derision, keeps a notebook entitled, "My Father in Dreams," which evolves into the novel we are reading.

Jed dives throughout his school years, but never wins competitions, only shows at best. After graduating from what we take to be Yale (Poverman is a Yale graduate), not knowing what to do, or not wanting to do anything in particular, Jed is sent to India by a do-good foundation. There he encounters what he was looking for: otherworldliness, the chance to be entirely self-sufficient, further rites of passage.

He sees people at an ashram, one that serves as a way station during the famine, and writes, "A novelist might have taken them, a cast of characters in a disaster, situated them under that huge spreading banyan tree and written an omniscient novel full if ironies, disasters, and separate ironic denouements, revealing all of their motivations and hopes against the larger counterpoint of the famine itself."

Yes, a novelist might, but isn't this a novel, too, written by a novelist? Poverman keeps bringing up the question he might not want asked: Why is this book a novel?

Though this volume contains many pages about Jed's father, there are only a few lines about Jed's mother. Since so much of Jed's life is taken up by his difficulties with women, one would surmise these problems may have something to do with his relationship with his mother, not his father; but this never occurs to him, though the "job" he ends up with is being an administrator with a "Family Service Center."

Nonetheless, the parts of *My Father in Dreams* are often quite arresting: the descriptions of prep school and the students and teachers are lively, accurate, and funny. The sojourn in India is always interesting, and the account of well drilling fascinating. And the last long relationship Jed has (before Gracie) with the alluring and provocative Darcy is both complicated and compelling, full of passion and power.

Often the form something is given makes it more than the sum of its parts; here the form checks the force each of the book's parts indisputably has. Mock autobiography is a genre that inspires indulgence, and Jed is already a young man who has known quite a bit of that. Darcy tells him, "There's something about men like you and you know it and you just get what you want with women and you're getting what you want with me. Don't pretend you don't know." And Jed does pretend, one feels, not to know. Something is staring him in the face, in his dreams, and in this novel he pretends not to see it.

"Show, don't tell" is good advice when writing fiction, but not necessarily the best advice when writing a novel in the form of autobiography. At the end we do know Jed (perhaps better than he knows himself), and we do feel the deficit he himself has felt—the absence of unconditional love from his father—as he begins life, not just as a son, but as a new father, too. *My Father in Dreams* is full of riches, but they are extracted at some cost.

DOUGLAS UNGER*

W ars have unforeseen as well as predictable legacies, and the people who live through them, this thoughtful novel shows us, are often left guarding "some small secret portion of history the rest of the world has forgotten."

The Turkey War illuminates a small portion of forgotten history, the story of German prisoners of war who spent most of World War II as laborers in a turkey-processing plant in South Dakota. It is certainly odd to read a novel by a relatively young American writer that praises German soldiers for their loyalty, courage, and "spirit," while depicting the local Americans as bumbling, corrupt, and loutish. Be that as it may, Unger's third novel—though not as affecting as his first, the highly praised *Leaving the Land*, or as direct as his second, *El Yanqui*—provides a clear, provocative chronicle of a time that should be remembered.

The tone and manner of *Turkey War* call to mind the proletarian novels of the twenties and the thirties, with their one-dimensional, working-class heroes. The working man of *Turkey War*, Mose Johnson, resembles his proletarian-novel predecessors in that he is never fully fleshed out and remains an implausible man. The fault, however, lies not so much with who Johnson is but with how Unger has chosen to narrate the novel; he adopts an unspecified voice from the present to tell the tale and mainly employs the rough, plain speech of his unschooled characters. Language of greater subtlety is found in the German that is liberally used—some translated, some readily translatable. It is there that we find the deeper nuances of meaning.

Mose is no Moses. From Unger's perspective, there is no Promised Land into which the proletariat can be led. The necessary cynicism of known history pervades the novel, as we watch Mose—capable and hard working—become

---

* First appeared in *Books, Chicago Tribune*, Nov. 13, 1988. Review of *The Turkey War* by Douglas Unger.

the foreman of the processing plant and the tool both of its avaricious owner and of the even more greedy army major who oversees the prisoners. The POWs turn into a parody of a desirable work force, skilled slave laborers who are motivated by their commanding officer, The Hauptmann—a twisted embodiment of the "good," pre-Nazi Germany, a Prussian officer whose heroism controls and emboldens his men.

Mose succeeds in raising production at the plant to a near-impossible five thousand turkeys a day, dressed and canned. Unger gives us a sense of the demanding work but does not depict it as intimately as one might expect— though what he does provide may be too graphic for some tastes ("every time men moved, their feet slipped and slid around on the greasy and bloody and wet cement floors"). Muckraking is not his intention; Unger is not Upton Sinclair observing Chicago's stockyards. But to the degree that the novel aims to be a psychological study of the nature of good and evil, it is damaged by the unlikeliness of Mose. Just as the proletarian novels of the twenties and thirties were seldom written by proletarians, *Turkey War* suffers from the fact that Unger hasn't witnessed what he is writing about.

As a reader would suspect, while hoping to be proved wrong, the novel's climax entails a confrontation between Mose and The Hauptmann—which results in the rebellion of the POWs and a general strike. But the war ends, men return to town, and the novel leaps and bounds over time, rapidly sketching the period of boom and bust: "Nowell was on its way to becoming little more than a ghost town . . . Safebuy Turkeys shut down its operations, moving them to turkey facilities in Minnesota. Then after a prolonged and painful labor dispute, it moved its turkey-processing business all the way to a brand-new plant already under construction outside Sao Paulo, Brazil . . . Safebuy stock rose dramatically on the American Exchange. Farms went broke. Banks failed. Schools closed. People moved away to parts unknown."

History of that sort is well known to us. But the bulk of Unger's novel is hidden history, the four years of the German prisoners' labor in a strange land. For resurrecting and preserving that tale, Unger deserves praise and readers. Admirable in intention, *The Turkey War* is often successful, if not totally satisfying in its ultimate effect.

RICHARD BAUSCH AND MARK PROBST*

These two accomplished, satisfying novels concern the contemporary half-family: a single parent and a child. Countering statistics, though, both parents are male: a widower in Richard Bausch's *Mr. Field's Daughter*, a divorced father in Mark Probst's *Winter Losses*. And both children bring menace and mayhem into their fathers' lives.

Bausch's protagonist, James Field, is senior loan officer for a bank, and the book's agent of destruction is his former son-in-law, Cole Gilbertson, a part-time drug dealer. Field's daughter, Annie, ran off with him when she was nineteen; she returns to her father's house five years later with a daughter, Linda, in tow. Meanwhile, Cole plans to reclaim Linda and to wreak revenge upon Field.

Bausch's prose is everywhere sonorous and engaging. Unfortunately, his least successful character is the title one, Annie, who remains a pleasing cipher. "I had just turned twenty years old," she tells us at one point, "and I was living in the home of a man I couldn't imagine anymore for the fright of knowing where we were headed."

He does a much better job of establishing her daughter, Linda, who is full of aspirations and needs. And one never doubts Bausch's story-telling power nor his wonderfully rendered sense of place (the book is set in the woods of northern Minnesota). All in all, this is a gripping piece of work.

The father of Mark Probst's *Winter Losses* is Philip Kreg, a partner in a Manhattan law firm, an expert on constitutional law and director of a grant-dispensing foundation. And most of the action of the book is woven into the fabric of big-city deal making.

Kreg's son, Adam, shows up with an attache case containing a million dollars he has stolen from his unsavory and now very angry employers, a pack

---

* First appeared in *Books, Chicago Tribune*, July 2, 1989. Review of *Mr. Field's Daughter* by Richard Bausch and *Winter Losses* by Mark Probst.

of international arms and drug merchants. Kreg spends a million dollars of his own money in an attempt to save his son.

Getting the money is never an issue; the characters of *Winter Losses* all have highly developed cash aesthetics. They are mostly in fear of the second rate: "He looked at his left wrist (a wafer Patek with a gold mesh strap"). Good taste is the only thing available to justify their wealth.

Probst certainly knows something of the world, and he is definitely making sharp social comments. The illegal enterprises of Kreg's son are meant to mirror the legal activities of Kreg. Business is business, and both sides meet in the gray world of overlapping profit taking. But Philip Kreg is the kind of man you would want to have on your side.

Both *Winter Losses* and *Mr. Field's Daughter* demonstrate that social and economic boundaries once thought to be insurmountable may no longer act as barriers at all. One person's shattered life is quite likely to infect someone—anyone—else's; all people are contagious now.

One thing these novels may not share, though, is the same set of readers, which would be a shame. Those attracted by the trappings of the glamorous, big-city novel might find much to like (and be excited by) in *Mr. Field's Daughter*. And those who look only to such overtly literary writers as Richard Bausch might profit from an encounter with the less polished, though more directly engaged, world of Mark Probst's *Winter Losses*.

HOWARD FRANK MOSHER*

A *Stranger in the Kingdom* is being compared by its publisher to Harper Lee's *To Kill a Mockingbird*. Almost twice the length of that 1960 novel and set in the far North (of Vermont) rather than the Deep South, Howard Frank Mosher's book does cover similar ground.

The story is told through the eyes of a precocious youth of thirteen, Jimmy Kinneson, although the novel's narrator is actually a forty-seven-year-old pretending to be thirteen, generating a false charm (complete with an "aw-shucks" diction) that is often more annoying than ingratiating.

Mosher's novel quickly becomes a tale of familiar romantic illusions, with its own stable of colorful cartoon characters who are real enough in their outlandishness and hyperbolic aspects, though never real enough to engage our deepest sympathies.

Here's a typical sketch of a minor character, seen by Jimmy:

> As I bounded upstairs . . . I caught a spicy whiff of bay rum after-shave lotion and clove-scented hair tonic. Farlow Blake, Kingdom County's part-time bailiff and full-time barber, and a veritable walking barbershop of aromatic suffusions himself, buttonholed me on the landing. "Greetings, young James," he said in his portentous courtroom tones. "Big doings this P. of M. Very big doings."
> Farlow gave me a canny wink.

This is a novel full of canny winks. Jimmy's is a childhood of endless bucolic pleasures, populated by the world's best father, a Betty Crocker mother, and a protective, home-run hitting, lawyering big brother. Jimmy and his father are out fishing, taking a break from unsavory business in town. "Instead of

---

* First appeared in *Chicago Tribune*, Nov. 9, 1989. Review of *A Stranger in the Kingdom* by Howard Frank Mosher.

Spam sandwiches, supper turned out to be roast pork sandwiches on homemade bread, two slabs of Mom's no-egg wonder chocolate cake, and two long-keeping apples she'd saved through the previous winter and spring. It was as pretty a spot as any in the county, as pretty as any I have ever seen anywhere, and for a time we ate in silence, enjoying . . . just being together after our great afternoon of fishing."

Though the good guys in Kingdom County are really good, the bad guys aren't so bad, either, however sociopathic they might seem to be, spending so much time carousing, boozing, and brawling.

But this story of lovable eccentrics and idyllic childhood days takes on its contemporary flavor and more serious subject with the appearance of Walt Andrews, the newly hired minister, retired RCAF officer and chaplain, and his teenage son Nat, the only black people to have lived in Kingdom County for fifty years.

The novel's plot has many twists and turns, but they are much better lighted than the treacherous back roads of Kingdom County. No reader will run off the curves. Into Kingdom County's world of folksy folks comes an equally picturesque French-Canadian girl and she is murdered in a way that interjects some of the late 1960s cartoonist R. Crumb's porno-detail realism into the Walt Disney style that hitherto prevailed in the novel.

The candidates for killer are many, but Walt Andrews, the black minister, is arrested. Jimmy's older home-run hitting brother, Charles, is the Reverend Andrews's defense attorney. The novel's culmination is one that would make the creators of Perry Mason's television courtroom confessions blush.

Mosher's novel may have its heart in the right place. It certainly has a Bush-era glow about it; he does give us a kindler and gentler image of our past, one people may well nostalgically wish to believe true.

THOMAS PYNCHON*

$\mathbf{V}$ *ineland*, Thomas Pynchon's first novel since the publication of his monumental World War II novel, *Gravity's Rainbow*, seventeen years ago, repatriates him, brings him back to America in both subject matter and style.

Pynchon reclaims the literary territory for which he was the point man, starting in 1963 with his first novel, *V.*—territory a host of others, from Robert Stone to T. C. Boyle, have occupied since Pynchon left it behind when *The Crying of Lot 49*, his second novel and his last with an American setting (until *Vineland*), was published nearly a quarter of a century ago.

Gravity's Rainbow, set largely in England and on the Continent, both Europeanized and internationalized Pynchon for readers, or, at least, the critical community. World War II, indeed, is the central fact of Pynchon's generation (he was born in 1937); it is the shaper of our contemporary world and Pynchon's sensibility and concerns: the bomb, the holocaust, the institutionalization of secrecy, the military-industrial complex, now expanded with its wholly owned subsidiary, the privatized intelligence-industry complex, were all products of, or created because of, the last world war.

Gravity's Rainbow was written by the publicity-shy veteran of post-war American prosperity; Pynchon's personality was created by the peculiar mating of the different cultures of the 1950s and 1960s, which produced a lot of strangeness, not the least example of which is Thomas Pynchon.

But the publication of *Vineland* fully reveals Pynchon for what he is: the long departed beatnik, the fifties bohemian, a talker extraordinaire in the manner of Lenny Bruce, Allen Ginsberg, Jack Kerouac onward, a mixture— once prized, but now largely nonexistent—of wild eclectic learning, plus unre-

---

* First appeared in *South Bend Tribune*, May 20, 1990. Review of *Vineland* by Thomas Pynchon and *Thomas Pynchon: A Bibliography of Primary and Secondary Materials*, edited by Clifford Mead.

strained anti-establishment scorn. *Vineland* is full of wonderful, dead-on, slightly manic hipster's speech.

Though *Vineland* takes place in 1984 and earlier, the novel might prove difficult to decipher for the new generation, not because the prose isn't made up of simple declarative sentences, but because it is full of nonstop cultural allusions (and illusions), history and reference, politics and science. And, for better or worse, to make much sense out of it, you need to know what he's talking about, have some passing familiarity with the late sixties and early seventies radical political groups and carryings-on. But, if you like the style of what follows below, a description of two low-rent film producers, Sid and Ernie, who have sworn off drugs, you'll most likely enjoy it all:

> Both men were nervous wrecks, covered with a sweat-like film of desperation to ingratiate themselves with the anti-drug hysteria leadership, suddenly perceived as the cutting edge of hip. Sid Liftoff, having owed much of his mately and vivacious public image to chemical intervention, often on an hourly basis, now, absent a host of illicit molecules in his blood, was changing . . . into the wild animal at the base of his character, solitary, misanthropic, more than ready to lift his throat in a desolate, transpersonal cry. Ernie, meanwhile, sat in a glazed silence that would have suggested his return, in this time of crisis, to his childhood religion, Soto Zen, except for the way he was unable to keep from handling his nose, with agitated fussing movements, as if trying to primp it into shape like a hairdo.

Vineland is simultaneously in and out of touch with the world around us. The novel takes place in California, between Fortuna in the north and L.A. in the south, and the complicated story is much like the highways that get you up and down the West Coast—scenic, but occasionally tangled and congested. It's a tale of seduction, betrayal, and revenge, populated by sixties radicals and their progeny.

Throughout *Vineland* Pynchon is not so much enraged as bemused. He is some laid-back California version of the fierce satirist Jonathan Swift. Pynchon is under the sway of glamour and power, and his paranoia has a utopian cast, where all the novel's bad guys, the forces of Big Brother, are not only omnipotent but efficient, too. Pynchon does seem to enjoy all the contradictions he illuminates and all the mayhem he depicts. He admires energy, something the twentieth century doesn't seem to lack.

But had Pynchon chosen to publish *Vineland* under a pseudonym (as Doris Lessing did for two novels and as Joyce Carol Oates unsuccessfully continues to do in order to see how their work would fare not freighted with their huge reputations—and what happens is not much), I am sure *Vineland* would have suffered the usual fate of a densely written, subversive book. It would have been largely overlooked. It's the lucky author these days whose latest novel is read in the context of all of his or her work, since most novels are usually greeted by reviewers and critics as orphaned strangers. This is not the case with Thomas Pynchon.

Academic critics are in need of large subjects and often find thoroughly contemporary American subjects (as is the case with *Vineland*) too confining. *Gravity's Rainbow* (1973) was the motherlode. Pynchon's first novel, *V.* (1963), as good as it was, would have been insufficient; his second, *The Crying of Lot 49* (1966), which also uses California as a setting, would have been too slight. *Gravity's Rainbow* is the sun around which the rest of Pynchon's work orbits, including *Vineland*, the newest satellite.

In order to get a sense of the academic Pynchon industry, one only need to turn to the newly published Dalkey Archive bibliography, which claims, rightly, that "No other novelist has generated as much criticism in as short a time." There are more than a hundred pages listing books, articles, conference papers, dissertations, and theses written on Pynchon and his books.

It is tempting to label Pynchon's generation of writers the last to comfortably bridge America's two cultures, the last to mix erudition and television, the last to have read the "great" books and, at the same time, been imprinted with all the bad movies and TV shows. The suspicion now is that you get one or the other, not both—and most likely you get the other.

I enjoyed *Vineland* as much as any novel I've read recently, and I found its history of the sixties and the years following more perceptive than most. I hope that nearly two decades don't have to pass before Pynchon delivers his next dazzling report on the state of the union.

LARRY HEINEMANN*

L arry Heinemann's raunchy and riotous new novel, his third, doesn't have
the word *Vietnam* in it (though that war is alluded to once), and he must
be pleased about that. His career thus far, like a number of other writers of his
generation, has been focused on the Vietnam war (or "conflict," as the Library
of Congress catalogues it). His first novel, *Close Quarters*, published in 1977 is
set there, and the excoriating *Paco's Story*, 1986, is even more intensely suffused with that war.

Paco's Story itself caused a minor skirmish in the literary wars when it
was nominated for a National Book Award (causing the *New York Times Book
Review* to at long last review it, after passing the novel by, the week of the cer-
emony) and, after actually winning the National Book Award, further caused
the *Times* to run articles about why that embarrassment (to the *Times*) had
occurred. The newspaper of record did not appreciate its judgment being so
thoroughly contravened by others, especially by an outfit as prestigious as the
National Book Award. The feathers flew for a few months. Toni Morrison's
Beloved, the *Times*'s choice, won the Pulitzer Prize. It was bruited about that
the *Times* was snubbing the Midwest's, or, at least, Chicago's, literary sons and
daughters—the flyovers being overlooked once again.

Cooler by the Lake is a Chicago book, as indicative of the Second (now
third) City as anything by Saul Bellow, Ben Hecht, Studs Terkel, or Mike Royko.
Perhaps the closest forebear from that city that Heinemann's book would call to
mind is Nelson Algren. Like Algren (as well as most of the aforementioned writers) Heinemann's speaks for the little guy, not the fake little guys like H. Ross
Perot, but actual working stiffs, the guys without connections, contacts, backgrounds, and easy luck. Heinemann's novel has a distinct working-class outlook,
which once would have been a compliment, but now is decidedly unfashionable.

---

* First appeared in *South Bend Tribune*, June 28, 1992. Review of *Cooler by the Lake*
by Larry Heinemann.

The novel spends a few rousing days with the Nutmeg clan (most of the novel's characters have names this side of cartoon land), an endearing bunch of hardworking layabouts, and charts the changes wrought in their lives by the discovery of a fat lost wallet. Along the way we learn a lot about Chicago—a running history of street names and place names is parenthetically provided. *Cooler by the Lake* is *the* novel of Chicago's human infrastructure, one that leaves the why and wherefore of that city's recently flooded tunnels no mystery.

In a not atypical illustration of the novel's style, Max Nutmeg, the con man discoverer of the mislaid wallet, is given a traffic ticket (one of many over a very short span) by Officer Bruno Hochmuth, who is reminded by Max of his "old man,"

> who for years wore himself out on the sign-washing crew for Streets and San. (the only municipal sign washing crew in the whole U.S. of A.—this back in the days when you couldn't kick a chair, Downtown, and not knock over some hack payroller), and always said that Mayor Richard J. Daley was the greatest human individual that ever lived, "and a great American"; his first words of working wisdom to his son, Bruno, were "Get a city job, kid, you can't beat it with a stick! It's cushy and the pay is terrific! It's the only nine-to-one, eight-hour day, Monday-through-Thursday, five-day-week job you're ever gonna come across."

What stands out about *Cooler by the Lake* is its infectious good-naturedness. Seldom has the wide spectrum of humanity (rascals all) that populates this book been looked upon singly or collectively with so much affection. What is further remarkable is the genuineness of the appraisal.

Vietnam-era writers are divided into two categories: those who have been in Vietnam (either as soldiers or civilians, mainly journalists) and write about it; and everyone else of the generation. The first category writers, though, are the only ones considered to be "Vietnam" writers. There is a price, it seems, for those writers: if they stray from Vietnam as a subject, the books are usually letdowns. Tim O'Brien is the best example: his books not about Vietnam haven't been successful. The same for Michael Herr, the journalist, whose book *Dispatches* is on most people's ten best list of Vietnam books. It is a new twist on the old idea that American writers don't have second acts in their careers. Happily, Heinemann escapes this fate.

How wonderful it must have been for Heinemann, after the Vietnam books, to write about something he likes—and loves. And wonderful for the reader, too. Reading *Cooler by the Lake* would make anyone a little cooler. What a relief.

ADRIAN MITCHELL*

Adrian Mitchell adds himself to a growing list of writers who are cautious prophets foretelling the near future. *The Bodyguard*, set in the Britain of Orwell's *1984*, purports to be the ramblings of the title character—a secular age's most ardent disciple—though that announcement is the author's washing of the hands, leaving us to decide the fate of the book's botched prose.

Len Rossman, a narrator so absent of human personality that every character trait is a non sequitur, is the voice of Mitchell's polemic fable. The author has a little interest in Rossman's case as a public defender who cannot find a name for a piece of evidence and labels it "Exhibit A." Consequently, he lacks even the zest of the average placard-bearing naysayer.

Mitchell's story line can best be described as a plot of mold at the end of a paranoid rainbow. Britain and the European Community are threatened by a movement called "the Rot." The government employs "the Yellows," a goon squad nicknamed because of the diseased color of their uniforms, to protect the country from "subverts," a group that seems to include anyone who has ever had a second thought. The bodyguard's (B.G.s) protect the venal successes of the establishment. There are ten thousand B.G.s already—but the narrator confesses, "The way the jungle mood of Europe's going, we'll end up with five times that number."

The novel proceeds with Len Rossman's *education macabre*. It takes him through episodic encounters, has him discover the home base of the Rot (their headquarters are in hollowed out centers of mounds of garbage). Finally, he is fatally wounded. His story concludes with an epilogue meant to be ironic—when a member of the Rot explains they are publishing his memoirs now, "in the Fifth year of the European Revolution, because it reflects some of the prerevolutionary England."

---

* First appeared in *New York Times Book Review*, Nov. 7, 1971. Review of *The Bodyguard* by Adrian Mitchell.

There are the faintest shades of Swift and Kafka lurking in this book, as if they had been supplied in a fiction-by-number kit. Rossman (the B.G.) is the classic *tabula rasa* moron, exposed to a number of bizarre experiences and rites in the manner of Voltaire's Candide, though Mitchell resembles Voltaire only as much as the *Whole Earth Catalogue* resembles the *Encyclopédie ou Dictionnaire Raisonné des Sciences, des Arts et des Métiers*. By default, this is a novel of ideas, although when Rossman comments, "I have always believed in learning from life, not books," one must conclude that would be absolutely necessary if he has only such books as this.

Rossman's monologue does not have the clinical interest of actual confession; it is a bedridden assemblage of current tabloid fears that Mitchell has drawn on to cover all possible bets. The youngest organization that Rossman infiltrates is modeled on the Weathermen and affinity groups, and his callow anarchists act like apprentice suicides. Each abrupt, theatrically shifted scene (Mitchell adapted Peter Weiss's *Marat/Sade* for London, Broadway, and the movies a few years ago) is a three-minute round of satire. Rossman's opponents are every cauliflowered social pug left on a street corner: government, clergy, academics, nudists, politicians, newsmen, brothels, and madames.

Mitchell uses the nightmarish future setting for no other reason than a stage director will change the time of a play of Shakespeare to twentieth-century London: an attempt to gain relevance. His vision of a totalitarian, completely evil world is so slickly arrived at that one is certain that if the danger can be so easily recognized it must be found somewhere deeper and less obvious.

The hintings at the dark collusions of media and technology in *The Bodyguard* come from the same impulse that speckles best-selling potboilers with brand names. Language such as "Erotic telegrams were tapped out" and "After computerizing the rhythm and the rhymes, I mentally rejected a couple of verses" is the shallow absorption of astronaut jargon. Mitchell, as noted, is not without invention. (In addition to contributing to the theatrical scene, he is a novelist, poet, and writer for television.) Unfortunately, his attempt to rework an old formula misses the mark, even as it offers the mixture as before—like altering Christmas red and green (in the name of progress) to orange and chartreuse. His book is not the allegory it wants to be, nor is it acceptable science fiction. It does not surpass its pulp title—or live up to it.

PATRICK McGINLEY*

$\mathbf{F}$oggage is a novel as odd as its title. The word (like the names of McGinley's two previous books, *Bogmail* and *Goosefoot*) looks familiar, as though its meaning were guessable. But the etymology is deceptive, for *foggage* preserves the Middle English meaning of *fog*: not mist, but the long grass left standing through the winter.

The novel plays a similar trick: At first glance it seems to be a realistic story of life in the Irish midlands; then it turns into a ribald and scatological comic fable; in the end, however, it is neither of these, but a variation on both, in keeping with the deliberate oddity of the title. For there is a fog in the novel, a pestilential cloud of the author's black humor; it settles on a quite realistic landscape and distorts it, but intermittently lifts.

McGinley's two earlier novels were praised for sharp renderings of Irish country life and astute handling of sexual peculiarities in rural characters. The quality of the prose was usually singled out for admiration. *Foggage* follows the pattern of its predecessors, but McGinley's chief concerns—Irish country life, lust and guilt—do not entwine gracefully here.

The story is simple enough: two forty-year-old twins (brother and sister) live with their ancient father. The brother, Kevin, tends to the farming; the sister, Maureen, cooks. Their days are full of nondescript activities, except for one: they sleep together. The sister takes both pleasure and pride in this arrangement, telling her brother: "I'll bet the neighbors see me as an old maid and you as a sapless bachelor. Little do they know that there's more heat in this house than in all the other houses of the townland put together."

McGinley does manage to portray their incest with some charm and naturalness, so much so that it made me question if this were not a peculiarly Irish *tour de force*, as though McGinley believes that brother-sister sex is the

---

* First appeared in the *Los Angeles Times*, Dec. 15, 1983. Review of *Foggage* by Patrick McGinley.

model for all domestic sexual unions in rural Ireland.

Sundry complications follows: Maureen believes herself to be pregnant. Kevin sets out to find a man to marry her and take the blame. Along the way are a handful of funny scenes; with the randy local vet and the gimpy hired hand; with the educated sister of Kevin's best friend, Murt, whom Kevin eventually marries. Only McGinley's crisp public-school prose keeps these characters from becoming clownish stereotypes. But that same lucid style makes the grotesque twists and turns of plot (trees conveniently falling on people, children drowning in water tanks, dogs being hanged) seem manufactured, even as it persuades us that the setting and characters are real.

Certainly McGinley has a talent for both plain and elegant depiction, but the portrait of sex and death in *Foggage* seems to have been drawn by a marvelous realist who has perversely taken up doodling cartoons. The result is unsettling, not morally, but aesthetically—as if two distinct talents were in opposition.

At times the novel appears to be heartfelt, sincere; then the fog descends, and the tone changes to rib-poking satire, and a reader hears—or, at least, I did—the author chuckling to himself offstage in a most condescending fashion. Unhappily I could not quite tell what McGinley was laughing at, or to whom he was condescending.

Foggage has its pleasures, especially if you enjoy coarseness served up in the most refined and stylish manner. But too often one feels the novel is an extended bad joke, a naughty limerick, although one set to lovely music and played by a symphony orchestra.

BERNARD MAC LAVERTY*

"Home from the war" is now becoming a peculiarly American expression, since in the late twentieth century it is chiefly Americans who come "home" from wars. In other countries the wars come to stay.

The Vietnam War, though, went on for so long that it seemed to be forever in our living rooms. And novels about Vietnam that appeared while that most televised war was still raging were read with some uneasiness, as if they were somehow premature, unfinished, since the war itself was not finished, over.

Novels set in contemporary Northern Ireland share some of this atmosphere of irresolution—indeed, the conflict in Ireland has been going on, in one guise or another, for almost the entire century, so long that it almost cannot be called a war. The Irish themselves refer to it as "The Troubles," a term that is surely the most dour of all Irish understatements.

Cal, Belfast-born Bernard Mac Laverty's second novel, provides American readers with the most affecting picture I've encountered of the conflict in contemporary Northern Ireland, of sectarian violence as experienced by its most humble victims and perpetrators.

The novel's story has the same stark simplicity as Mac Laverty's prose. The language he employs is consistently charged, as it must be to become superior writing, by a poetry of perception: Cal "was crouched at the window of the cottage replacing the hardboard with glass and putty . . . the pane of glass in his hands. It was remarkable how clear it was, yet the cut sides were dark green. The difference between a bucket of sea and the sea itself."

Cal, a motherless Catholic teenager, street-educated rather than schooled, lives alone with his widower father, a slaughterhouse worker, in a small, almost wholly Protestant town in Ulster. When the novel opens, Cal has just quit the

---

* First appeared in Michiana Magazine, *South Bend Tribune,* Jan. 13, 1985. Review of *Cal* by Bernard Mac Laverty.

slaughterhouse job his father arranged for him and is on the dole.

While idle, Cal falls in love, at an adoring distance, with a librarian, a young widow possessing education, beauty, and a small child. Once smitten, Cal visits the library regularly, though only to take out rock-'n'-roll tapes and to stare at his love object; at length, Marcella, the librarian, does manage to put a book in his hands. Cal later discovers that Marcella is the widow of a man he helped the IRA to kill.

Cal is an entirely successful novel up to the moment when Cal gains Marcella, his dream-woman—though his daydreams of her become mixed with the nightmares of his participation in the murdering of her Protestant husband, a member of Ulster's Police Reserve. Once won by Cal, Marcella becomes for the reader more of a figure of fantasy than she had been when Cal merely fantasized about her, and the novel's vivid reality becomes blurred.

Mac Laverty stacks the deck in this romance: Marcella, unlike her dead husband, is Catholic, but not a product of Ulster; she is more a cosmopolitan type and informs Cal, not knowing of his complicity, that her murdered husband was a brute whose death left her little moved. Cal's and Marcella's union is too neat, too pat, and since the novel gets its great strength from its convincing verisimilitude, the stage aspects of their love affair strike at the novel's core.

Nonetheless, *Cal* reveals powerfully the harsh actuality of the lives Mac Laverty depicts, the nature of the young man's almost inevitable connection with the terrorist wing of the IRA, and the everyday chain of circumstance, consequence and blame. Cal and the Protestant who manages a farm (owned by Marcella's Protestant in-laws) where Cal has found work, discuss their respective versions of the cause of The Troubles. Cal asks the older man,

> "What's so terrible about a united Ireland anyway? One island, one country.
> "And be ruled from Rome? A state told what to do by priests and nuns. Sheer voodoo, Cal, Mumbo-Jumbo. Ulstermen would die rather than live under the yoke of Roman Catholicism . . . I'm serious, Cal, I would die rather than let that happen."
> Cal believed him and settled down to silence.

There are other explanations that would suggest Northern Ireland's plight to be more complicated than that; and it is. But to the characters in *Cal*, who represent the ordinary men and women and children of Ulster enduring and continuing the conflict, it is just that clear-cut. And such deafening—and silencing—clarity sits at the heart of the problem, as this exceptional novel shows.

WILLIAM TREVOR AND FAY WELDON*

Like caviar, the modern short story often has its peculiar taste: slightly bitter, but rich. William Trevor and Fay Weldon, both short story writers who also publish novels, write rich, but slightly bitter, tales. They share some of the same Anglo-Irish settings, though Trevor regards his world with somewhat more seriousness and with far less of Weldon's sense of retributive sacrilege. Taken together, Trevor's twelve and Weldon's eleven stories (she and her publisher have thickened her volume by reprinting her first novel, *The Fat Woman's Joke*, published in the U.S. in 1968) do not so much amplify as echo one another.

What is often a virtue in a novel is a vice in a collection of short stories—a novel, though written over a number of years, still hopes to be seamless, whereas short stories are often discrete landmarks throughout an author's career, and, in volumes such as these, a writer's themes, obsessions, ideas, characters, can be placed much too close to one another, creating a crowding not altogether happy. What is quite innocent taken separately becomes a flaw when looked at together. In both writers quite different characters share certain common names (though Trevor is the more careful writer); and in Weldon's case an annoying number of the same phrases turn up in various stories, speaking of the same type of event, as if she had only one way of describing it.

Neither Trevor nor Weldon is much concerned with extending the boundaries of the contemporary short story, "pushing the envelope," as test pilots put it. Both are content to write within the well-established tradition, and both show a not entirely suppressed fondness for ghosts and unexplained madness, though their stories are, for the most part, firmly grounded in realism. Trevor exploits the fact that the "predicament" is a natural shape for a story; his characters are either escaping a nervous predicament or wandering into one: the

* First appeared in *Book World, Chicago Tribune*, Feb. 14, 1982. Review of *Beyond the Pale* by William Trevor and *Watching Me, Watching You* by Fay Weldon.

embarrassment of an untidy scene, or the humiliation of a quirk of circumstance, is at the center of his stories. In "The Bedroom Eyes of Mrs. Vanisittart" (all of Trevor's names are ironic; a tired saloon is named "Paradise Lounge"), a loyal wife is thought to be a flagrant adulterer when a waiter, mistaken for her gigolo, knocks on the door during a dinner party; in "Mulvihill's Memorial," Mulvihill dies at work, leaving behind a cache of pornographic films in his filing cabinet that create posthumous predicaments for a number of characters.

Trevor is a skillful delineator of the mundane, and when he writes about the rigidly middle class or the rich he does it with the fascination of Henry James but none of his sycophancy. In the title story, "Beyond the Pale," an English foursome makes an annual visit to a vacation hotel in Northern Ireland, and the wife of one couple encounters an Irishman who engages her in conversation and then commits suicide. The experience makes her "a little dicky," as her pompous husband puts it, and she causes scene after scene (a very low-grade, British hysteria, but enough to shatter the establishment's false decorum). The story is narrated by the wife of the second couple, mistress to the pompous husband of the first: through her observations of the distraught wife we hear the suicide's sorry tales of recent Irish history, the pathetic facts. The odd and intriguing thing about Trevor's story is the point of view, laced with dotty ambiguity, coming as it is from the rival woman's mind. It is as if Trevor wishes to relieve himself of the responsibility of judgment while allowing for criticism of everyone concerned. The story's effect is both unsettling and frivolous.

In one of the collection's lesser stories, a woman, silent and shy at a party, after speculating privately on the lives milling around her, wonders "what would happen if she revealed what she had thought, if she told them that in order to keep her melancholy in control she had played about with their lives, seeing them in childhood, visiting them with old age and death." And, more so even than the young woman at the party, this seems to be Trevor's intention: to keep his melancholy in control, he has written these stories, steeped as they are in pale, nostalgic disaffection (especially those with Irish locales), of misunderstood people, always troubled and in trouble, visiting them with old age and death. His stories are the sort that lead you to seek out more.

Fay Weldon is more of an interested tourist than an intimate visitor—rather than Trevor's mournful, but steady, gaze, we have in Weldon a sharp, some would say superficial, observation, a quick (to come and to depart) curiosity. Weldon's style would be called, in derogation, breezy; in praise, urbane. Her characters are entangled in the fringes of glamour (whereas Trevor's are often the warp and woof of ordinariness): playwrights, fashion designers, ad men and women. Both Trevor's and Weldon's stories are contemporary reports;

they pretty much cover the seventies. But Weldon's depiction of feminism is quite apart from what we have in the States. All her women are saturated with what here might be suspiciously thought feminine wiles and glances, attributes that Weldon's English women would be loath and hard put to deny. In fact, what seems a tad reactionary is Weldon's unquestioned contention throughout her stories that men and women are separate species, quite unable to speak to each other in the same language.

The predicament most often seen in Weldon's stories is familiar: the husband leaving a wife (perhaps a second wife) for a younger woman. The men, though uniformly without virtue, have enough money, status, good looks, and so on to accomplish this exchange with ease. The women who are left, though uniformly lovely, conscientious, bright, hard-working, and so on, usually have a single flaw that the men discover and pick at, a loose thread that quickly unravels their unions.

The most successful stories ("Christmas Tree," "Alopecia," "Geoffrey and the Eskimo Child") are funny, mordant, irreverent—there is so much irreverence that it keeps Weldon's stories from ever being too moving. Laughter, thankfully, always interrupts pathos. When Weldon speaks with ironic scorn of "the dreary world of established spouses," we feel there is less sympathy than appreciation in that remark. From her stories alone, one is forced to conclude that what is really established in Weldon's world is marriage-divorce-marriage-divorce-marriage, with its intricate web of social connection; and that this very complex interconnection shows how valuable and necessary divorce and remarriage is to modern life, in the relatively claustrophobic London that Weldon, at her best, so clearly and amusingly describes.

IRIS MURDOCH*

I t is difficult, if not impossible, to find any American writer who writes novels the way Iris Murdoch writes them. A comparison in production could be made to, say, Joyce Carol Oates. And Murdoch's training as a philosopher stitches elegantly through her novels the way, for instance, Andrew Greeley makes use of his theology to sew his rougher romances together. Indeed, to find the same sort of writer one would have to blend Greeley and Oates, and the freakish result would most likely turn out to be an Iris Murdoch character.

The Book and the Brotherhood is, in many ways, the least lurid and most realistic of her novels. In the fashionable spirit of theatrical revivals now possessing Broadway, the experience of reading it is similar to seeing a smartly done production of an old play (a Kaufman and Hart, though, not Chekhov).

The plot of her twenty-third novel is less unwieldy than intricate, because it involves only a small circle of friends, and while complicated, it works within a tiny enclosed space, has the same pleasing simplicity of a ship in a bottle. The entanglements are all romantic, sex and death near at hand, though Murdoch spends most of her energy lingering over the deaths and not the physical encounters. She remains the most genteel of writers, though some of the couples actually enjoy sex.

The novel, essentially, is about friendship, particularly the sort that originates in college and then continues to dominate adult lives, a formula often resorted to in novels (Mary McCarthy's *The Group*) and films (*The Big Chill*). How many permutations of romantic relationships can you manage with a set of friends? Murdoch exhausts the possibilities.

Her group convenes at a midsummer ball at Oxford University that serves as a reunion, and the coming together is not unmarred by a crisis. David Crimond (*cri mond*, cry of the world), the character who functions as the linchpin

---

* First appeared in Tribune *Books*, *Chicago Tribune*, Feb. 7, 1988. Review of *The Book and the Brotherhood* by Iris Murdoch.

of the group (and the novel), induces one half of a couple to leave her husband and go off and live with him, after pushing the husband into the river Cherwell.

Crimond, to make use of the jacket copy's heated, albeit accurate, tone, is a monomaniacal radical genius who is being supported by his wealthy friends, since he seems to be the only one not in possession of inherited wealth. The "Book" of the title is the one Crimond is being financed (for some three decades) to write. The "charismatic" and multisexual Gerard Hernshaw is the maitre d' of the group; he is always arranging how they get together. Then there is, quoting the jacket copy, "Rose Curtland, who has loved Gerard in silence for years; Jenkin Riderhood, the saintly schoolmaster who is the group's moral center; Tamar Hernshaw, Gerald's tormented niece," and a few others, also breathlessly described.

As one would expect from Iris Murdoch, the book has passion, murder, a suicide pact, a quite well done and lovely skating party. There are Christmas teas and quiet evening discussions among friends. And there is a mother-daughter relationship that, given our times, competes in its ferocity and ugliness with any I've read in contemporary fiction.

Since the novel takes place in the environs of Oxford University and is peopled with its graduates, the author does have direct access to her own society. Murdoch exists not so much in an ivory tower as an ivory world. Even though she is up to date about the way successful people behave, she is not under any pressure to change, another attribute of success.

The novel does touch on politics (Crimond's long awaited masterpiece is a revisionist Marxist "synthesis, it's immensely long, it's about everything") but the outside workaday world only exists in *The Book and the Brotherhood* the way it is felt in *Wuthering Heights*—as a pernicious mist. Rose, still longing for Gerard, can say late in the novel, with Murdoch intending no irony, "She held onto his warm dear hand which mattered so much more than any book, more than the fate of democrative government, more than the fate of the human race."

Murdoch is at her best, paradoxically, with her younger characters, rather than with her elderly ones. Buzzing around the older central core of friends are a few bright young people, acolytes and messengers, agents and victims, and they provide occasions of liveliness in the novel.

Iris Murdoch is nearing seventy, and she is such a fact of the literary landscape that carping at her methods seems as superfluous as complaining about an outlandish but long appreciated statue in a public park. (In 1987 she was made a Dame of the Order of the British Empire.) Succumb to her spell and there is a good bit of enjoyment to be found. No fan of Iris Murdoch will suffer disappointment here.

Studded throughout the novel are witty, though arch, remarks, evidence that Murdoch actually enjoyed writing this book, rather than producing it dutifully: "It is possible for a girl to have a too long a neck, and Lily's could be said to be on the border between the swan-like and the grotesque"; and "One can get away with being a mediocre tennis player or a moderate cricketer, but skating is like ballet, unless one is fairly good one is contemptible"; and "Handwriting can tell a tale of joy or of fear well before it is connected with a name." There are many more, and you won't find their like in homegrown romance writing. Murdoch is much more an incisive novelist of manners than a writer of philosophical novels.

The Book and the Brotherhood contains a recurring lament: "No novel pleased her now with that glad feeling of escape and refuge . . . No one reads books of imagination now . . . they want facts. Rose could not do with facts, but the other things had gone too. Was she becoming, like the century, illiterate?"

This complaint runs through the novel, a frequent aside to the melodramatic turns of plot, and it becomes clear that Iris Murdoch does not see herself writing, as one stern critic has complained, "Harlequins for highbrows," but something even more impossible: romances as they were written before the age of television, when fantasies of soap opera proportions would only play in the mind's eye, be given life with words, not electrons, and be read by an audience that would eagerly grant her the time it takes to appreciate her multilayered tale-telling and all the deliberate needlepoint that goes into her elaborate characterizations. For all such who endure, her novel does supply "that glad feeling of escape and refuge."

D. M. Thomas*

D. M. Thomas, the English author who made a great commotion in 1981 with his surprise best-seller, *The White Hotel*, has more quietly brought to a conclusion a "quintet" of novels with the publication of *Lying Together*, which was preceded by *Ararat, Swallow, Sphinx,* and *Summit*.

Lying Together, like all of Thomas's fiction, makes free and easy use of important historical figures and events. But where *The White Hotel* acquired some dignity from its subject matter (Europe before and during World War II, the early years of psychoanalysis, the Holocaust), the new novel suffers from an utter lack of dignity—even though, in all his novels, Thomas's method remains the same.

Each of his fictions is a pastiche of letters, poems, journals and narrative. Done (or noticed) the first time, this can leave the impression that one is an innovator, as some critics believed him to be in *The White Hotel*; done endlessly, it becomes the hallmark of an amateur.

No longer is it enough for Thomas to make use only of characters from history; he now makes use of himself. In *Lying Together* he claims (as character and author) that the first four volumes of the series, as is this one, were collaborations with a number of contemporary Russian writers who weren't free to publish in the pre-Glasnost Soviet Union. Some of the Eastern Bloc characters in those novels, who appear in *Lying Together* as themselves, now come together for an international writers conference at a posh British hotel and announce to Thomas their intentions of making their roles public:

> "We'd like our friends to know we weren't entirely inactive these past few years," said Masha with a smile. "Are you pleased?"
> Actually I felt acutely alarmed. I tried to show pleasure at their decision and at the same time annoyance that our contract simply

---

* First appeared in *Books, Chicago Tribune*, July 15, 1990. Review of *Lying Together* by D. M. Thomas.

wouldn't permit it. I felt grateful to my publisher for their insistence that we guard against any change of mind by my secret collaborators—unlikely as that had seemed in the frigid era of Brezhnev.

Lying Together has a few moments of droll comedy when some of the foreign writers and the one English writer present, Don Thomas, mistake an undertakers conference for their group and unwittingly engage in non sequiturs about each other's work. This joke pops up later on when an undertaker arriving late mistakes the literary conference for his and reads his paper on new embalming techniques, which the literary crowd applauds as a superb piece of fiction.

Thomas's entire literary career has been tied to Russian literature, principally Soviet poetry. He has translated Akhmatova, Pushkin, and Yevtushenko. He calls this quintet of novels "Russian Nights," in homage to Pushkins's narrative fragment "Egyptian Nights," which Thomas translated and used as the core of *Ararat*.

In the new novel, Thomas gathers with the Russian writers every night of the conference to improvise, à la Pushkin, the novel at hand, *Lying Together*. The puns of the title tell the story: sex, betrayal and mutual, make-believe storytelling. The facts of the plot are revised as different characters take turns improvising the story; unfortunately the cleverness of the method is more interesting than the result. Thomas entertains ideas instead of making ideas entertaining.

Lurking around *Lying Together* is not so much the ghost of Freud (though he puts in an appearance) as the spirit of Tom Clancy, because one aspect of the "improvised" tale concerns a Soviet nuclear submarine captain who, bothered by his homosexuality and beset with AIDS, plans to blow up England.

For a man who is presumed to know a lot about Russian literature, Thomas offers us contemporary Russian characters who rival those in the pulpiest of pulp fiction. The most famous Russian writer friend of Thomas attending the conference, Victor Surkov, is, we are informed, the lover of both Raisa Gorbachev and Margaret Thatcher, and he has been invited, albeit prematurely (the novel is set right before the 1988 U.S. presidential elections), to read a poem at the Dukakis inauguration. However amusing that might seem to be—especially the idea of the Russian's early-morning liaisons with Maggie—Thomas does seem a bit underwhelmed by his own subject matter. Indeed, one agrees with him when he writes, "I . . . thought there was very little likelihood that our chaotic improvisations could make a successful novel."

In the final analysis, Thomas seems to have the mind of a screenwriter trapped in the body of a well-read pedant. He is often heavy-handed with everydayness, whereas his depictions of great atrocities, as in *The White Hotel*, can be quite lyrical and light.

Thomas's fiction needs great historic events to gain power, just as people often scramble to be near celebrities in order to absorb warmth from their glowing fame. Unfortunately, he appears to think that both writers conferences and the killings at Babi Yar are celebrity events. *Lying Together* is an example of how some writers can be mock-wise about the past but perfectly silly about the present.

IV

NONFICTIONAL TIMES: AMNESTY, TRIALS, PROFILES, CENSORSHIP

REMEMBERING TO FORGET*

> **amnesty 1.** *Forgetfulness; an intentional overlooking 1592.*
> **2.** *An act of oblivion, a general overlooking or pardon of*
> *past offences, by the ruling authority 1580.*
> —The Shorter Oxford English Dictionary

1

The quest for amnesty contains a significant paradox. In order to forget we must remember; in order to heal we must irritate. Amnesty's first cause is necessity; it shares the same Greek root as *amnesia*: even our bodies practice it. Amnesty is the antithesis of shock; it does not make us unable to feel, yet it allows us to forget. This is not the repression of unexpressed fears or guilts but a salubrious remembering to forget.

The opponents of amnesty (including, but not limited to, the Nixon administration) have instituted their own kind of de facto amnesty. They want the problem forgotten as quickly as possible; they refuse to acknowledge the dimensions of the issue, the numbers involved, or the significance to the people and the country. For good or ill, millions have already declared their own separate amnesty over the war in Vietnam. They want to forget; indeed, it is such an imperative that it is a truism.

The search for amnesty raises ghosts already put to rest. The war is fought once again; the specter of body counts walks when so much time is spent arguing over the numbers who are affected. More than seven thousand convicted for Selective Service violations; nearly forty thousand cases being reviewed by the Department of Justice for possible prosecution; indictments in

---

* First appeared in *Rights*, May-June 1974. Citations and footnotes have been dropped in this printing.

existence for about six thousand more. More than thirty thousand deserters (from out of 495,689 cases from August 1964 to December 1972) still at large. An estimated forty thousand exiles in Canada and elsewhere. A half-million less-than-honorable discharged soldiers, Vietnam-era veterans. Numbers numb.

The 1972 census reports that an estimated 10 percent failed to register for the draft when they reached eighteen. And, most strikingly, out of the teeming draft pool available to the armed forces during those years, only 11.1 percent of the men examined were actually inducted and served.

The reasons, motives, and methods of the large majority of men who did not serve would be as numerous as the individuals. Luck, stealth, accident of age, occupation, parents, position, wealth, health, location of draft board, and so forth.

Amnesty debates, both for and against, are inexorably interwoven with those about the Vietnam war. The history of that war, and the history of its domestic front—the resistance—are parallel; the mirror image of escalation in Vietnam, and protest and repression in this country, is eerie in its duplication. The claims of historic precedents for amnesty—each one enlightening in its way—are not sufficient. As J. G. Randall remarks in his introduction to J. T. Dorris's *Pardon and Amnesty under Lincoln and Johnson* (1953): "It [amnesty] is a broad subject which the 'history books' do not cover, nor the 'law books' either."

Amnesty is the solution to a number of complex problems, which, like the many serpents of the Medusa, cannot be killed one by one but must be severed collectively, at the base.

2

Amnesty is something winners give to losers. The *Encyclopaedia of Social Sciences* (1937) understands it to be "an act of the legal sovereign conceding, from grace, a voluntary extinction from memory of certain crimes committed against the state." A defective but prevalent explanation of amnesty, found in *Amnesty? The Unsettled Question of Vietnam* (1973), further characterizes it as "strictly an act of grace on the part of the state. That is to say, the state in no way concedes thereby that its laws are unenforceable, or that they may be violated with impunity. Amnesty, if it is granted at all in a given case, partakes rather of the character of charity . . ." The extending of "from grace" to "the character of charity" is unwarranted. *From grace* is more a legal term than a theological one, as in Days of Grace, the period allowed by law for payment of a bill of exchange; or, as in an instance of favor; an exceptional favor, a privilege, a dispensation (*Oxford English Dictionary*). The need to imply the high virtue of "charity" to amnesty stems from an argument against its use: that in some way it is forgiveness (and thereby charitable to forgive). President Nixon prefers this incorrect definition. In *Burdick v. United States* the Court's definition of amnesty noted its use when it was "deemed more expedient for the public welfare than prosecution and punishment." *Expedient* is not usually accepted as a synonym for *charitable*. The grants of amnesty in American history were governed more by common sense and expedience than by acts of grace and the character of charity.

According to the *Encyclopaedia of Social Sciences*, amnesty is used to "erase civil strife from memory by the imposition of legal oblivion." After an open rebellion, the solution that will adequately heal such a breech is an amnesty. The first American pardon/amnesty was conferred on July 10, 1795, on the Whiskey insurrectionists. Pirates who fought in the War of 1812 were pardoned by President James Madison. The Civil War brought about the most sweeping amnesties under three successive presidents. The bulk of precedents leads to a startling conclusion. The protests against the Vietnam War and the subsequent Selective Service and military and civil violations would have had to result in a true insurrection in order for an amnesty to be swiftly declared. In order for amnesty to be implemented, the offenses would have had to be greater, because it is absolutely necessary in order to achieve and retain the equilibrium of the state. Those who argue against an amnesty by citing flaws or lapses in historic precedents are guilty of the perverse (but sometimes expressed) reasoning of the physician who declares the disease must get worse before it can be cured, or the officer who suggests that the village must be destroyed in order to be saved.

Winners bestow amnesty on losers because there would be no victory without it; amnesty follows traumatic civil strife because the vanquished and the victors must live together. (In the case of the amnesties following World War II, to avoid a permanent garrison state; in the case of the amnesty that President Theodore Roosevelt gave in 1902 to the Philippine insurrectionists, to diminish continuing rebellion.)

The divisions in this country that were demonstrated or created by the Indochina War have often been compared to those that were exacerbated by the Civil War—if not in kind, at least in intensity. The primary reason was superficial: it seemed that half the country was opposed to the other half, and that the division was neatly drawn—hawks versus doves, the North versus the South. The reaction of the people of this country to the war in Vietnam is the chief historic precedent to ponder in discussion of amnesty (that alone would include at least a decade of observed cause and effect); the arguments opposing amnesty that are based on the fact that such an amnesty as would be required has never occurred (thus tacitly acknowledging that the nature of the problem is without precedent) are as empty as the arguments of those who discounted manned flight until it was accomplished.

The Spanish-American war, according to the Congressional Research Service, created the pressures that resulted in a universal amnesty bill that was finally enacted in 1898. The atmosphere of the country during that war oddly echoed our own time. "Remember the *Maine!*"—the slogan that stirred the country into what commentators refer to as war "hysteria"—was created by an explosion aboard the USS *Maine* in Havana harbor as shrouded in mystery as to its origin and causes as were the circumstances which led to the Gulf of Tonkin Resolution in 1964. Teddy Roosevelt's "Rough Riders" in Cuba were the eager Green Berets of the last years of the nineteenth century. "Anti-expansionist" rallies were disrupted by mothers of sons fighting in the Philippines. The acquisition of the Philippines, Guam, and Puerto Rico was hotly contested in the Senate, and the peace treaty with Spain was passed by a one-vote margin.

The historical precedent of interest is not the universal amnesty but the state of conscription. A contemporaneous essay serves as a bellwether for the direction conscription would take, as well as a summary of its history. The history of conscription in this country is critical to the amnesty question. Conscription serves as an impetus to volunteering. The Spanish-American War, which caused much the same distress in its day as the Indochina War in ours, was fought by volunteers. Calls were put out for "volunteers" spurred by a possible threat of conscription; but, most importantly, the war had to be "sold" to the public. And it was. Organized religion contributed to the clamor for intervention; the Hearst *New York Journal*, the Pulitzer *New York World*, and other exponents of the yellow press harangued for intervention. The reluctance of the McKinley administration was one of the few pockets of prudence, but that was overcome. Since the war was so brief and fought by regulars and volunteers, the problem of amnesty did not become crucial; but it can be presumed that a country that passed a universal amnesty bill that very year would not maintain a vindictive policy towards those who resisted conscription. Nor was there, at the turn of the century, anything like the "dossier dictatorship" that would dog one's past and make it one's present. That period in American history has often been referred to as the beginning of a "new era" that may well have found its conclusion in our own.

Much has been made by opponents of amnesty that there was none following the Korean War. It is not difficult to see why. The post-World War II baby boom did not produce the first eighteen-year-old crop until 1963, and the military still retained its World War II credibility at the time of Korea in 1950. The UN was involved; Truman characterized it as a "police action." The cold war was two decades away from detente. It was not fought in the living room on the six o'clock news, and, most significantly, it lasted three years, not twelve. (It seems that in all American wars the government is given the benefit of the doubt, and even in Vietnam evasion and desertion did not begin in earnest till after the war had been on stage and on trial for a number of years.)

The war in Vietnam was an unprecedented though not unforeshadowed experience, and the actions taken because of it, including amnesty, must therefore be unprecedented. The need for amnesty is attributed not only to the Vietnam War but also to its agent, the Selective Service System (SSS). The system had been allowed to fade away (like old soldiers) on March 31, 1947; but two important precedents before that date must be noted.

The Selective Service Act of 1917 was passed only *after* the United States declared war on Germany on April 7, 1917; and it was only *after* Pearl Harbor in December 1944 that the Selective Service Act of 1940 was amended to permit the removal of restrictions as to where men could be stationed (hitherto they had to remain within the confines of the United States and its territories and possessions). After World War II, President Truman proposed a system of universal military training, but Congress chose instead to reinstate the expired draft law. When the Korean conflict was at its height, Congress extended the Selective Service Act, and the draft became a part of the American way of life. A few contemporary senators objected to a peacetime draft and the contradictions it presented. The "draft" has now ended, though the SSS is perpetuated and registration continues.

The draft made possible the shadow standing army used during the cold war. The so-called Truman Emergency has never been repealed, and in effect this country has been in a state of national emergency since 1950. The act was the reverse Magna Carta of the cold war and has served as legal underpinning for various acts. For example, it called for "a strengthening of American military forces to meet the threat of world conquest by Communist imperialism."

Since that time, the philosophy and use of conscription have ceased to be that which the framers of the Constitution had envisioned and which the public has come to expect. In effect, a new kind of conscript has been created.

It is not just a truism of history to say that those who fought the war did not bring it about. Vietnam was the bloody capstone of the cold war, and the servicemen who were sent there were more displaced than the refugees caused by the war. The fact that mercenaries prospered in Vietnam only serves to show what kind of war it was. Even the most callow of youths must feel they are serving a purpose, defending their country. If the horrors of war can be reconciled (and history does not so attest), they must be buttressed by the deepest kind of commitment, however irrational that commitment may be.

The war in Vietnam, and the draft, divided the country, but in an even deeper way than public protests showed. The Selective Service System (SSS) in effect during the war (and whose provisions were so often violated and now require amnesty) had, according to Richard Flacks (*The Draft*, 1967), "the apparent virtue of permitting a partial mobilization for wars as large as Vietnam without substantially increasing the militancy of the population, without developing a major war fever."

This schism had profound consequences: it contributed to general public's detachment and divided the country, not in the simple hawk-dove contrast, but in just who was affected by the war and who wasn't. It literally touched, along with those in the military establishment (including enlistees), only those who had to go and their families—specifically, that 11.1 percent who were inducted (the percentage of those young men who served after being drafted, not the country's entire population; there are more than 220 million Americans—2.5 million served in South Vietnam during this period).

This "apparent virtue" of the method of conscription during the prolonged Vietnam conflict was one of the most ignored, but destructive aspects of the war—and even now hampers any movement for amnesty. The majority of Americans were remote from the war when it was occurring and are now even more distant. The war that many have said was the most immediate (since it was fought on television) was at the same time the most removed from the daily concerns of Americans. The perversion of the uses of conscription, which required neither a militant population nor a "major war fever," was in large part responsible. (It is ironic that only following "peace with honor" does gas rationing become a possibility.) It is in the setting of these historical precedents that the issue of amnesty must be discussed.

3

Though our Constitution forbids "cruel and unusual punishment," the military is able to cripple a life forever by means of a less-than-honorable discharge. A felony conviction of the jailed draft resister and the lot that faces the exile are no more or less than a stigma. And it is cruel and unusual that such a condition rises more regularly than a phoenix, especially in our time of a reigning "dossier dictatorship." The SSS has instituted a filing system that any totalitarian ruler would envy.

Ours is a credentials society, and black marks create an automatic response in a computer's brain. A less-than-honorable discharge prevents the men it labels from even taking the most hesitant steps toward self-advancement. It excludes an individual from this society's mainstream as effectively as the bells worn by lepers in biblical times. Branding is a trait well established in our country's culture and economics (consider, e.g., *The Scarlet Letter* and cattle ranching).

A half-million Vietnam-era veterans are branded with less-than-honor-able discharges. There is something pitiless in taking a young man and marking him for the rest of his life. These less-than-honorable discharges are (for the majority) handled administratively; the men are "fired" from the army. The charges make a dreary litany: drug abuse, bed-wetting, apathy, general "bad habits." The practice reveals the pervasive need for amnesty when it becomes clear how many veterans require it. It does not take long to determine who are the victims of these discharges: the poor, blacks, Puerto Ricans, rural whites, the ill, or the noneducated. The military scorns them as misfits, bad apples; but before they throw them back into society to sink or swim they tie the lead weight of a less-than-honorable discharge around their necks.

There is one remedy, other than amnesty, that would solve this problem—if no distinction were made in the type of discharge given to a veteran. But that would run counter to the "dossier dictatorship." What past history would be more likely to produce a future felon: the governorship of Maryland or a less-than-honorable discharge?

The deserter from the Vietnam War is quite different from the popular stereotype: a man shirking under fire, leaving his fellows in the lurch; "bugging out," as President Nixon has put it. Yet desertion from units in Vietnam constitutes a minute percentage. Before a Senate subcommittee an assistant secretary of defense submitted the names of 228 deserters who were considered "military absentees who go to a foreign country because of suspected political motivation." Of the 228, 11 absented themselves from units in Vietnam; 9 of the 11 failed to return from Vietnam from "rest and recuperation" in Japan. In other words, 2 of the 228 actually deserted in the popular sense; and there is no information that even these 2 deserted from front-line units. The vast majority of deserters/AWOLs absented themselves before they were to return for a second tour or before they went at all. Their desertion was *ex post facto* evasion.

The "typical" resister and deserter are in many ways opposite but equal. The stereotypical picture of a resister is, by and large, correct: some college education, if not a graduate, white, hovering around the middle class, and, significantly, older, having possessed for a time some type of deferment. They had time to think about it, often a few years. The "average" deserter, though, is more often than not a high school graduate or drop-out who has enlisted in the army, with little experience or exposure to the world. The armed forces served as the place of his matriculation. But there the differences end, and the similarities, the questioning, begins.

Had Socrates been eighteen when asked to choose between hemlock and exile, both the reasoning and the outcome might have been different. Yet compulsory conscription presents every American male with the same dilemma. Though there are other spurs to serious thought, the draft has served for this generation. It is the first experience men have with their government; it is equivalent to getting to know someone by first becoming acquainted with their garbage. The inequities of the draft are common knowledge, yet opposition to the draft does not stem entirely from a reaction to the faultiness of the methods of selection; it occurs in proportion to the lack of support for the immediate purposes of conscription.

Daniel Webster wrote: "Who will show me any constitutional injunction, which makes it the duty of the American people to surrender every thing valuable in life, and even life itself, not when the safety of their country and its liberties may demand the sacrifice, but whenever the purposes of an ambitious and mischievous Government may require it." In one form or another, that question has been asked by even the least sophisticated of eighteen-year-olds. The SSS wished (and presumably still does) to have a continually replenishable pool of nineteen-year-olds to choose from. It is an example of their cynical realism.

The military has always been an unhappy alternative education offered to the poor. But now, since large numbers have partaken of mass education, the burden of conscience has shifted away from those who have evaded to those who have gone into the army, asking each of them for a positive reason for a choice that heretofore had hardly been considered. Once in the service, many find few positive reasons to be there.

The military has classically been a place to escape to (e.g., the Foreign Legion) or an opportunity to begin again with a clean slate (as in the offer to a young offender of the choice between going into the army or a stretch in prison). It is not insignificant that the most famous young officer of the Indochina War, Lieutenant William L. Calley, Jr., volunteered for the army when he was stranded in Albuquerque, New Mexico, after his car broke down.

The so-called resister outside the army evaded by getting into the National Guard or the reserves, finding a job that brought a deferment in the national interest, being the only means of support for his family, or by uncovering a legitimate medical impairment—in short, any kind of socially acceptable means of evasion. (It should be recalled that the SSS examined 15,612,487 young men from January 1, 1965, through December 31, 1972. Only 1,727,608 were inducted.)

The much-praised conscientious objector exemption benefits the military more than anyone else. The C.O. deferment (until the most recent court definitions) was a legal nicety used to dismiss fanatics (e.g., Quakers and Mennonites) from the service much as any processing machine will reject a misshapen package. But when this provision was seized by those looking for a way out, who did not fit the proscribed orthodoxy, the weakest link was discovered (the military's own version of amnesty: overlooking them intentionally), and it was here, upon C.O. classification, that the most stress has been placed.

The members of local boards, by all reports, those who make up these home-grown symposia deciding on C.O.'s, have the theological and philosophical depths of a beauty-pageant jury: what they look for is "sincerity," the elixir that settles any bad case of the doubts. In the draft's last hours a lottery was reinstated, acknowledging the transfer of human responsibility for who shall perish in war back into the hands of fate and the gods—in this case, a bingo-parlor Olympus.

Throughout history the rich and educated have been able to find their way clear of conscription (once it was possible simply to buy one's way out, and indirectly, it is still possible). The military, with the tutoring of antiquity, settles a basic conflict by separating officers from enlisted men. The "grunts" are taught to fear and follow orders; the officers are instructed in the art of giving orders and instilling fear.

The vindictiveness of those who oppose amnesty flows not from their respect of law and order (for the legal basis for amnesty is well established) but from a much darker spring. The real grievances held against evaders and deserters are twofold. In William Rusher's brief against amnesty (in *Amnesty?*) these classifications are established: (1) "the gravity of the offense" and (2) "the attitude of the offenders."

After what is referred to as "scarifying arithmetic," this conclusion is reached: "it follows that the defection of those 60,000 draft-dodgers [an almost arbitrary figure] resulted in the deaths of at least 1,500 of their fellow Americans who would otherwise be alive today, and the wounding of 10,000." This is the dark equation that works in most minds when draft evasion and desertion are considered.

Evasion and desertion are not balanced by the young man who has used the military as an escape from a hometown, a rite of passage, or a time of maturation and acquiring of discipline. An evader or deserter is equated with a dead soldier. Even taking the "scarifying arithmetic" at its face value, there is only one constant in the equation used: the figures for the dead and wounded. Those will not change, no matter the percentage of evaders or deserters. According to the argument's figures, one out of thirty-nine evaders or deserters must bear—so the argument goes—the responsibility for one death.

There is something nonsensical in this mathematical morality. Two million men were drafted (again, according to the argument's figures) in this period; 600 thousand of them went to Vietnam. It is presupposed that every evader, if he had been inducted, would have been sent to Vietnam. But that is not so: each inductee had roughly a 25 percent chance. But it is spurious even to dispute the calculation. What is totally wrong is the placement of the blame. It will ease many a conscience to say the deaths in Vietnam were caused by draft evaders and deserters, but that is an affront to the facts. It is not unusual for supporters and originators of wars to establish evaders and deserters as the low creatures of their imaginations, since they have fouled them with their own guilt. They are scapegoats. And if evaders and deserters are amnestied, the blame will have to fall on other shoulders.

This branding of those who protested the war or refused the draft, as shirkers and cowards who only cared for their own skins, was one barb that spurred the escalation of antiwar protest. Some of those who were daily slandered wanted to prove that they valued their lives no more nor less than the average soldier. Bombings, trashings, and other acts of physical violence were meant to signal—in part—that they were not cowards.

The only conclusion to be drawn from this mathematical morality is that the proper and just amnesty would be some version of Russian roulette, where—after a more precise figuring of odds—a man would spin a cylinder with so many (thirty-nine?) empty chambers and one loaded one, and, if he did escape, he would be allowed to go completely "free." To account for the wounded would take a much more elaborate system. There are many primitive tribes that would applaud such a method.

No one gets off scot-"free" though. That is a concept that chills the foes of amnesty. The idea that an individual escapes the most cruel caprice of fate bitterly disappoints some people. Congressional hearings in 1968 revealed how the average deserter goes "free": he is subjected to "(a) the great disadvantage of less-than-honorable discharge upon his future life; (b) the present plight of absentees in Europe is not enviable; (c) that absentees have a hard life ahead of them as a result of their failure to adhere to military discipline."

This analysis emanates not from a humanitarian organization describing the hardships of a deserter's lot but from the United States military. And the life of the exiled young American evaders is not one marked conspicuously by freedom's virtues. For the most part they live marginal existences; and the best of these, those with college degrees and skills that make them highly employable, are the exception, not the rule. These men are forced exiles, and they live in a gray, unresolved state. An amnesty would allow them to make a decision about returning, free from the constant coercion of their predicament. President Nixon would require them to pay a penalty ("Those who deserted [their country] must pay their price"). No one will be let off scot-"free"; everyone will have to pay.

4

Amnesty applies to a class of offenders. It is general, not particular; the general lawbreaking was caused by the war and the vast opposition to it. Amnesty would not necessarily apply to state law violations. There are many

Americans who now have some sort of court record because of petty violations associated with a peace demonstration. These violations stem from one cause: the Vietnam War. Those who cry for the jailing of draft evaders or deserters do not care about individuals; they are speaking about a class of offenders, precisely to what amnesty applies.

The arguments for a partial amnesty on a case-by-case basis serve only to reveal the need for general amnesty. Now, with the current alteration in the C.O. statute, many evaders and deserters could qualify. The powers of discretion allowed to both military and civil courts are wide and far ranging. Similar cases have completely dissimilar results; there is no equal application of justice. Two federal district court judges ruled in January, 1974, that 153 men charged by the government in 1972 with draft evasion had been deprived of their constitutional "protection against false accusation." They found that the indictments "seriously infringed upon the rights of individual defendants" and that the cases had been "allowed to languish in the files" for many months. Future dismissals based on delay in bringing cases to trial are to be expected. The government, in its own interest, keeps diminishing the number of men who benefit by an amnesty. That is still another reason in favor of it.

Amnesty is also opposed on the basis of a new but equally discredited domino theory. That is, if an amnesty is granted, no future armies will be able to be raised. The last amnesty granted in this country, by President Truman (1952), applied to all persons convicted for having deserted between August 15, 1945, and June 25, 1950. Despite that, armies *have* been raised. Those who have evaded or deserted never did so with the expectation that amnesty would be granted; and, for the most part, they are not the ones calling for amnesty now. It would take the most obtuse misunderstanding of social dynamics to believe that in this single instance history would not be allowed to repeat itself.

The cast of mind that functions when the deserter is considered is best expressed by the military form USAFPP194-356/73. It is a "bounty" form (the "6/73" refers to the latest updating), reminiscent of old Wild West "wanted" posters and runaway slave circulars. What is especially striking is the amount of the reward. It is $25 for the apprehension and the delivery of an AWOL/deserter; but only $15 if he is apprehended and merely detained. The callousness of this form and the tiny reward make one believe that it is simply featherbedding for the MPs who must accompany the prisoner to the lockup (though many civilians have availed themselves of this additional income). The size of the reward reveals the military's insignificant interest in the problem.

Unless the untenable logic of one-evader-equals-one-dead-soldier is accepted, evasion is a victimless crime. Desertion (and thereby evasion) is traditionally considered a political offense. It is a negative crime, choosing *not* to do something. This unwillingness to participate is accepted as being entirely different from the "every day, garden variety felony."

If there is a less abstract "victim" it is the "people," and that is why it seems most appropriate for Congress to legislate amnesty, though it can be decreed most swiftly by the president. Senator George McGovern, as the Democratic candidate for the presidency in 1972, said he would grant "full and unconditional amnesty to draft evaders abroad or in jail." The 39 percent of the electorate that voted for him has, in effect, ratified this amnesty. Polls taken late in 1971 showed a majority of Americans favoring "some form" of amnesty.

The draft dodger of popular imagination, usually cartooned with bent paper clips and pencils stuck in an ear, has faded almost entirely. The Vietnam War produced the oxymoron "conscientious evasion and desertion," but it is just this "conscientiousness" that troubles those who oppose amnesty. The military, in explaining the large number of deserters to Congress in 1968, contended that only "one person in 28,000 who served in the Armed Forces during the period" [June 1, 1966-May 17, 1968] who "went to another country, or attempted to do so," did it "for stated or suspected political reasons." Conscience and politics are uneasily linked in the minds of the military and by the opponents of amnesty. The quoted congressional report discloses that in fiscal 1967 "one man in 32 was absent without authority at some time during the year." Action taken against 40 AWOLs/deserters during that time "reveals a wide range of punishments . . . from a $15 fine imposed for a 7-day absence to Sweden, to a general court-martial sentence of bad conduct discharge and 2 years' confinement at hard labor for a five-month absence to Canada."

The results of individual "case-by-case" solutions are apparent. In a celebrated case of desertion, John David Herndon's, the army did not court-martial him but cashiered him out of the army administratively, with a less-than-honorable discharge. Opponents of amnesty fear that a few deserving of punishment will escape under the cloak of a general amnesty; but it is clear that there would be more cases of justice miscarried in a case-by-case amnesty/pardon than there would be under a general amnesty.

The "attitude of the offenders" (in Rusher's phrase) is the larger offense, and that is what rankles opponents of amnesty. Such a young man is characterized by Rusher as "defiantly hostile to the American society in general" and "essentially rebellious," a person who has developed a "profound alienation from the traditions, values and general direction of the American society." Opponents of amnesty ask: Why accept these malcontents back? It is better that they have deported themselves—or, as former Attorney General John Mitchell is reported to have said, it would be better to trade a few good Communist bureaucrats for the likes of them. Indeed, hostility to amnesty is based not on what has been done but on what is feared will be done.

Those who would benefit from amnesty directly are considered to be—by those who oppose it—radicals, agitators, and dangerous subversives. This distorted view is the chimera the cold war has left fastened on the minds of the generation which fostered it. The military's own figures for so-called political deserters are minute, yet amnesty is withheld because of the fright this mare's nest awakens in their hearts.

The facts tell another tale. To listen to the profile of the "ordinary" deserter reported to Congress is to hear a roll call of the disadvantaged, the misused, and the unfortunate: "80% of the absentees (in a random sampling of those gone more than 30 days) were in pay grades E-1 and E-2 [the lowest] . . . 83% were in the lower mental groups, while 59% had 9 years or more of education . . . 82% had a prior military disciplinary record and 20% had a civilian record . . . 69% were *under 22 years of age* and 67% were single" (emphasis added).

These are the young men defiantly hostile to American society in general. They are the have-nots, the wily subversives we must keep from our borders. The typical evader would show, as has been noted, a different profile; but to label them as "un-American" would demonstrate a blindness to history. Deserters and evaders share a common condition: they were caught in a juggernaut of circumstances that presented them with unacceptable choices. It was the setting for tragedy.

5

The responsibility for amnesty rests with the American public. Only with sufficient support and pressure will a president or Congress be moved to grant it. And it will most likely have to await the presidential campaign of 1976, when sufficient attention can be focused on it as a separate, distinct issue, apart from impeachment, inflation, Watergate, and the various "emergency" crises. The turbulence of the moment obscures the necessity and worth of amnesty. "Wherever the government feels itself insecure [amnesties] are of doubtful worth. In fact, from the standpoint of the group in power, amnesties are politically expedient only when the regime is safe from further violence, and when clemency may not be mistaken for weakness," notes the *Encyclopaedia of the Social Sciences.*

Yet, 1976 may be an especially appropriate time, since an amnesty traditionally signals an end to one period of history and the beginning of another. Our country's bicentennial would be enhanced by such a commemoration.

Some matters involved in amnesty will always be moot. Lincoln, the statesman of binding wounds, so often quoted, serves again: "Blood can not restore blood, and government should not act for revenge." The emotions that swirl around amnesty will never completely settle. But now that the war has "ended," the draft has "ended," the POWs have returned; now that the country may act, it is no longer necessary to await history's luxuriant verdict.

JURY DUTY*

1

Stepping out of one's "normal" existence into two weeks of jury duty causes a minor case of emotional whiplash. Personalities constrict or expand—a decompression caused by being hoisted too quickly out of the usual environment. Gregarious individuals become positively giddy and solitary figures deeply sullen. In a few days the large jurors assembly room takes on a shipwrecked-island atmosphere, which remains until the sail of dismissal appears on the horizon near the end of the second week.

In New York City, New York State Supreme Court at 60 Centre Street, despite a lofty name, handles unexalted cases. When called for jury duty you may be drafted to serve on criminal trials, but the common fate is civil cases. The first day you will encounter a line as long as any hit movie's along Bloomingdale row. You have your summons, which is the ticket to the jurors assembly room, where you wait . . . and wait. The only scheduled entertainment is the court clerks who watch over you. The most amusing of this group—he does schtick between the calling of names—resembles a lumpen William Ronan. The comparison is not just physiognomical; he calls the shots. He treats the chosen like the infantile bumblers they are; with rare exception (the recidivists) they are ignorant of procedures and therefore at his mercy. Most are content to be herded, giving themselves up into the arms of regimentation. He is the first to acquaint the laity with the rituals of jurisprudence, and he has been made testy, as is anyone whose job is to impart the simplest information, over and over, year after year.

I had a number of misapprehensions. I thought as soon as I was found unfit by an attorney—as I expected to be—I would be released. No. The clerk chooses panels of thirty-odd, and these are questioned individually by the two

---

* First appeared in *American Rag*, vol. 1, nos. 2-3, 1980.

opposing attorneys, out of the presence of the judge, in a small room with a mock jury box. If you are rejected it is not terminal; you return to the jurors assembly room and wait to be called again.

New York City juries are reputed to be the most sophisticated in the country, and lawyers often try to void this fact; but, in the first panel of thirty for which I was called, there was a familiar name. Jason Epstein, the author of *The Great Conspiracy Trial* (aka the Chicago 7). What were the odds, I wondered, at getting two authors of conspiracy trial books in a random panel of thirty strangers? Epstein resembles a mischievous *Through the Looking Glass* character (much more Tweedledee than Tweedledum); his corporate vice president's pin-striped suit is offset by a waggish pink bowtie. When I introduced myself, his expression seemed to confirm the view that the jurors assembly room was a circle of hell reserved for authors of trial books. Was that Murray Kempton huddled in the corner? Decca Mitford asleep in a pew? Epstein was examining the titles of the "library" provided for the expectant jurors: tattered newsweeklies and eccentric house organ magazines left by hookey-playing employees. Convinced by the presence of a Random House vice president, I made a reference to the egalitarianism of the jury system.

Epstein scoffed: "You don't see David Rockefeller here? Haven't you heard of the Sheriff's jury?"

I had not, but I learn. The Sheriff's jury is a good-ole-boy club of New York's establishment rich; it is self-seeded through nomination by sitting members. The cost is around $400 a year; its historic function is to decide mental competency cases, but the highlight of the year is a dinner at the Biltmore.

"Perhaps it's worth the money," Epstein mused, looking around the dusty assembly room. "They present each other with gifts," he said, chuckling, "money clips, and such."

2

My name was called and I joined the line straggling out of the jurors assembly room. I passed Epstein and he asked what "part" (judges and cases are assigned by a system of divisions and parts) I was headed for; I told him and he raised an eyebrow, made a roguish face, full of promise.

The *voir dire* (the truth to say) of the jurors for this suit was conducted in front of the judge because of the nature of the case. Seventeen lawyers sat around a table; they were a banquet of disputation. From the questions of the lawyers and the remarks of the judge, the circumstances of the case were revealed:

Two men were in a hammock on the terrace of an apartment in the West Fifties of Manhattan. One end of the hammock was secured to a chimney. The two men were not alone in the hammock. There were an equal number of women. According to an attorney, they were alleged fornicators, this foursome. (Whether this would be substantiated awaited testimony.) Whatever their exertions, they were sufficient to pull down the chimney on top of them—killing the two men. (A fellow jury candidate remarked how well that spoke for the missionary position as protection for life and limb.) The unhappy widows—they were not the women in the hammocks—made doubly unhappy by the circumstances of their husbands' demise, decided to sue everyone with the exception of the two young women who were revealed to have been secretaries at Benton & Bowles, where one of the unfortunate males toiled as a "creative writer." Seventeen attorneys, three for the plaintiffs, fourteen for the defendants, were diverse: the chimney-owning landlord, insurance companies, his and theirs, construction companies, the owners of the new skyscraper adjacent to the smaller apartment building, the architects of the skyscraper, and so on. The incident had taken place in 1967 but needed nearly a decade to reach the trial stage. The widows were in the courtroom and were introduced to all the prospective jurors en masse, in case any should know them (they looked injured but proud). A daughter of one widow, now eight years older than at her father's death, stood with her mother: she glared harshly at the collection of citizens who had become, out of chance and the action of the court, sanctioned voyeurs of this particular example of fate's quirks. It was the seventh day of jury selection, almost unheard of for civil cases; hundreds had been dismissed. They had empaneled six jurors, but needed two alternates. A first alternate juror had been selected, a prison guard, a type more desired by the defendants than the plaintiffs. My name was soon called and in that short walk-on to the box where gait is taken to be the calling card of character, I marched resolutely, composed, a grave set to my lips, and sat down on an abbreviated captain's chair, which—to my surprise—tilts backwards beyond reason, throwing my legs and feet into the air.

"We almost lost a juror," one of the lawyers remarked.

Since I had unintentionally broken the ice, everyone relaxed. Jury selection has become a minor psychological sideline science; lawyers develop an empirical ability, by now a pseudo-exact set of principles, that can be applied to the best and worst possible juror for a variety of cases. Lawyers try to arrange the best possible jury for their clients, and the more people they see the more likely they are to achieve it. In this suit, the seventeen lawyers had a good number of preemptory challenges (where a potential juror can be dismissed without any specific reason) and, losing those, they could attempt to have a juror removed for "cause": obvious prejudice, preformed opinion, other physical (impaired hearing), emotional, and intellectual limitations. One woman was previously bounced by the defendants, who considered her to have "natural" sympathies and who had once worked, coincidentally, as a secretary in a large advertising agency. Another woman was excused earlier for cause after she announced that the collapse of the smiting chimney, an ample phallic symbol, had been an act of "poetic justice" against the unfaithful spouses.

First questioned by the plaintiffs' lawyers I mentioned the Harrisburg book. "Harrisburg? What? Is that in Pennsylvania? Berrigan who?" the lawyers at the table muttered to one another.

The judge had asked prospective jurors if anything had occurred in their lives that had made them deeply cynical about law and the courts. I offered, unasked, that my level of cynicism was equal to, but not necessarily greater than, that of lawyers and judges. There was a general rueful smirk, and the judge said that cynicism is not reason enough to be excused.

The standard question, couched in various forms, was asked: Would I accept the judge's instruction on the law, whether or not I believed it to be a "good" law? I replied that I could not give a simple yes to that proposition, that in extraordinary cases a jury should exercise its function as part of the checks and balances of our system to protect against a runaway judiciary, that the framers of the Constitution wanted juries to be strong, free from the tyrannies of Star Chambers and English appointed judges, that in extraordinary cases a jury should act as the most accessible referendum to redress bad law, but the such action is, and should be, rare and I would, in this case, have no worry about following the judge's charge.

The lawyer who asked presented me with a pained expression. The judge broke in upon the silence, saying, "That's a point well taken, but it should only apply in criminal cases; this is a civil case . . ."

"Your Honor," I said, "unless the law was gross I would have no trouble in accepting it . . ."

"All right; go on with the questioning."

The corporation's lawyer asked if I would favor an individual over a giant corporation, a David over a Goliath?

I pondered a second—not a reaction that comforts an attorney. He elaborated, saying just because the corporation had a great deal of money, why not give some of it to any person who lays claim to it?

"Any adverse feelings I have about corporations would not affect my judgment in this case," I said.

Another attorney asked if I could describe, "in one word," what my novel (that had recently been published) was about.

"Indecision," I said.

"Just like *Hamlet*," the judge offered.

"Exactly, Your Honor."

The defendant's attorney with the least polish and the widest tie arose. Having put together *Left* from the title of the Harrisburg book, the fact that there was a Vietnam veteran in the novel (they had finally asked for more than one word), and the way I looked, he fixed me with his best HUAC stare and asked, "Do you believe in the capitalist system as it is now practiced in the United States of America?"

It was such a B-movie performance that I burst out laughing and said, "I don't have to answer that . . ." There were better answers.

"Of course you don't have to answer that," the judge said. Indistinguishable murmurings between the judge and the attorneys resulted in my being excused. I didn't learn if it was a preemptory or for cause.

Regardless of the experience I had with federal courts, I had only seen swatches cut from the great bolt of the daily practice of law.

Here, at 60 Centre Street, is the rag and bone shop of justice. The lawyers attending upon the well-known cases of the past decade would not fill a middling-sized testimonial dinner. But here are their faceless colleagues. The culture that breeds the gaudy spores: the pinky rings, the Vegas sharkskin suits, the shyster lawyer. Sixty Centre Street is the legal ghetto that spawns the prejudicial stereotype.

3

William Kunstler, I heard, was next door at the federal courthouse, defending a man accused of extortion. During lunch hour I was able to attend, catching the prosecution's closing argument. The trial received little attention in the press, with the exception of the *New York Post*, it being a noonday kind of trial. An author, one John Van Orsdell (his chief distinction as a writer being that his novel is the first to begin with the word *shit*), was charged with being the "mastermind" behind a plot to extort $320,000 from the Concord Hotel. The threat was to spike the hotel's water supply (thus, eventually, the chicken soup) with LSD. The interesting thing about this Mad magazine plot was that it was successful—after a fashion. The money was obtained, much to the FBI's chagrin, at a drop located in the ladies room of Grand Central Station; even though it was staked out with the best FBI overkill, a young woman accomplice of Van Orsdell was able to pass through their net. The money, alas, was fake. And this was to be expected, if you believed Van Orsdell (who was referred to constantly during the trial as "Van Arsdale," after the more well known taxi boss) since his defense, at one time, rested on the basis that his motive was corrective, wanting to reveal and stop a shabby practice of the FBI: its use of phony money, which placed the victims of extortionists in compromising positions. Van Orsdell let it be known that he wanted to be considered "the Ralph Nader of the FBI." He then, out of either pique or motive, pressed this reasoning by taking ads in newspapers mocking the feckless Feds; finally, Van Orsdell sought out Jack Anderson, whose imprimatur seemed required for an authenticated exposé, and presented Anderson with the evidence of his own guilt and the FBI's cupidity. Anderson ran a column. Luckily J. Edgar was dead, L. Patrick Gray was twisting slowly, slowly in the wind, and Clarence Kelly was too busy interlocking computers to worry about Van Orsdell's tweaking the bureau's image. The local office was not happy—that bungled money drop (there had been only two successful in the last twenty years, they boasted) touched their self-respect. Van Orsdell's supposed scheme required him to be caught and tried, and he was and was. The FBI, by means of a tap on Jack Anderson's phone, located him.

His two young accomplices gave evidence against him; the *idée fixe* shifted even after the trial began, though the prosecution never strayed from its charge of simple greed. Van Orsdell's accomplices had been told fortune was the object. Much to Kunstler's distress, Van Orsdell suggested another motive: a mysterious government official put him up to the whole thing; he was merely taking orders from a public telephone booth. The mysterious government official, strangely, if fittingly, resembled, perhaps a bit too closely, the hero of Van Orsdell's novel *Ragland*, who was president of these United States in a futuristic fantasy tale. (Had the novel been about the garment industry it might have been more successful.) Van Orsdell, the day of summations, wore a gold corduroy suit and the high cowboy boots of the urban rustler.

Van Orsdell's extortion scheme was to run a bit bigger than the Concord, though: the aforementioned novel let Orsdell play at being president, negotiate with world powers, bring the earth to the brink of destruction. A wooden Tinkertoy construct, but one of his own design; but the only World that was destroyed after publication was World Publishing, which put out the book; it was swallowed by a corporate maw, and *Ragland* caused not an indifferent belch. Van Orsdell turned to screenplays and founded Excalibur Productions; but here again, the sword of success was not to be pulled from the rock of failure, and it went into bankruptcy: a legitimate form of extortion where his investors were concerned. The only scenario to see the light of day was the present case, playing to a small house in Whitman Knapp's courtroom.

Van Orsdell expected his scam to cause a sensation, provoke a wave that would cast him on a shore with the flotsam of film rights, book contracts, admirers—propel him into the financial paradise that his novel had failed to provide. Along with a lawyer, he came to court with an agent. Now in our time, the courts have produced as many writers as did Paris in the twenties. But baiting the FBI had been done by Van Orsdell's betters. LSD and chicken soup did not make the most savory ideological dish. The crowds were never drawn.

Kunstler took the case because of the tenuous FBI connection. Knapp conducted his court with the paternal, but firm, control of a session with an uptown psychiatrist. He found time to compliment Kunstler.

Kunstler's summation to the jury ended with Stephen Vincent Benét's famous line "*Bury my heart at Wounded Knee,*" which caused at least one spectator to question if Kunstler knew which courtroom he was in. "Think about it," he finished.

Van Orsdell took the stand in his own defense and gave a monologue reminiscent of country and western *Sprechstimme* patriotic recordings. He spoke about his love for his country and the FBI, exhibiting the ambivalence of the pariah longing for acceptance. After the solo on the stand, he queried an acquaintance about securing a copyright of his testimony, so no one could pirate his eulogy.

Van Orsdell was found guilty and sentenced by Knapp to two years in federal prison. Kunstler was quoted as describing his client's actions as "quixotic."

4

Jurors know the least about the case they decide. There is always one group that wants to protect another from the corruption of too much knowledge. I was eventually chosen for two cases. I was kept by not protesting too much. The first was declared a mistrial before opening arguments. The trial that proceeded to a verdict was a breach of contract suit, an architect claiming nonpayment of fees.

A gentleman blushing beneath his Puerto Rico-acquired tan, who characterized himself as a "boy from the Bronx," had the notion to move from his rental business into construction. Time had taught him the lure of long-term leases, the delight of equity, the security of property, and the finagling of clients. He proposed to Allstate Insurance Company that he would build them a building after their own specifications and lease it to them at reasonable rates. During the wooing period, this entrepreneur persuaded an architect "friend" to accompany him to proposed sites and draw sketches of a possible building. He did this for two aborted projects and a third, which was accepted by Allstate; his friend, accompanied by two other partners, removed the architect entirely from the enterprise at that time and offered to pay him roughly five percent of what the architect demanded. The Allstate building was built, more or less, as designed by the dumped architect. The affair made its tiresome journey towards trial, the plaintiff's original attorney dying along the way. The amount of the suit was not large, the total hovering around twenty thousand dollars. The architect was a svelte man of European heritage who had received his Masters of City Planning from the University of Berlin in 1938; he made his way to America via Istanbul and Australia in the early fifties. While I wondered if the attorney for the defendants was going to ask if he knew Albert Speer, it was disclosed that his biggest project of recent years was a building in Munich that was to house Radio Liberté. With the trial but a day old, the Nazis and the CIA were poking their heads into the courtroom. But, keeping an open mind, I concentrated on the facts. I had nothing at stake in the proceedings, and judgment is often best ushered to its seat by indifference.

All trials are reduced at the end to a juror's paraphrases. During the periods we jurors were together, we didn't talk about the case, though some champed at the restriction. OTB and sleep, the weather and employment, the quotidian topics of the bored. I didn't expect total agreement (for civil cases five out of the six is sufficient), but that is what we had. There was a professional on our all-male jury (a social scientist), and, either counting or not counting myself, the others were all working stiffs. I had thought that they might object to the high rate of payment, the large amounts an architect could earn for a short period of time: no, they even had a certain reverence for the creative ability of the architect, that it was his design that was used (though the case had nothing to do with any copyright infringement: indeed, as a matter of law, this was not to be considered). Knowing a little about the creative process and also about working for so-many-cents-an-hour (I had just been laid off from a construction job), I found this respect both touching and disturbing. It was also commented upon, during our deliberations, how well dressed the plaintiff was and that the fees he wished seemed to be commensurate with his haberdashery.

That he deserved to be paid and had a contract with the defendants seemed plain enough, though they denied it. Their arrangements, they testified, were just so much loose talk. He was to be paid after a job was secured; all the other work was done on "spec." It was an interesting display of self-chastisement when the defense lawyer, an affable man with a penchant for painted ties, described in detail how many lawyers function with the same system of payment.

There did seem to be a basic misunderstanding between the two parties, but it was more fundamental than one telling the truth and the other not. It was the difference between a boy from the Bronx (that oft-repeated transformation of street gamin to dapper urbanite)—a builder manqué and boy-on-the-make—and European politesse, the aristocrat who sinks towards wheeling and dealing, but in no way is willing to be left high and dry. In the end it was chutzpa versus the Hapsburgs.

The architect kept records, copies of correspondence, lists, and journal entries. The boy from the Bronx, while trying in his fly-by-night way to fly first class, produced only one letter offering to arbitrate the architect's fees. It was, as they say, self-serving. They worked together as friends for three years, and during that time the corporation to which the architect addressed his bills and correspondence did not actually exist.

Jurors try to make sense of the whole, and it is just this pursuit of the comprehensible that sometimes makes them bend facts against the forge of the possible. How did this happen? Woe to the plaintiff or defendant who refuses to tell them.

There was the suspicion expressed by my fellow jurors that some sort of cover-up had occurred, since the deposed corporation produced no records of any sort, save the one letter. "Just like Watergate," the humblest of our number said. The distillation of that affair was still potent enough to spike the judgment of this lowly case.

The neighborliness of the Constitution, its provisions for trial before members of the community, often lost in federal cases since venue is chosen strategically or politically, was demonstrated: two of the jurors had used the facility the architect designed.

We asked for all the exhibits and got them, including the plaintiff's yearly diaries. Between the entries relating to the case, there were clues to his character not evident in the courtroom. At intervals a woman's name would be the sole entry for an afternoon followed by an exclamation mark(!).

The architect was dumped on the recommendation of the third partner, an Irishman who didn't warm to the touchy superciliousness that the architect showed; besides, he knew of a firm that could get the work done faster and at less cost. The president of that concern testified in the defendants' behalf but not to good effect. He boasted that his firm built everything from "toilets to skyscrapers," and that remark figured in the plaintiff's attorney's closing argument, asking us to decide which of the two structures the man had the most experience in.

That the case went on and on, finally coming to trial a half decade after the events, seemed to testify to the wounded pride of the plaintiff, the betrayal he suffered by his friend, the boy from the Bronx. He was stubbornly looking for vindication. When we gave it to him, deciding in his favor on every point, he was no longer sitting at the table with his attorney but in a pew in the gallery. As the court clerk intoned the affirmative "For the Plaintiff," the architect began to weep. And that sight, of someone in tears, made clear once again what is at stake when justice is either carried forth or denied.

MICHAEL HARRINGTON*

W hen you meet Michael Harrington, socialist and author, for the first
time, you might be reminded of a line from Clement Moore's holiday
rhyme about St. Nicholas: "And laying his finger aside his nose." Harrington's is slightly bent to the left, as if he had laid his finger aside his nose one too
many Christmases and it stuck. The rest of him resembles the educated mariner:
lean and weather worn, his salt and pepper hair stuck under a watch cap.

I had not read any of Harrington's five books until I read them all at
once; it was like rummaging through a relative's attic. Harrington's *The Other
America* (1962) and his autobiography, *Fragments of the Century* (1973), serve
to bracket the swollen sixties. At the close of 1960, according to the U.S.
Office of Education, there were 3,215,544 Americans enrolled in institutions of
higher learning; by 1971 there were 8,948,000. That unprecedented increase (it
had not even doubled from 1919 till 1960, much less tripled within a decade)
has had as profound an impact on our country as did the mid-nineteenth-century
immigration.

Incubating in educational ghettos was a new class: students, the youth
mob. Madison Avenue gave them cohesion, a common consciousness; communications let them experience the same nervous system. Harrington, in many
ways, served as an older brother to that generation.

The Socialist Party had elected more than one thousand members to public office in this country by 1912; but the Russian Revolution (and World War
I) severed America's European roots—made them dangerous and suspect—and
the hysteria rolling over all things socialistic, from the Palmer Raids till the present, has tarred the very word.

The sixties saw an entirely new kind of "radical" born; but the youth
mob can wear either Janus face comfortably: the tragedy of Kent State or the
comedy of Woodstock. There were many catalysts that stirred the movements

---

* First appeared in *Soho Weekly News*, vol. 3, no. 6, Nov. 13, 1975.

192

in which Harrington took part. The most significant, perhaps, was that the generation took its designation, "postwar," literally and not figuratively.

Harrington published *The Other America* in 1962; he went to Europe the following winter and waited for the transformation most writers think will come after they invade the Library of Congress. But nothing happened. Harrington was glum; but then, becoming an exception to the rule that helped perpetuate the Cinderella myth of authorship, something did happen: a long review of the book by Dwight Macdonald in the then fledgling *New York Review of Books*. More reviews than books are read, and that review brought Harrington considerable attention. It was talked about; Jack Kennedy noticed it. Harrington became an expert, enlisted in the war on poverty, became friendly with the Shrivers. This was heady stuff for a thirty-six-year-old socialist (who still wears the lank rayon hosiery that seems to be socialists' trademark), a former member of Dorothy Day's Catholic Worker pacifist-community of the voluntary poor. These contradictions, as he recounts movingly in *Fragments of the Century*, contributed to tearing him apart and to an eventual nervous breakdown.

Writing joins hands with commerce in varied ways. Critics have power because their scribbling sells something: their prose is the coinage of blurbs, and they find they have more to spend. The traffic in ideas is not so fast and not as lined with silver. Harrington's book created a new product, the first in a series: Poverty Studies (followed by Black Studies, Woman Studies, etc.). He discovered the yellow brick road of the lecture circuit.

I asked Harrington if he had any reflections about the Symbionese Liberation Army, the organization that for a brief moment helped remind society of the vast numbers of hungry (through the food-distribution debacle sponsored by the Hearsts). *The Other America* was poverty's well-mannered introduction to polite society; the SLA were the bizarre gate-crashers.

He said he was "hostile to terrorism." Indeed, it was a bad time again for the poor; his book had argued that the poor were made invisible by relative affluence, but because of the "energy crisis," rationing, and threats of rationing, a whole new cycle of have-notism has been fostered. He said that the white working class now concludes that it is the true poor, and the humanitarian impulse (no matter how suspect) that accompanied the Johnson-era war on poverty has now been removed and the poor are again villains for being poor.

Harrington was asked whether he thinks Watergate has been politically "good," and his answer echoed the divisions that separated the Socialist Party from a large portion of the antiwar movement (later referred to by the Socialist party as "New Politics Liberals," a phrase picked up and used with the same scorn by George Wallace). Vietnam had seemed to many (including Harrington) like a bad acid trip that the country is only beginning to get over. It distorted and sidetracked all the progressive programs that could have been pursued; it allowed for a reactionary president to be elected and for a new triumph of the Dixiecrat-Republican alignment. The Left was in a trance of despair from which it is now just beginning to awake since the daily incantations about the Vietnam war have stopped. And, at the center, the unhealed sore of the New Left's less-than-"progressive anti-communism" rankled. That had lead to Harrington's original break with the inchoate Students for a Democratic Society (SDS) at the time they were being financed by the League for Industrial Democracy.

The Democratic Socialist Organizing Committee (DSOC), with Harrington as its chairperson, was founded October 13, 1973, after an acrimonious split from its progenitor, the Social Democrats, USA (formerly named the Socialist Party Democratic Socialist Federation, formerly the Socialist Party, USA). It was with hand-rubbing relish that Harrington urged at the DSOC founding convention that "It is time for the democratic Left to close the books on the differences of the 1960s." On with the show!

Harrington demured that Watergate is good politically, but offered the "energy crisis" as an event which augurs well. (The reasoning is parallel: Watergate equals New Politics Liberals; energy crisis equals workers without gas.) Watergate has been too much the glare of a sun god, easily idolized, but only deflecting serious inquiry and solid work. The energy crisis, he argued, is personalized and direct, suffusing every strata. "Radicalizing" has left the campuses and has moved onto the truck stops, a development that Harrington wants to capitalize on.

His lifelong association with institutions has marked him no less than it has marked the men of the Nixon administration. Corporate man is now a glamorized image, and even a man as independent as Harrington finds an organization with which to identify. Perhaps it is because of the jettisoned Catholicism. Once brought up in Mother Church, it is hard to be adrift in the world without succor, and Harrington's biography never shows him to be bereft of a parent organization: St. Louis University High School, Holy Cross College, the University of Chicago, *The Catholic Worker*, the Socialist Party, chairman of the board for the League of Industrial Democracy, advisor to government, and now—not least or last—chairman of the DSOC.

Perhaps the key is contained in the remark Sidney Zion made when he tried to make sense of the vitriolic attacks aimed at him for disclosing Daniel Ellsberg as the source of the Pentagon Papers. Zion reasoned that he was assailed because he was not working for anyone, any news service, magazine, newspaper. He was on his own, and that, in our corporate age, is the home for pariahs. Harrington requires the structure of an organization that—differing slightly from the Mafia's—serves as an emotional and personal front.

Harrington recited the beginnings of the DSOC's brief demographic history. They began with 840 members, the largest concentration being in New York City. At the start there was one member in Wichita, Kansas, and three very active members in Alabama. Their original goal was a modest 2,000 members.

The internecine battles among the factions of the Left help establish their identities—if we can expel people, we must exist. To keep straight the cause and effect that splinters "Fringe Political Movements" (as the *New York Times* indexes them) requires the interest of a paleontologist. The word *socialism* still possesses its own chilling effect, so much so that the early leaders of SDS would not ascribe to it, thinking that this country's basic institutions could stand reform (after a few failures, such as the Economic Research Action Project (ERAP) projects, SDS adopted an "if you can't join them, beat them" stance). The agrarian Charlie Manson wanted to show that his "family" could live on the garbage America produced, and radical organizations live on the more tidy excess their members or friends have amassed in other ways. Harrington's life is necessarily contradictory, since he espouses a world in which he does not exist.

The Socialist Party, USA and the Democratic Socialist Federation merged in March 1972 after a thirty-five-year split. They became the Socialist Party Democratic Socialist Federation (SPDSF) and set as their primary goal the defeat of Nixon in 1972. And that campaign, in the continuing paradox of the Left, split them apart once more. The raucous and intemperate 1972 Democratic convention was an accurate picture of what this country is like, and the Republican convention was just as correct a picture of how it is run.

After Nixon's re-election the SPDSF convened in late December 1972 and changed its name to the Social Democrats, USA (SD, USA). The Young People's Socialist League (YPSL), the youth wing of SD, USA, led the attack against the "McGovern takeover" of the Democratic Party, chastising the "supercilious antilabor elitism" of the "New Politics Liberals." The YSPL platform then went on to denounce "upper-middle-class youth who flamboyantly rejected materialism, embraced voluntary poverty, espoused oriental mysticism or more recently became Jesus freaks" and continued that "implicit in the counterculture is a repudiation of the aspirations and struggles of ordinary working people."

The "resolution" containing those remarks was written by a professional political speechwriter. It didn't take a Weatherman to see that Michael Harrington might find it hard to stand up for the new line of the YPSL and the Social Democrats, USA.

Harrington protested, at the time, that the newly baptized Social Democrats, USA might not "mean simply the abandonment of a name but of a tradition and, in an attempt to become more acceptable to the American people and the American trade unions, it would result in our giving up our Socialist content. I think the Socialist Party should forthrightly stand for socialism."

Harrington broke away and formed the DSOC, taking some two hundred former members of the Socialist Party with him (the Social Democrats, USA were claiming around eighteen thousand members). Harrington outlines his reasons for his split in *Fragments of the Century.*

When asked if he carried any personal bitterness about the split and the actions of the participants, Harrington shook his head negatively while he clenched his jaw affirmatively.

Harrington said that the DSOC wanted to involve people who didn't "share our memories." An interesting objective, though I suspect that what Harrington doesn't want them to share are the past failures, disappointments, and betrayals.

Harrington remarked that the DSOC expected membership turnover, but they wanted solid numbers, and he referred to the problems of individuals who were members of the Communist party for six months and then had to live it down the rest of their lives.

He pointed out that Robert Strauss, chairman of the Democratic National Committee, had said that the Wallace democrats had something to add to the party—"ten million votes," I interjected unkindly, and Harrington half-smiled and winced. But, nonetheless, Harrington wanted Strauss to say the same thing about the Socialists. ("We must go where the people are, which is the liberal wing of the Democratic Party," he said at the DSOC founding convention.)

The DSOC at its initial stage is the type of organization where one out of fifty members is on the national board. The romance has been rekindled with the worker in America. Students and youth are being jilted. Harrington's hopes for a socialist presence in this country rest on a coalition of labor, student-youth, and a not-yet-organized light-blue-collar class, which is "middle class in its education and income, but often subjected to a production discipline like that of the workers."

He was asked what fiction he has been reading and he replied that he had finished Dan Wakefield's *Starting Over.* The title seems to have hooked him, for that is how he sees himself, starting over.

"How can a man feel," he replied, "starting life over again at forty-five? You do what you can."

WILLIAM SLOANE COFFIN, JR.*

I f a man publishes one book in fifty-three years and it is a memoir, a single conclusion can be reached: the life is known more for deeds than writings, for its public side, rather than the private. And the Reverend William Sloane Coffin, Jr. is known more for his acts: an activist Yale chaplaincy, freedom rides, Peace Corps, the antiwar movement, the Spock trial. Coffin's life has always been full of elegant contrasts, and now there's another: the release of his memoir—an effort at summation—just as he sets off on an entirely new chapter, his service as senior minister of Riverside Church, New York City's symbol of liberal and ecumenical Protestantism.

The oddest thing about Coffin's memoir, *Once to Every Man*, is that the first half of his life now stands revealed as more interesting than the second, though it is the later half that has made him a national figure. In his pages the young reverend-to-be appears as William Sloane Zhivago, dashing through war and clandestine revolution, and, given this background, the events of the sixties acquire a parochial air.

Publishing a memoir, Coffin said in the Blue Bar of Manhattan's Algonquin Hotel, was like "throwing your life away—you're done with it and now you have to get a new one." As with most things, that notion seemed to please and displease him. A memoir, I offered, is often criticized more for what it doesn't say than for what it does.

"I have been knocked for lacking an interior life," he responded, looking away; and then, finding something to smile about, he said, "Someone called it 'All Iliad and no Odyssey.'"

"Who?" I asked.

"One of my ex-wives," he said with genuine sheepishness.

Yet that one remark gave one of his two ex-wives more flesh than anything that appeared in the book.

---

* First appeared in *Politicks*, vol. 1, no. 5, Jan. 3, 1978.

Memoir is traditionally a less heated form of autobiography, and this does disappoint some critics: *memoir* stems from *memorandum*, providing personal views of public events. It can be a delicate form, and, at times, Coffin's version reads as if a man with thick fingers is laboring to repair the innards of a watch. Coffin was trained in the pianoforte, not the violin.

Since his departure from Yale at the end of 1975, Coffin has had a fling with Esalen and the human potential movements, but this has not made him confessional. His stoicism and general WASP-ish repugnance at any "shameful display of emotion," well described in the memoir, has not eroded. The press delights in great swings of behavior (Rennie Davis selling insurance and serving a young maharishi; Eldridge Cleaver being born again; Mark Rudd coming home) but does not find them in Coffin. His pendulum is not swinging in wide arcs; it is settling, becoming composed. Protest movements have kept expanding, hoping to enlist more members; they have now coalesced into the human rights movement, to which no one can avoid allegiance.

Coffin has returned recently from a short trip to Latin America, and, while there, he was impressed with the Catholic Church's stand on human rights. He is convinced that "the human rights issue undercuts national sovereignty" and that is why totalitarian countries fear it. Coffin explained to me that, before accepting the senior minister position at Riverside (he was the first choice of the thirty-member board of deacons, replacing the Reverend Ernest T. Campbell, who resigned last year), his original plan had been "to live three months in Latin America, and get Spanish down cold, and then come back and tour the religious communities in the United States and see who was up for what. Particularly in the public interest, and then, sort of see what I would do at the end of that process."

It has been reported that Coffin saw himself as becoming a "chaplain of the world," a characterization he loathes. Taking the position at Riverside, Coffin recounted, "at first represented a kind of failure of nerve on my part—having broken with a base to have found a new one so quickly, as it were. But, on the other hand, to turn down a place where, perhaps, you are able to work in a community that's really dedicated, with all kinds of talent, that wants to work with you—it would have been kind of stupid not to make too much of it."

Coffin's life, as he recalls it, in many ways has alternated between action and reflection. "Since the ninth grade I had never studied for more than three years at a stretch without a break," he has written of his mid-twenties. "Given my temperament, it was natural that I should be longing for action. But this time the action I wanted [joining the Central Intelligence Agency] may well have been less to express myself so much as to avoid myself. Once again I was longing to escape by dutiful WASP self. When studying, I hardly ever played.

I had had only two dates in the last three years. It was as if the prodigal son—the passionate one—and his older brother—the dutiful—were both living inside of me and had never gotten together to work things out."

Passion and duty may have begun as antithetical states to Coffin, but they finally melded into a passion to duty and a dutiful passion. There was a great conspiracy to make Coffin a success, and he did not escape it, though choosing the ministry saved him from its gaudier aspects. Conversion is an impossible argument, and in his memoir Coffin provides little explanation for his elevation. (Though Erik Erikson appears in the book, Coffin never applies any of Erikson's techniques of psychohistory to his own life.) Coffin's father died when he was nine years old, leaving his family in somewhat reduced circumstances (but with no diminishment of Coffin's sense of self), though none of the many father figures that are important in his life made doctoring or lawyering appealing professions. With his experiences of World War II and the CIA serving as horrendous parentheses around his training as a minister, he returned to his calling, and it is there Coffin-the-dutiful and Coffin-the-passionate can reconcile.

Becoming senior minister at Riverside, I asked, wasn't it like coming home again? He agreed and elaborated: "San Francisco [where he worked on his memoir] to me is the most beautiful city in the world, but to be educated by the best minds in your particular trade—that takes place in New York. If you're lucky enough, as I will be, you can pick up the phone and call anybody, and say, 'Teach me, will ya?' and they probably will."

Coffin is engaging, a good mimic, talking with his hands, which are held apart, palms opposed, in a pre-praying position, and he has the nondescript handsomeness of WASPs: the features are so refined they lack salience.

"One beautiful thing about Riverside is that it changed in the most interesting way; it's now about 35 percent black and they're not at all middle class. A lot are poor folk who are genuinely happy to be members. Almost all of which, in a way, is made possible by Mr. Rockefeller's $40-million endowment; now poor folk can run the church because you don't have to raise that kind of money to keep the church heated."

Coffin's first service occurred on November 6, and the crowd was large enough to prompt one parishioner, it was reported, to remark: "I don't think even Jesus could get such good billing."

"I hadn't been here a day," Coffin recalls, "before I went down to see Al Lowenstein [the United States delegate to the United Nations Human Rights Commission], and while I was there I saw Andy Young, and two minutes later I had Andy lined up for a human rights service at Riverside on December 10. I sort of pictured all the flags of all the countries coming down the aisle—it's great to have a big liturgy. And the next day, I get a call from the director of the

U.N. Symphony Orchestra, and he says, 'How would you like us to take part in that service?' And I realize, 'Hey, I'm really lucky I know a lot of people in this city.' It won't really be that hard; I've always just picked up the phone and called somebody—and it works!"

In just that way, Coffin brings to mind a story about Robert Kennedy. Asked why he got so far so fast, Kennedy is said to have replied: "I always got the top job." And Coffin always goes to the top (his memoir is redolent with examples), though he has not yet phoned President Carter.

"I'm afraid, for all his compassion and hope, President Carter is fundamentally a manager of a deteriorating status quo; and he ain't got the plans for saving America, anymore than Kissinger had the plans for ending the war. Because they are not realistic; they won't recognize the conditions. And when things don't get better, will he have the imagination and compassion to resist getting defensive and be able to come through with something else?

"I think we're very much in that situation: facing the unacceptability of unpleasant truth. Everybody knows this isn't working, but nobody really wants to face it. You see how torn we are on the Panama Canal, which represents a very strong transition from America the all-powerful, to America taking its place among other nations of the world. If there was something really credible as an alternative with the kind of passionate leadership that brings people to it, we might be able to accept a little more of the necessary changes, which, if we don't accept them, are going to produce a violence. It's a terrible, dangerous strait, and the fact that we don't know it makes it doubly so.

"It is certainly important not to root one's protest in one's own guilt. Never mind if we are guilty or not. Never mind rooted injustice; let us root ourselves in justice. What does justice demand now, say, vis-à-vis the Panama Canal? I think a lot of protest aims for guilt, and that makes people mean as hell. That's something that I'm not sure Gandhi quite got to the depths of. And if you do arouse the conscience of the victimizer he might just kick you twice as hard."

Coffin is no pacifist (of his early childhood, he recounts fistfights when he is not recounting splendor), and he still is troubled over the appropriate use of force. Vietnam was, for him, a question of the just and unjust war. His memoir's title, *Once to Every Man*, though not referred to in the book, is taken from another prominent WASP, James Russell Lowell:

> Once to every man and nation comes
> the moment to decide
> In the strife of Truth with Falsehood
> for the good or evil side.

Lowell was speaking, in 1844, of slavery. Choosing sides is very important to Coffin, and he has done so more than once.

In his memoir, for example, Coffin discusses, for the first time, his activities in the fledgling CIA; but in the first draft it wasn't mentioned.

"I wasn't going to write anything about the CIA. And then after all the disclosures [the Rockefeller Commission, Senate hearings on CIA intervention in Chile, drug experiments, et cetera], I realized I would be knocked out of the ballpark—and rightfully so—for not mentioning it. The typical WASP-Ivy-League-club-rules. So, I went down to see my old buddy in the CIA and went for a long walk with him—he's pretty high up—and I said, 'What would you do?'

"And he said, 'I'd write it all up.'

"'You mean, how we recruited and dropped them in the Soviet Union?'

"He said, 'Yeah. In the first place, we're not doing it anymore; in the second, it's all known in general, and third, if you write it up, it would be the best press we've had in years.'"

The CIA is wrong again; it isn't the best press it's had. Coffin's picture of himself, as one of the best and brightest, recruiting spies and sending them to their deaths, is ultimately pathetic. Coffin writes of "Serge," whom he trained and who, he is sure, had been "captured, tortured, and executed":

"Maybe we had been too impatient. Maybe we should have told him to bury the radio and SW equipment near the DZ and to come back for them after he had established himself."

Maybe. Maybe! They drop a spy by parachute into the woods outside a small town, where he is supposed to settle inconspicuously, a stranger walking down a road with a suitcase full of radio equipment. Today, the CIA would still rather be thought of as evil than idiotic.

Coffin further explained: "My old buddy said, 'Are you going to submit it to the Agency?'

"I said, 'I don't like to do that.'

"And he said, 'You did sign the paper.'

"But he showed the book to our former boss and they both had no quarrel with it, so that was the end of that."

It would be quite a task to create a fuller life that scaled as many peaks of social history over the past five decades. And so, at this juncture of both endings and beginnings, Coffin looks forward to more peaks (the nearest being the odd "neo-eclectic" tower of Riverside Church). The church will undoubtedly be back in the public eye with Coffin at the pulpit. We talked of some of the illustrious moments in Riverside's history, including James Foreman's "Black Manifesto," calling for $400 million in reparations (later whittled down to a Fund for Social Justice that has given out nearly $400 thousand to minority group programs). Coffin offered a more recent example: "Ernest Campbell [the man he is replacing] did an open letter to Billy Graham; it was very moving, very fine. The folk there know there's a great tradition to be called on. So, in that sense, I think that people are really eager to do something."

Though it would be hard to imagine that the people are more eager than their new senior minister. "It's kind of a fortuitous thing," Coffin reflected. "Because of marital reasons, I never thought that Riverside would even ask me to come."

OF JUDGES AND G-STRINGS*

I have always been struck by the two faces of Indiana's Highway 31. The avenue that ushers the southbound motorist into Indianapolis is an imposing corridor of costly real estate; the road that leads northward into South Bend is a gauntlet of dives and rundown retail outlets. Each face is meant to be intimidating. Both remind one of who is in control, because both strips are about money: who has it and who doesn't.

The Kitty Kat Lounge does not stand alone on South Bend's welcoming thoroughfare: there's the Torch Lounge, Peaches, the Ace-Hi, and, a bit further down, the most whimsically named of all, Ramona's Car Wash. Nearby, but off 31, close to the decaying Studebaker corridor and the buildings of South Bend Lathe, hard by the police department's credit union, is the Gloworm. Its proximity to the industrial base of old South Bend is telling, for there is something commonly working class about all these establishments, something that suggests good jobs, decent pay, men in groups, a certain type of blue-collar culture that is actually, for a host of reasons, nearly extinct in South Bend.

Go-go bars are to burlesque shows what massage parlors are to bordellos, or what the Golden Arches are to restaurants. The demise of burlesque theaters (and the crumbling of America's urban industrial base) helped pave the way for go-go bars. High-overhead theater operations went under and factory jobs disappeared. If the neighborhood is denuded of the industry that gives rise to working men's bars, then the bars must be filled with nudes to keep them from closing. Blue-collar men's bars turn into go-go bars; they become strip joints franchised.

Admission into the U.S. Supreme Court's chambers is gained through many portals, but one of the strangest entryways is the front door of South Bend's Kitty Kat Lounge, which is resplendent with an unsigned painting of a woman in a leopard-like cat outfit, a mixture of flesh color and black-dotted

---

* First appeared in *Arts Indiana*, April 1991.

burnt sienna, executed in the rather unforgiving medium of housepaint and ply-wood. Thanks in part to the Kitty Kat, the Supreme Court since early January has been pondering the following: "Whether nude barroom-style or 'go-go' dancing is 'speech' protected by the First Amendment. And, if nude barroom dancing is 'speech,' whether Indiana's general public-indecency law is unconstitutional as applied to such dancing." By summer, if not before, the Supreme Court will decide *Barnes v. Glen Theatre* and provide us with answers.

The Indiana case began when two dancers filed suit in 1985 challenging the constitutionality of Indiana's public-indecency statute. Gayle Sutro and Carla Johnson sought to avoid arrest and prosecution for dancing nude at the Chippewa Bookstore in South Bend. Previous to their suit, there had been approximately eleven arrests and five convictions for violating the Indiana public-indecency statute at the Chippewa. The dancing took place behind glass panels; customers sat in booths and inserted coins into what court documents refer to as a "timing mechanism."

At the time of the suit's filing, Sutro had yet to dance at the Chippewa but had been scheduled. Sutro is a professional actress, stunt woman, and ecdysiast, and she has studied acting, dancing, speech, and language (so the Memorandum and Order of the Chief Judge of the U.S. District Court, Northern District of Indiana, describes her). In an affidavit, Sutro claims that her nude dances are appropriately choreographed and an attempt to communicate as well as to entertain.

Later, another dancer, Darlene Miller, along with JR's Kitty Kat Lounge, joined the case; so consolidated, the "bookstore" dancing and the "barroom" dancing have pirouetted onto the Supreme Court's stage.

Strange as it might seem, for a number of years the Supreme Court has wanted to decide this issue: Justice Byron R. White, in a 1986 dissent, stated that he believed that it was time for the court to address the question because the state courts disagreed over the reach of the First Amendment in this area.

Indeed, the Glen Theatre-Kitty Kat Lounge case is the sort of First Amendment battle that often turns up. Many, though, might prefer not to see it that way. After all, it isn't exactly the Nazis in Skokie, which lost the American Civil Liberties Union so many members when the ACLU defended the right of ragtag neo-Nazis to march through the Chicago suburb; it isn't even the performance art of Karen Finley or the photographs of Robert Mapplethorpe, which have created such difficulties for the National Endowment for the Arts. The world of dance has not risen up in support of its less-fashionable sisters (and brothers). It is not a glamorous enterprise, this outpost of First Amendment freedoms, the short runway whereon the Kitty Kat dancers strut their stuff.

It was Gayle Sutro and Carla Johnson's fear of being arrested if they danced nude that led them and Glen Theatre, Inc. (the bookstore owners) to bring suit against South Bend's chief of police and Michael Barnes, the St. Joseph County prosecutor. The case worked its way through the appeal process; the Seventh Circuit judges of the federal appeals court decided in Chicago on May 24, 1990, in favor of the dancers and their employers.

It appears that Indiana hadn't labored too strenuously, at that point, in its efforts to rid the state of nude dancing. Judge Richard Posner, concurring with the majority, comments on the state's brief:

> [It is] four and one half double-spaced pages in length, and is replete with grammatical and typographical errors. It contains no explanation of the evil at which the statute is aimed, and its analysis of the constitutional question is limited essentially to the following passage: "Entertainment which did not contain expressive content—e.g., cockfighting or bear-baiting—could presumably be regulate [*sic*] or prohibited by the States. Entertainment per se is not protected; entertainment that is a form of expression is." It is not obvious, however, that just because people can be forbidden to incite animals to kill each other, striptease dancers can be forbidden to remove all their clothing. There is [Posner aptly points out] a missing link between blood sports and erotic dancing that the brief does not attempt to supply. A psychiatrist might find the juxtaposition fascinating.

One should take a look at the law that is being challenged. Indiana Code 35-45-4-1 provides in full:

> Public Indecency
> Section 1.
>   (a) A person who knowingly or intentionally, in a public place:
>   (1) engages in sexual intercourse;
>   (2) engages in deviate sexual conduct;
>   (3) appear in a state of nudity; or
>   (4) fondles the genitals of himself or another person;
>   commits public indecency, a Class A misdemeanor.
>   (b) "Nudity" means the showing of the human male or female genitals, pubic area, or buttocks with less than opaque covering, the showing of the female breast with less than a fully opaque covering of any part of the nipple, or the showing of the covered male genitals in a discernibly turgid state.

What this boils down to is Indiana's staunch support and promotion of pasties and G-strings. Barnes et al. are opposed to nudity, though, as one can see, "nudity" so defined puts any number of people at risk for prosecution: women in clothing less than opaque, breast-feeding mothers, and males—adolescents, primarily—say, at swimming meets, where hormones and the excitement of the race may get the best of them. No boys have been arrested at any swimming meets, to my knowledge; no women in diaphanous evening gowns have been handcuffed; no mothers separated from their nursing infants on buses, and so forth; all of which goes to show how selectively the law is enforced.

You must keep in mind that the Kitty Kat Lounge case does not turn on obscenity. That isn't at issue. All sides stipulate that what is being dealt with is "nonobscene" nude dancing. The question is whether nude dancing is "speech." Judge Daniel Flaum, writing for the Seventh Circuit majority, says, "The State in effect advances the proposition that the dance involved loses its expressive qualities as the dancers lose their clothing. It is well established, however, that 'nudity alone does not place otherwise protected material outside the mantle of the First Amendment' [*Shad v. Mt. Ephraim*]. Nor does the fact that the dance is sexual remove the mantle of protection: 'Sexual expression which is indecent, but not obscene is protected by the First Amendment' [*Sable Communications v. FCC*]." One of the questions the Supreme Court will be dealing with is the phrase "otherwise protected." Is nude dancing "otherwise protected" because it is "speech"?

The State of Indiana and the dissenting Seventh Circuit judges argue that nude dancing is not speech, not protected expression. Judge Frank Easterbrook's dissent flatly states, "Go-go dancing is not 'speech,'" and he goes on to say, "James Madison would have guffawed had anyone suggested public nudity as an example of 'freedom of speech.'"

But bad law makes for strange reasoning, so much so that the dissenting Seventh Circuit judges avoid, for the most part, discussing the speech issue; instead they concentrate on the nude dancing's consequences. And it is likely that the Supreme Court's Justice Antonin Scalia will be taking a similar position; earlier Scalia decisions point to an analysis of nude dancing as a form of "pandering."

But there are laws against pandering, there are laws against prostitution, all the things that the dissenting judges claim nude dancing leads to. Can you claim that nude dancing is not speech, not expression, to prohibit what you fear it leads to?

Judge John Coffey, in his dissent, exercises some up-to-date rhetoric: "Most importantly, a real consequence of nude dancing is the loss of human dignity for the female performer and sometimes even those who observe the performance." The loss of human dignity is certainly a problem, and claiming that nude dancing is not speech is certainly a way to strip a dancer of her or his dignity.

What follows? Violence towards women follows, it is held, though it can as easily be shown that shelters for battered women report their busiest hours are those that follow the Super Bowl (see "The Super Bowl and Wife Beating" by Rachel Lurie, *Village Voice*, Jan. 19, 1991). The it-leads-to argument is often used by conservative jurists and lawmakers, but seldom do they apply it quite so vigorously to football. Or to gun-control legislation (even though it is less debatable that having AK-47s leads to shooting children in schoolyards).

Be that as it may, though our culture is riddled with the perceived menace of sex and violence, it should be obvious that violence has won the day. If pasties and G-strings are the bulwark that is holding back the tide of violence, somebody needs to save us.

The word *ballet* is much bandied about in both petitioners' and respondents' briefs. In the discussion of dance, ballet is held up for esteem, go-go or barroom dancing for derision. But two differences that aren't discussed are central.

In nude dancing, obviously, flesh is the main attraction. In ballet—classical ballet primarily, but some modern ballet, too—flesh is the enemy. First it must be disciplined, often trained to the point of pain. And the flesh must be encased—in leotards, tights—because what dancers and choreographers are interested in is form, not flesh. Ballet shoes are designed not just so dancers can stand on their toes, but so the foot will be disguised—not an appendage flat and pointing out in the wrong direction, but one elongated to become part of the leg, part of the line. Male dancers' dance belts are constructed to disguise whatever "turgidity" might be present. There are some ballets and companies that make use of nudity—they are cited in the respondents' briefs—but the majority of people associated with ballet go far beyond pasties and G-strings. They want the flesh covered and made firm and uniform.

Nude dancing, barroom style, as mentioned earlier, is not old, but it does have a tradition. It is a populist art, a folk art. (That, of course, exposes it to censure. Things that cost a lot of money, which are consumed by the middle and upper classes and require capital and leisure to achieve, are granted a good bit of protection. Things that are low in capital outlay, do not require years of training, and are consumed by the lower classes, are afforded much less.) Populist art has a quality of spontaneity, naturalness, in it, in other words, you can do it—perhaps not well, but nonetheless do some semblance of it—almost immediately. Play a comb, a bottle, hit a tambourine, sing songs, dance. You get better at it by emulation and practice. It can provide employment without training. People learn from one another. Instruction is not institutionalized.

Because go-go or barroom dancing is not descended from the ballet, because it does not have a tradition of formal, institutionalized training, it is not respected. But nude performance dancing is not mere social dancing. It is extremely difficult to dance in the nude without appearing ridiculous. Any of the judges who are deciding or have decided on this matter might give it a try.

The appeals court was provided with a videotape of three dancers dancing, filmed by the respondents' South Bend counsel, Charles Asher. The judges were not overimpressed. They described the dancing in deprecating language and decided that "these striptease dances are not performed in any theatrical or dramatic context."

One might ask how well versed the judges are in theatrical and dramatic contexts. Go-go dancing is minimalist burlesque, and just as plays since the 1960s (at least) have stepped down from the proscenium stage, so too has burlesque. Have any of these judges been in an off- (or off-off-) Broadway theater in the last thirty years, seen a cast mingle with spectators, observed the Theatre of Cruelty (or the Ridiculous)? The Kitty Kat Lounge is its own theatrical context. It is theater. The dancers are interactive; not only their dancing speaks but they themselves speak to the audience. (They certainly did the night I paid a visit to South Bend's newest tourist attraction.) An evening at the Kitty Kat is theatrical, even if the customers are cast as unwitting members of the troupe.

It is this interactive nature of the performance that the dissenting judges fear. Judge Daniel Manion serves up the most graphic language of all the Seventh Circuit judges. (Conservatives often like to wallow a while in what they denounce.) He quotes Supreme Court Justice William H. Rehnquist writing in an earlier, different sort of case (*California v. LaRue*): "Customers were found engaging in oral copulation with women entertainers; customers engaged in public masturbation; and customers rolled currency either directly into the vagina of a female entertainer, or on the bar in order that she might pick it up herself."

But Indiana's case is about speech, not obscenity; it is about, as the Glen Theater, Inc. brief puts it, whether nude dancing, performed as entertainment indoors and before a willing adult audience, is expression entitled to First Amendment protection. Just as live and "legitimate" theaters have trouble developing and keeping audiences (since the popular culture is so "tube tied"), the Kitty Kat Lounge exists as a theatrical service catering to an audience that enjoys the social experience, rather than the abundant options available in private video viewing. And when such places are called "tawdry" and their acts "sordid," the critic is often describing not the show, but the audience.

Most of the judges on both sides tend to sidestep the fact that this case involves—indeed, it started—at an establishment quite unlike a go-go bar, one that didn't serve or allow liquor, the Chippewa Bookstore (which burned down in 1988). It was the dancing behind glass panels, the money deposited in the "timing mechanism," that began (and despite the fire continues to be part of) this case. One can see just how stark that setting is—a woman dancing nude behind glass—and how speechless it has rendered thus far all the judges who have contemplated it. Such a place as the Kitty Kat provides a lot to discuss; but only the stark and elemental condition of nude dancing as speech confronts the jurist behind glass panels at the Chippewa Bookstore.

In many ways, the Kitty Kat Lounge is its own underground theater; it certain does not espouse mainstream taste (anti-Spandex as it is), forced now, even to its surprise, to be the latest sorry battleground for First Amendment combat. Behind the Kitty Kat's bar, there is a flashing electronic sign announcing an upcoming attraction, Fast Freddy's Playgirls. After Fast Freddy blinks by there is the injunction: SUPPORT THE FIRST AMENDMENT. The effect overall is somewhat like the circus (another populist art), insofar as there are a number of things to choose from going on simultaneously. But the center ring, the main attraction, is the dancing.

Each of the women who dances at the Kitty Kat (at least the night I went) provides something different. The dancers select their own music (which is evidence of expression, speech). One had her own tape, but most punched their choices into the jukebox, the music arranged (again evidence of expression) to reflect their own backgrounds and aesthetic preoccupations and tastes. One, a thirtyish blonde from Kentucky, danced to a redneck repertoire of country-western songs. Her "outfit" was the closest thing to street clothes any of the dancers wore: a modern minimalist cowgirl ensemble, feathers dangling from a straw western hat. Another woman, heavy set, wore the more traditional costume, half negligée, half gown.

It was clear that each dancer was engaged in speech, because each dance expressed something entirely different—to me. Again, we return to the audience question. If a go-go dancer is dancing nude in the forest, and nobody sees her, is she engaged in constitutionally protected speech? If a tree falls and so forth? Art always involves an audience question, and none of the judges deciding this matter so far seem to be too up on reader-response criticism, much less traffic in the disassembled audiences of the deconstructionists.

Judge Easterbrook's dissent reasons thusly: "Our problem involves conduct, and to know whether to treat conduct as speech we must ask whether it shares the communicative aspect that led to the protection of *real* speech."

Easterbrook goes on to quote an earlier Supreme Court decision:

"In deciding whether particular conduct possesses sufficient communicative elements to bring the First Amendment into play, we have asked whether 'an intent to convey a particularized message was present, and [whether] the likelihood was great that the message would be understood by those who viewed it.'"

The district court found that the dancers are not trying to express an idea; the dancers agree. Our court does not say otherwise; it holds instead that a message is not necessary to expression because "eroticism and sensuality" automatically qualify as speech. Can other emotions be far behind? Despite the court's claim that its holding covers only "dance as entertainment," the majority does not identify any kind of entertainment that contains neither ideas nor emotions . . .

Pervading this opinion is a belief that states may draw no lines where art is concerned. Sophisticates go to the museum and see Renoir's *Olympia* or to the opera and see a soprano strip during the Dance of the Seven Veils in Strauss's *Salome*. If the First Amendment protects these expressions, the argument goes, Joe Sixpack is entitled to see naked women gyrate in the pub.

Why does this follow? That a dance in *Salome* expresses something does not imply that a dance in JR's Kitty Kat Lounge expresses something, any more than the fact that Tolstoy's *Anna Karenina* was a stinging attack on the Russian social order implies that the scratching of an illiterate is likely to undermine the Tsar.

I suppose the dancers could, after a fashion, Mirandize themselves, as police must tell an individual his or her rights immediately upon arrest. Each dancer, before dancing, could announce or title the dance, Jules Feiffer style: "Ode to Spring," or "Ode to Jesse Helms." Judge Easterbrook would then be silenced. Each of the women dancing recently at the Kitty Kat expressed a great deal, even beyond "eroticism and sensuality," beyond the notion filed in their Supreme Court brief that claims their "nudity is a dramatization that sensuality is not shameful." They were revealing a psychosexual map of themselves, however sketchily drawn. They were displaying, describing, as all artists do, who they are: not, perhaps, completely, but in a fashion they find expressive in performance and that an attentive audience finds particularized speech.

I talked with one of the Kitty Kat dancers the night I visited. She told me, not unexpectedly, that she enjoyed the dancing, that it let her work off tension, that she liked doing it well, was stimulated by how performing made her feel. She was the one with her own tape. The dancers collect money from the patrons to pay for their tunes: "Got a dollar for the jukebox?" There are moments of silence when the jukebox finishes one song and goes to another, and most of the dancers have yet to incorporate silence into their dances—John Cages they're not—but since she had a tape there wasn't the usual number of awkward periodic hiatuses (though once she did need to flip the tape over).

Since the case is still pending, the women were stripping not completely but only down to Indiana's sanctioned pasties and G-strings (though one would be hard put to say the "buttocks" were not completely exposed—just as they were recently on the Phil Donahue show that featured the South Bend case and dancers). Asked if the Kitty Kat held a special place among other similar establishments in the neighborhood, the dancer said, "Yes. They dance nude here." Would she, if the Supreme Court permitted it?

"Oh, no," she said. If the Kitty Kat returned to nude dancing she would dance elsewhere.

"Dancing nude? That's," and she lowered her voice, "you know, too personal."

More or less, she put her finger on it: dancing nude is personal, a most personal form of particularized expression, speech; so personal that a five-year-long parade of black-robed male jurists (and at long last, one woman) have been deciding, and shortly are going to decree once and for all, whether it is speech anyone should be allowed to hear.

WILL THE COURT BARE ALL?*

T his summer the Supreme Court will deliver a decision in *Barnes v. Glen Theatre*, as the case will be called in legal shorthand. It, like many others, is a small-town case making good. So good, the local prosecutor in St. Joseph County, Indiana, Michael Barnes, whose name the case bears, flew to Washington to attend the argument before the Supreme Court on January 8. "I initiated this," the *South Bend Tribune* quotes Barnes as proudly proclaiming. "I wanted to be there." But Barnes didn't quite initiate this First Amendment case; lawyers and a dancer for a South Bend establishment called the "Chippewa Drive-In and Bookstore" started it by challenging the constitutionality of Indiana's public indecency statute. What Barnes had been doing was prosecuting nude dancers.

Indiana has a rather broad public indecency law, which holds, among other things, "nudity" to be "the showing of the human male or female genitals, pubic area, or buttocks with less than opaque covering, the showing of the breast with less than a fully opaque covering of any part of the nipple, or the showing of the covered male genitals in a discernibly turgid state." The local authorities had been using that law to enforce selectively (no nursing mothers have been handcuffed on buses yet) the state's notions of public morality. No one is charging obscenity here; it is nudity that causes the problem. The wearing of pasties and G-strings is, it seems, a required badge of public morality in Indiana. Such minimalist outfits are sexual euphemisms, and authorities often prefer strategically placed euphemisms to naked reality.

Gayle Sutro, a dancer booked to appear at the Chippewa, holds nude dancing to be speech; in an affidavit, Sutro claimed (I am quoting from the district court's memorandum and order) "her nude dances are appropriately choreographed and are an attempt to communicate as well as to entertain." Sutro and Glen Theatre, Inc. (owners of the Chippewa) attained an injunction in 1985

---

* First appeared in *Nation*, vol. 252, no. 24, June 24, 1991.

against the threatened application of the public indecency statue. Six years later Michael Barnes got to travel to Washington.

During those years, another establishment joined the case: the Kitty Kat Lounge, a South Bend go-go bar, one of a number along a strip leading into the south side of town. All these bars exist in the shadows made by empty factory buildings (Studebaker, Wheel Horse, and South Bend Lathe, among others) of the city's rapidly disappearing industrial base.

The Kitty Kat Lounge and the Chippewa Bookstore are different sorts of establishments. At the Chippewa, Gayle Sutro planned to dance nude behind glass panels. No liquor is served or allowed. Patrons could watch her dance by inserting money into what court documents call a "timing mechanism." In the various hearings and court appearance, the dancers (Darlene Miller represented the Kitty Kat) weren't the most articulate spokespersons for their art. Sutro's affidavit lists her credentials as a "professional actress, stunt woman and ecdysiast" who "has studied acting, dancing, speech and language," but she is not quoted in court documents further elaborating any notions she might have about dance as expression. Miller stated that she sees herself as "just entertaining, just dancing." Such laconism on the part of the dancers has led the judges involved to a great outpouring of language on the subject. On May 24, 1990, the U.S. Court of Appeals for the Seventh Circuit decided seven to four in favor of the dancers, ruling that nonobscene nude dancing is entitled to limited protection under the First Amendment and that Indiana's public indecency statue was accordingly unconstitutional.

For some time the Supreme Court has had an interest in deciding this question, because state courts disagree over the reach of the First Amendment in this area. In a 1975 case (*Doran v. Salem Inn*) the Court held that "although the customary 'barroom' type of nude dancing may involve only the barest minimum of protected expression . . . this form of entertainment might be entitled to First and Fourteenth Amendment protection in some circumstances." The status of nude dancing had remained unsettled, and that is why the Supreme Court took on the South Bend case.

Judge Richard Posner, one of the Seventh Circuit's majority, writes, "I am less interested in particular decisions than in fundamental principle. If the only expression that the First Amendment protects is the expression of ideas and opinions, then most music and visual art, and much of literature, are unprotected. This would be a shocking contraction of the First Amendment as it has come to be understood. If the only way to exclude nude dancing from the protection of the amendment is to exclude all nonpolitical art and literature as well, the price is too high."

The Seventh Circuit's dissenting judges claim (here quoting Judge Frank Easterbrook) that "go-go dancing is not speech. James Madison would have guffawed had anyone suggested public nudity as an example of 'freedom of speech.'" James Madison would also have laughed himself sick at the idea that women should have the right to vote, and he very likely wouldn't have contemplated the idea of dancing as speech, either. (The State of Indiana clung to its position when the case was argued before the Supreme Court. When Justice Anthony Kennedy asked if go-go dancing lacked protection because the dancers were not good enough, Deputy Attorney General Wayne Uhl replied, "Go-go dancing could be good or bad, but in neither case is it speech.")

Writing for the Seventh Circuit's majority, Judge Joel Flaum said, "The State in effect advances the proposition that the dance involved loses its expressive qualities as the dancers lose their clothing. It is well established, however, that '[n]udity alone does not place otherwise protected material outside the mantle of the first amendment.' *Schad* (1981). Nor does the fact that the dance is sexual remove the mantle of protection: 'Sexual expression which is indecent, but not obscene is protected by the First Amendment.' *Sable Communications v. FCC* (1989)." A lot of the verbal dueling will be and has been done in the not-so-empty clearing that the phrase "otherwise protected material" carves out for itself. The dissenting judges do not see nude dancing as an activity that warrants protection.

Judge Posner, in his concurring majority opinion, attempts to understand the dissenting judges' motives; he writes, "The true reason I think for wanting to exclude striptease dancing from the protection of the First Amendment is not any of the lawyers' classification games that I have been discussing, such as expression versus nonexpression, ideas versus emotions, art versus entertainment, or speech versus conduct. It is a feeling that the proposition, 'the First Amendment forbids the State of Indiana to require striptease dancers to cover their nipples,' is ridiculous." I think Judge Posner is being a bit too understanding of his colleagues. "Lawyers' classification games" do play a large role; important questions of behavior and speech, conduct and manner are hotly contested constitutional terrain. Dissenting Seventh Circuit judges quote Supreme Court Justice Antonin Scalia often and admiringly: "The more limited guarantee of freedom of expression," Scalia wrote in *Community for Creative Non-Violence v. Watt* (1984) when he was on the District of Columbia's U.S. Court of Appeals, "does not apply to accidental intrusion upon expressiveness but only to purposeful restraint of expression. It would not invalidate a law generally prohibiting the extension of limbs from the windows of moving vehicles; it would invalidate a law prohibiting only the extension of clenched fists." Scalia would have the dancers clench their fists.

Nude dancing is not the sort of First Amendment activity that ignites much public outrage at the thought of its potential curtailment. There has not been an outpouring of support for nude dancers from the dance world or from the arts world in general. Gayle Sutro is no Karen Finley. The friend-of-the-court briefs filed in behalf of the dancers have been few: the A.C.L.U., joined by the Volunteer Lawyers for the Arts, offered one; as did the Georgia On Premise & Lounge Association, Inc., a trade association; along with a third filed by a group headed by People for the American Way.

When nude dancing is done in a high-rent zone (opera or ballet, for example) it is afforded some respectability. In the lower courts' opinions there is a good bit of class derision in the language used, with scoffing comments about "hoi polloi" and "Joe Sixpack." The audience for nude dancing is derided as much as, if not more than, the dancers.

But at the Supreme Court, Justice Kennedy asked Indiana's Deputy Attorney General about who decides what forms of dancing are constitutionally protected. "Who's to do this?" he said. "Is the legislature to do this? Are we to do this?"

Even if the Court upholds the Seventh Circuit's opinion, which is likely, it will nonetheless probably fashion language for states to use in order to write laws that would not only prohibit nude dancing but could further whittle away the protection of expression in general by expanding (if by no more than the size of a G-string) what can be labeled "conduct" and not "speech." And if the Supreme Court goes all the way and declares nude dancing not to be protected expression, it will be drawing a line—not in sand, as George Bush did, but in flesh. And, if they get their ounce, how long will it be before they come for their pound?

FREEDOM AT RISK*

Three years after its publication, this book is more timely than ever. Anyone reading this collection (from diverse hands—journalists and academics, principally) of twenty-five insightful, alarming, and informative articles the year it was published would have encountered (in Richard Delgado's article, "The Language of the Arms Race: Should the People Limit Government Speech?," first published in 1984 in a law review) the phrase "collateral damage" long before it became a buzzword of Desert Storm briefings (and also would have been able to predict, even without the invasion of Grenada, how the press would be handled in Saudi Arabia). Eight years of Reagan-Bush, continuing into the first Bush-Quayle term, has seen the determined undermining of individual liberties and the First Amendment, and now the sinkholes are everywhere starting to appear.

Freedom at Risk's first essay is an overview, starting at the appropriate place, "The State of the First Amendment as We Enter '1984,'" by Thomas I. Emerson. However, its concluding sentences (and sentiments), "Nevertheless, on the whole, the First Amendment lives a powerful life. If we can keep basic economic, environmental, and other social conditions from overwhelming us, keep warfare from destroying us, and keep faith in the progress we have made, the symbolic year of 1984 need never arrive," if written now, might not be so rosy.

In 1974 a precursor volume to *Freedom at Risk* appeared, entitled *State Secrets: Police Surveillance in America*, which collected a number of articles devoted to the government's Nixon-era flirtations with secrecy. Then, there was enough sunlight on the topic that a commercial press published the volume. Today, the rethronement of the secrecy cult is something of a secret itself, left to the more secluded audience of an academic press book. Three years later,

---

* First appeared in *Rights*, July-Aug. 1991. Review of *Freedom at Risk: Secrecy, Censorship, and Repression in the 1980s*. Edited by Richard O. Curry.

only two national circulation, non-trade publications have reviewed *Freedom at Risk*: the *Progressive* and the *Village Voice Literary Supplement*.

Attempting to summarize the contents of *Freedom at Risk* is a decidedly gloomy task, but this collection is an indispensable compendium for anyone who wants to speak cogently about such issues and events of the 1980s as changes in libel laws, immigration policies, drug testing, recent conspiracy trials, disinformation, the FBI and domestic surveillance, the Sanctuary movement, the CIA at work, the politicization of international educational and cultural affairs, and the First Amendment itself. But no review digest is adequate; reading the book is required. Within its pages are found the hard peas hidden under the many soft mattresses of Reagan's brain.

One could ask, though, how could freedom not be at risk today? How could the cult of secrecy not be in firm control, when, for the first time in our history, the president of the United States, ascending to office after eight years of loyal service as vice president, is the former head of the government's own secret intelligence agency? Bush's CIA leadership has not gone uncommented upon, but its import is seldom fully felt, only because it is so terrible a circumstance.

In an article reprinted from the *Nation* (1985), "Beyond Westmoreland: the Right's Attack on the Press" by Walter Schneir and Miriam Schneir, the authors write,

> We should by no means regard the New Right movement with any sense of inevitability. Events are moving rapidly. In the next four years the New Right could field its own presidential candidate— Helms, for example—in the Republican party, or it could be a powerful third party movement. [*Wishful thinking?*] Or it may overreach itself, peak and decline. [*Swaggart, et al.?*] William Rusher has admitted, "Any development that revives and inflames the old division between haves and have-nots in the producing segment of the society could quickly disrupt the New Right coalition." With a blue-collar and lower-middle-class constituency, the New Right quails [*What a prescient pun they unwittingly made*] before class consciousness and conflict as vampires recoil from sunlight or a crucifix.

And it is wan indeed to recall in the waning days of the 1988 campaign, when Dukakis finally began highlighting class differences between the two parties, that George Bush spoke out against such divisive tactics by Dukakis, that Dukakis had the temerity to raise the chimera, the bugaboo of class division, which, Bush held, does not exist here in the U.S.

The 1980s witnessed a turnabout that is currently part of the conventional wisdom: as conservatives complained about the dark damage of the "Warren Court" now liberals are merely suffering the flipside of such ideological unhappiness. The "Rehnquist Court" may yet be as vilified (with less effect) as the Warren Court. Such seductive symmetry is often offered as a picture of fairness: first one side has its way, then the other. Winners and losers. It is still difficult to picture the government and the Constitution as a ball game, though the American public would be better served by the press if the press reported the government's doings as well as it reports sports.

As Delgado's law review article reminds us, "Even short of censorship and secrecy, government controls the content of news by working with the mass media to set social agendas. According to some communications scholars, the crucial characteristic of mass media is their capacity to shape social reality by setting the agenda for public discourse. The media may not always succeed in telling people what to think, but they are highly successful in telling them what to think about."

The Reagan years and *Freedom at Risk* also point up another submerged and sour fact: how much certain individuals shape policy. Change the person, change the policy. Edwin Meese as attorney general, Charles Wick running Voice of America; William Casey heading the CIA; Ollie North and Secord; O'Connor, Kennedy, Scalia, Souter on the Court, and so on.

The conservative shibboleth, get government off our backs, is always half quoted: off our backs and on to someone else's. And, with the most recent Supreme Court decisions, it is the backs of have-nots, especially women, that the Rehnquist Court has decided to ride. Articles about Robert Bork in the *Nation* (1983-84) by Jamie Kalven (reprinted in *Freedom at Risk*) may have helped bring about Bork's nonconfirmation to the high court, but Justice Scalia and former Judge Bork must have spent a lot of time patting each other on the back when they both served on the U.S. Court of Appeals for the District of Columbia, since Scalia often duplicates the Borkian line regarding political speech being the only sort that deserves protection. But since this year's ignominious *Rust v. Sullivan* decision, which allows the government to dictate what doctors at federally funded health clinics can and cannot say, the clearest line drawn is that speech that is paid for can be restricted by whomever pays for it. Recall Reagan angrily saying, when a microphone was going to be turned off during the 1980 campaign, "I paid for this!" With the *Rust* decision, the almighty dollar has become more almighty.

The privatization of information keeps popping up like a stubborn rash throughout a good number of *Freedom at Risk*'s articles. That trend is especially troubling (amongst a large selection of troubling developments). Privatization makes more valuable the knowledge of those in control and also makes what they claim as knowledge less open to refutation. The *Rust* decision is only the most egregious example of this privatization of knowledge, albeit one found in an unlikely context. The overall attempt is clear: to make the opening up of government during the sixties and seventies an aberration. The Pentagon Papers were the secrecy cultists' Bay of Pigs, and the White House tapes were the Tet Offensive in the demystification of the power holders; indeed, almost everyone, even critics, thought, hoped, that the talk in the White House was more thoughtful than it was.

George Bush's 1988 campaign strategy called for gaining and implementing yet more social controls, to stymie what he called the "deterioration of values." He is getting them—often through the Supreme Court: witness the recent case banning nude dancing, *Barnes v. Glen Theatre*, which was decided in favor of police power, not artistic expression. As Byron White wrote in dissent, "That the performance in the Kitty Kat Lounge may not be high art . . . is hardly an excuse for distorting and ignoring settled doctrine." What has gone on the last ten years regarding the reinstitution of secrecy and the weakening of the courts as defenders of free speech is the intellectual equivalent of the S & L "crisis." We will all be paying the bill for a long time; *Freedom at Risk* will at least tell anyone who cares what went on and why it happened.

V

TIME FOR ONE STORY

THE MAGGOT PRINCIPLE*

I do two things each day that I hate to do. I go to sleep and I wake up. Knowing this, it is not as easy to rail against that which I do that I have no wish to do. We are all extorted by chance, though the guise makes a difference, and it is not unusual to come to a place and find yourself engaged in an enterprise opposite your original intentions.

A small town is different from a large city, in that any grotesques you see, you are likely to see again, as in a recurrent bad dream. And this is not even a small town but a summer resort, the bait on the tip of this hook of New England. When winter comes, those who remain are the stragglers any traveling thing leaves behind. You may think of touring circuses, fairs, religious zealots with tent compounds, or a retreating army, and that is close to the situation. There is a meanness in the shut-up buildings: plywood over the windows as if the glass has grown cataracts. What makes people stay is the same inclination that brings them to the lip of an extinct volcano or a notable man's grave.

Through the winter there is only one institution that functions; it is the Fish Factory. It appears another ruin, cited for extinction. Listing walls notwithstanding, it still prospers within. The building is kept together by what it is: three floors of cold storage is its center and the ice gives solid structure. If the freezers were shut off, it is said by those who have worked there longest, the building would collapse. The ice is like anger, which steadies men.

The employees of the Fish Factory have a grim cheerfulness that comes to people who are glad to have a job, any job. The manager who hired me, seeing drawn across my face a map of midwestern industry, advised me to take other employment if I could find it, though his expression was that of the only grocer in town who tells you to buy your produce elsewhere if you don't like the price.

---

* First appeared in *The Transatlantic Review*, no. 44, Autumn-Winter 1972.

The stench, the unskinned odor, though never gotten used to, becomes familiar and then unrecognized. My training began in the packing room, where lobster tails are weighed and sorted and put in packages ready for stores. One thousand frozen lobster tails smell like caged white mice. Stainless steel tables, a cement floor, Toledo scales, gray plastic pans, and cartons of frozen lobster tails from South Africa. Who packed these across the Atlantic? I wonder as I crack a block of frozen lobster tails across the edge of the table. It shatters, an ancient clay pot filled with coins, into fifty little tails.

Could any machine equal the chaotic precision of four people sorting lobster tails? Flinging them, after checking their weight, into eight stainless steel pans, separated in two by wooden dividers. The air is as full of flying lobster tails as the sky above Kennedy Airport is with planes.

Casey, an aging lesbian who does the final weighing, has masculinized every woman in the room by circumcising their names. Alice is Al, Lucy is Lu, Freida is Fred. Casey is boss of the radio, a tiny plastic thing that sits on a crate. Its cord snakes up the wall to a high socket as if the music coming from it held it erect like a summoned cobra.

Frozen lobster tails hit pans sounding like cutlery dropped in a sink. The windows are covered with polyethylene; a few late summer flies cling to it. Furry, they evolve short cilia against the cold; and it is cold in the large room. A heater suspended from the ceiling comes on at intervals suddenly, like a man bolting up from troubled sleep.

There are the stuffers, usually four, lobster tails piled in front of them. The tails come wrapped in cellophane, and the stuffers put them into boxes and then onto a conveyor belt that brings them to two elderly women who select an additional lobster tail from one of the pans I and another have been filling, which will bring the weight up to what is marked on the box. From there to Casey and then through a machine that seals the ends of the cardboard boxes. The air is filled with the smell of melting wax. An old man, Sammy, takes them into the freezer, where they wait to be shipped out. On the wall is taped the record amount of lobster tails ever to be packed in a day.

Four of us, poker-faced, stand around a table, dealing lobster tails into pans. Each tail is given an inspection, a multiplicity of single observations of identical articles. Having seen each for a second, you have seen one for eight hours. The dark brown carapace that is spotted with reds and greens is no longer a crustacean's but an insect's. The white meat of the lobster is the starch inside a withered twig. The little fins folded over in death across its belly are the hands of children in their abbreviated coffins.

At the end of the day, when the room is filled with fluorescent light, a giddiness sets in, a hilarity takes over. After a spurt of feverish activity, crackling laughter. I have seen it happen elsewhere, this spasm of silent activity ended by laughter. The infirm have it, as do the insane and the employed.

"Oh, look at this, Casey," a small Portuguese woman says upon finding a lobster tail brown with eggs. The women gather around her as around a newborn. "They should have thrown her back in, the damn fisherman," Casey says, "I've seen them sit on the dock during summer and scrub off the eggs so they could sell them. They'll kill them all off." The women continue to coo over the lobster, halved as ever the babe would have been if Solomon had carried out his intentions.

I keep forgetting these are corpses. Dismembered ones at that, since they're frozen, hard little shards of ice. Sometimes, through excessive handling and being in a lot that is unpacked but not repacked, and then returned to the freezer to come out again and not find its way into a finished package, they get to be a little limp. But these are supposed to be terminally discarded.

There is a break at ten after beginning at eight in the morning. The men go for coffee, the women into a room that has benches. The packing room empties and takes on a coldness that is present whenever humans depart, like a fire gone completely out.

There is an hour for lunch. Atop a nearby firehouse a siren screams out noon. A generator that is hooked up to nothing, and its wail is mechanized frustration. It gives a split-second warning of its coming, a mere electrical click, and as I walk away from the factory to a luncheonette, I put my gloved hands up to my ears. It takes fifteen steps for it to end. Every day at noon; a reminder, a flag at half-mast; whatever machines are buried in me mourn with it.

I worry for the first week that my work in the Fish Factory will brand me. That the stink will be too odious to those not directly involved with the work. That my uniform of boots and sweaters and coarse coat with a cap pulled over my hair will ostracize me, make me stand out, put the town off-limits. But the populace surprises me and takes no notice. Even when I get to the luncheonette, the stools next to me are not vacated, even though I smell of death and flounder. Soon I have no sense of shame.

Walking the one main street of town, I see the daily grotesques. The man with his hair shaved away from two sullen lumps that show the remains of their stitches like the teeth marks a child leaves playfully on your arm. Some hack's proud work, though I cannot know what ill caused the surgery, though the man has an addled smile. The main street of town is the common recreation area for a number of lost homes. There is the man with the nervous disorder who has to generate more stationary thrust than a Saturn rocket before he can propel himself ten feet. Then he rests against the fender of a car. He once asked me a question and spoke so fast that I had to learn to listen to him. By slowing down his speech, a seventy-eight record to thirty-three-and-a-third, I could understand him. But then the only answer his question required was "No." By the time I reach the luncheonette the parade is half over, though usually at the counter there is a gentle spastic who is having a cup of coffee, continually stirring his sugar, sounding all the while through my desiccated meal like he is calling a meeting to order.

The Fish Factory system can assimilate anyone immediately. Without notice, one afternoon the packing room empties out, and we file through the door, up narrow steps attached to the outside of the building. High tide is in, right up to the pilings which begin where the building stops. There is a long wharf extending into the bay. Next to the Fish Factory is a boat-restoring yard, and a large fishing boat lies beached on its side, a peeling underbelly exposed like an obese patient waiting for an injection. The steps we climb continue over the roof and up to a high third floor to which I have never come. From here everything is motionless, stilled by distance, and silent except for the squalls of the gulls who perch around and along a track that descends to the wharf. There is a large cage that is run on cable, ascending now, loaded with fresh fish. The trap slams against a metal tank and then the load of fish drops. Hollow sounds, distant, far-off explosions. The cage descends again as we enter the room, leaving the gulls to rip the fish that make a path of carcasses underneath the cage's track.

Machinery, water on the floor, mounds of ice go undiminished in the cold. Cartons thrown down a hole in the ceiling; Dominic, the foreman, herds his gang together, the old women beside the conveyor, herring comes over the elevated ridge on one belt like an unexpected assault and flops into cartons that are to hold fifty pounds each. They are sent down over rollers to be weighed and then transferred to carts, and when fifteen are stacked they are hauled to the freezer. I lift them from the weighing table to the carts. Round silver scales stick to my black gloves. Soon they are covered by this soft mail. The boxes of herring get backed up. "Stop the belt!" Dominic yells. Herring spills over the filled boxes onto the floor, sounding like strokes of a tired whipping. They are scooped up later with a shovel. It is hard work and doesn't slow down unless the belts stop. During the pause my wrists ache, the delayed burning that cold produces when you just start to get warm. The body gets used to it, new rhythms are learned. I keep forgetting the fish are dead, I pay such little attention to them, lost to the rapid motions that are required to keep up. They do not have whites to their eyes, but are clear. All their small mouths are open. Thousands and thousands of herring. My feel slip on the ones fallen around me. The iron wheels of the cart flatten them. My heels gash open orange bellies. I get used to the queasy footing.

Three young men are clustered around the end of the initial conveyor belt. They wear thick aprons and gloves, shoving boxes just filled down the line. At times they find an odd fish among the school of herring and they are discarded into one large box. The monster box. They look like excited physicians throwing spare organs back over their shoulders.

Sarge trips the cage, releasing fish into the tank. There is a fury behind the work that is always present during a siege. The long whine of the steel cable, the crash of the cage against metal, the thud of two hundred pounds of herring. They drop onto the fish below, which are continually slithering out a small opening onto the conveyor belt. In their convex and concave mesh they resemble the race of the sperm for the egg, down the narrow channel, each forcing the other with helpless collaborators' weight. Cattle do the same thing in their stalls that lead to slaughterhouses. A Judas goat is not necessary in every case. Confined numbers can cause deadly momentum.

We get caught up. More than two hundred barrels of herring packed. Dominic, now bored with driving the crew, descends to the floor beneath, and I wander over to see the beginnings of the process of which I am the end. I pass the monster box like a cemetery a young boy encounters unavoidably at night on his way home. A spiny fish that still breathes like a tattered bellows. A starfish adhering to a pink stingray like a sea spider. A squid twisted around a scup. Kelp forms a reticule around the ooze. The monster box: a synopsis of a nightmare.

There is a tank into which large cod have been thrown that were caught with the herring. One cod has already been gutted. Its emptied carcass, which is now nothing but a wide flat head and a long handle of backbone, stretches out on the cement like a lost shovel you find rotting in the ground after a winter's snow had gone and uncovered it. The two filleted sections rest atop a crate. They are washed off and very white.

In the tank are the sleek cod, so huge they seem after the herring, which never got beyond eight inches. Big-mouthed, an olive-drab color without any of the iridescence of the herring. Some of the cod have, stuck halfway out of their mouths, three or four half-swallowed herring. Death has prevented the cod from consuming them. A macabre *in flagrante delicto*. Stories to inspire chastity in my high-school youth leap to mind like spawning salmon. During a retreat, a gray priest telling of two "fornicating youths in the back seat of a car, crushed by a brakeless truck, found by their parents and the authorities still locked in their carnal embrace, their sin embossed in death, their guilt preserved as surely as by the lava of Vesuvius."

I picked up one of the cod from whose mouth four half-swallowed herring protrude, and in death his startled eyes give back some excuse of innocence, like all the heads at the boys' school seemed to want to extend by the amused and shocked shaking of their heads. *Somebody stuffed them in my mouth. I can't even breathe. . . .*

I try to pull one herring out by its tail, till its reluctance overwhelms me, so tenacious is their graved epoxy, and I drop the cod back in the tank. I had begun to get an erection.

It is seven-fifty in the morning, and I am the first to leave tracks in the snow. As I come around the corner of the pump house, a man leans out the window and pours a coffee can full of steaming water over a pipe's frozen valve.

May, an old woman who is very short and whenever she looks at you to speak she turns her head, so it appears she's looking at you from around some nonexistent corner, says to me as I weigh lobster, "Maybe they'll give us medals depending on how many lobsters we get done."

How could people have worked eighteen hours a day? The same incomprehension as a soldier has viewing the armor of a knight. Finally five o'clock comes; it is terrible; the death wish of killing time. We file from the room each day like surgeons who keep losing their patients under the knife.

The men who assemble near a truck in the early morning, cold vapors seeping from their mouths, the departing cast of their slumbering hopes, come rubbing their hands, standing near the empty trailer like seconds who arrive early for a duel in order to survey the clearing.

The resignation of men before they take to their jobs. It is the same, regardless of the task, as long as it is one they have resigned themselves to. Shrugged shoulders, jokes made, bitter as coffee grinds that collapse garbage bags. They shame reluctance by action. We are used to earth's passings, its relays, its handings-over.

So we load the truck. The freezer door swings open onto the loading dock. Aluminum tracks are set up down the middle of the empty trailer, the truck driver and myself at the far end. An air conditioning unit sticks out, for this truck carries perishables, the cold air channeled down the length of the trailer by a canvas tube that hangs close to the ceiling. It is primitive but works, something Archimedes would have figured out. The truckdriver and I do not introduce ourselves, but the speed with which we handle the cartons describes us to one another, the archaic dance of manual labor. Midway, he tells me his name and asks for mine; and because I am ten years younger than he, and youth will be forgiven most anything, he overlooks the length of my hair, and because I will take eight cartons to his seven (a subtle dowry I have to pay because it is *his* truck). The others he has met before, and for the sake of good comradeship they recall him, or if not exactly him, a truckdriver they did remember, as if it is good enough to say kind things about a member of the species if not the exact individual.

The truck fills up completely, a queen bee brimming with eggs, and for a while we are somber with the idea of procreation, stacking the cartons, but it wanes.

"Boy, whoever it is that runs that coffee place, is that a man or a woman?" the truckdriver asks.

I reply it is indeed a woman but in a voice full of regret at her mannishness, the same tone a hunter uses when he speaks of a favorite coon dog that has lost the ability to follow the scent. With this cleared up, other testings go on, exchanged assurances in the muted air of the trailer as we pile up frozen whiting.

"You don't exactly clean up around here," Sammy had said. Clean up. Hygiene. Money douche. Five-dollar ablutions.

Sarge talks like a motor that will never quite turn over. Short, breathy sentences that end completely before they are finished, then start up again, only to end. He tells about an old man who would pay money for your socks, the mangier the better, which he would stuff into his mouth. Sarge makes movements with his hand like he's tossing peanuts in between his teeth. The truckdriver tells about a friend of his who would walk twenty miles through a blizzard if he knew there was a sure piece of ass waiting for him. Sarge, because of his excited speech, seems to bubble, telling about a retarded girl who has to be taken out of school because she would remove her clothes in class.

"Slap. Her titties." Sarge using his hands like there's fluttering wash hanging below his chest. "Hump. Around in. The aisles." Sarge juggling his three hundred pounds around the loading dock as if he were offering his thrusting middle to a fire hydrant. Common men load trucks and we are common men.

Who saw the first one? Behind me, at the table of stuffers, someone says quietly, "Is that a maggot?" Lippy, who sounds like Radio Free Europe jammed by the Russians, replies, "Naaaahissparrtaadulobstir," and brushes aside whatever it is.

It is a bad day for lobster packing; the law of averages had given us the wrong sizes, too many big ones, too many small ones, not enough medium-sized and the correct weight was hard to come by. A computer could figure the variations possible to get four separate lobster tails to weigh out to an average of 6.8 ounces and it is easy if you have all different sizes; but a preponderance of one will impede the natural selection, and boxes are rejected, and the race of 6.8-ounce boxes of Cap'n Ahab's South African Lobster Tails will die out, disappear from the face of the earth, if the balance in sizes is not restored. Boxes would come back and be emptied out, repacked and sent back again—not many, but just enough to make it a bad day, like yesterday, when the same thing happened. There was a box of lobster tails that had been put back in the freezer the day before that had begun to thaw out and so there would be today.

"Look," Casey let out with an unaccustomed girlish screech, "there are maggots!" She held up a blue box on which could be seen a small silhouette climbing along one wall, like a mountain climber descending a sheer cliff.

The stuffers pushed aside the pile of lobster tails, and there on the top of that stainless-steel table are about a dozen maggots. Maggots! Though on top of the bright silver table they look like shoots of wild rice. Their backs hump like babies flexing little fists.

"It's these loose ones," Casey yells, holding up an almost completely thawed lobster tail that bends over in her hand like a man collapsed across barbed wire.

"I told Dominic they were getting no good, but he wanted to get rid of them," Casey goes on exultantly, glad to have her day's grumblings vindicated. Maggots in the lobster tails! That'll show them!

Maggots. An American housewife, fresh from Food World, comes into her kitchen, puts down her brown sacks, takes off her car coat, sets aside her new checkbook which pictures in color the first A-bomb explosion on each check, and gets out a box of Cap'n Ahab's Apartheid Lobster Tails, tearing its quickzip opener to thaw out her hors d'oeuvres for tonight's pre-bridge dinner party, and out crawls a maggot. Her throat parches. She steps back, irises widening. She puts out a hand to reach for the absolute axis that Food World spins on, and finds it gone! Stumbling, only to knock over her Osterizer, which trips the switch that sets growling her disposal, and finding nothing to cling to as the terror of that vision becomes entire and lucid, cracking open an evil that falls onto her Teflon mind like a black egg, she grabs her Arctic Chest's door handle, reeling, swings it open and collapses at its feet, slowly being covered with ice cubes from the mini-igloo-icemaker till she revives.

What must she think we are? We who have packed MAGGOTS into her lobster tails. That our factory is a geodesic dome of cobwebs. Our lobsters hauled in fetid garbage cans. She sees not ground zero, but the periphery, the sores, the ooze, the tracks left by the skittering rats which imprint the new cuneiform on the clay tablets of Mesopotamia!

But all the while, it is just our Fish Factory. This room quiet as a battlefield when they come to strip the weapons from the dead. Clean, brightly lit, the cement floor washed as spotlessly as front walks by summer gardeners. And on the silver table the dozen grains of wild rice.

Casey is still yelling, vilifying Dominic, as if he is the First Cause, the uncaused cause, the harborer of spontaneous generation.

I hear a faint rambunctious tapping. I look over to the window covered with cloudy plastic, and trapped in there are several hairy flies, one of whom, knocking against that plastic, sounds as proud as an old man who has been accused of being the impregnator of a young girl thought to be virginal. A Joseph fly.

Dominic comes through the door, his upper and lower jaw meshing badly, the missing teeth cause his bite to be sinister. He grumbles against the elements, that it is not his fault, that it is the general policy to use lobster tails if they have thawed out a bit, possibly exposed to contamination by our little club of flies. He rips open sealed cartons and discovers no maggots in them, but Casey takes a box and finds a maggot perched on a tail.

Dominic's broken face for a minute resembles Robert McNamara's as he stares at the pile of boxes ready to be taken into the freezer. A whole day's work! His brow knots into an abacus, cost accounting, tabulating, the number of employees, wages, hours worked, cost of recycling, and makes the humane, the only decision: Check all the boxes! Open them up and check them and repack them all. He continues to mutter against the cosmos and quits the room, a king who chooses not to see the execution he has just decreed.

We all set to the sealed boxes. Savagely tearing them open, transfixed smiles as we ravage the work we did, a chance to open what we heretofore had only been able to close. The battered boxes we empty lay at our feet like the fruit that falls too soon from the tree and is trampled by the pickers. Young men grunt as they rip into large cartons, which contain the smaller baby-blue boxes. The first minutes of this are elating, then the dark zeal abates and the monotony that is our true condition reclaims us. No other maggots are discovered.

Casey looks at the rising pyramid of repacked cartons with a bitterness that I know can only mean she let one contaminated box through, to lurk on the shelf of Food World, under the frosty breath of their air conditioning, which continually bathes the produce with a white eminence like the red glow of a sacristy lamp. The unsuspecting mother will pick it out and take it into her home and finally unwrap for herself a putrescence that even if hell were our three floors of freezers could not be preserved forever from her gaze. We deal in perishables.

The repacking resumes its usual pace. Any lobster tail that is even partially thawed is discarded. The work is done. The day over. Sammy hauls the last load into the freezer.

"Maybe we should tell the Board of Health," May whispers around her invisible corner, but the refrain is not picked up. If someone tells, and they do something about it, if they close this place down, then we won't have jobs, and anyway, nothing really happened. The maggots were here, but they didn't get through; the maggots didn't get into Food World. If they got into Food World and crawled along America's kitchen counter, that would be one thing; but they were stopped *here*, where they began. At the Fish Factory.

Afterword

I. Edward Dahlberg Times 5

Edward Dahlberg, Teacher

This is the "earliest" piece in this collection. I wrote it in the summer of 1967 when I was twenty-one. Dahlberg had told me that Jonathan Williams was preparing a volume and that if I wrote a recollection it might be used. In 1970, my friend David Black came into McSorely's saloon and said he saw my name on a list of contributors for the next issue of *TriQuarterly*. I didn't know what that could be, so I called Charles Newman, then the magazine's editor, and asked him. He told me it was my piece about Dahlberg. In the three years that had passed, I thought I had developed quite a bit as a writer, and I asked if I could edit the essay. Newman wasn't too happy with that, but agreed and he sent me galleys. I cut out about three pages of prose that seemed too heated to me. What remains still blazes.

Dahlberg's The Olive of Minerva

I had published two books by 1976, both with Nick Ellison as editor at T. Y. Crowell. Dahlberg was without a publisher at the time. I told Nick about Dahlberg and arranged that they meet. Unbeknownst to either Nick or me, Nick's biological father, long deceased, was a friend of Dahlberg, a man who had actually supported Dahlberg. This coincidence bonded them, and it didn't take much to persuade Nick to publish Dahlberg's new book, *The Olive of Minerva*, and to take my suggestion of an omnibus volume of Dahlberg's early novels. I wrote the jacket copy for both books (getting the plot of *The Olive of Minerva* wrong in the bargain). There was not a great rush to the bookstores, something I anticipated, but Nick, self protectively, found the lack of interest surprising.

Edward Dahlberg 1900-1977

I wrote this shortly after Dahlberg's death. The *New York Times Book Review* occasionally ran this sort of tribute. I sent it to them through Joan Raines, my agent at the time. She reported back that Harvey Shapiro said that they get "dead author" articles frequently and couldn't run them all. It took me over a year to find a publication for it, whereupon it was subtitled, "On the Occasion of the First Anniversary of His Death."

The Wages of Expectation

Charles DeFanti and I became friends through our mutual friendship with Dahlberg. DeFanti ends his biography with a quotation from my writing, an unnecessarily gallant act of self-effacement. The biography would have been fuller and longer had it not been his Ph.D. dissertation. His involvement with Dahlberg was further complicated by the paradoxical nature of his Boswellian role.

The Causes of Immortal Conceptions

It was Steven Moore, the senior editor of the *Review of Contemporary Fiction*, who first noticed the Dahlberg line at the end of *Darconville's Cat*; he brought it to my attention and suggested I might like to write about a Dahlberg/Theroux link, for a special issue half devoted to Alexander Theroux. Moore knew of my connection to Dahlberg. Dalkey Archive Press, which is connected to the *Review*, had published Dahlberg's *Samuel Beckett's Wake and Other Uncollected Prose* in 1989.

II. The Literary Life and Hard Times

The Literature of Place and No Place

The editor of this volume, David Hoppe, commissioned all of its contents. David works for the Indiana Humanities Council, which sponsored the book, and, before that, he ran a reading series at the Michigan City Public Library, where I first met him. Since the number of writers who are well known nationally grows smaller, states are taking more interest in their writer-residents, though they might not be any more well known to their more immediate neighbors.

The Night the Ghost Didn't Get In

This is the lightest piece I have ever written. I was struck by the coincidence of the events which paralleled so closely those in Thurber's famous stories. This piece profited from editing by Daryln Brewer of *Poets & Writers* magazine. It was made as short as it could be, thereby improving it.

Catholics Coming of Age

I was asked by the magazine *New Catholic World* to write on the subject. The magazine printed it as I wrote it. I assume I was asked because of my reviews in *Commonweal* and the fact that I taught at Notre Dame. The presumption was that I was a Catholic author, a category I never considered for myself, though, given the literary situation, one had better fit in somewhere.

Ellen Frankfort's Voice

I knew a few people who wrote for the *Voice*, including Ellen Frankfort. I read the book with interest and sent the review to *Commonweal*, which ran it. Subsequently, I got to know Ellen Frankfort much better. She was incisive, at times madly brilliant. She was a battler, but lost her own battle and killed herself in 1987.

Difficult Women *and* Minor Characters

These two memoirs intersected in an interesting way: both were looking forward (to their future careers) as well as back. Plante successfully inserted himself into literary history as a youthful American link to the aging Auden group. Joyce Johnson spun out of the Beat orbit into the publishing world, playing a handmaiden role to literature in a more direct way, as well as writing books.

On Becoming a Novelist *and* Panic among the Philistines

This, perhaps, should have been titled "On Becoming a Philistine and Panic Among the Novelists." The Panic book was an example of Reagan-era fashion (yuppie conservatism, Dartmouth lit-crit, Yale Literary Magazine aesthetics) spilling onto writers on fiction. Gardner left another posthumous how-to book, *The Art of Fiction*, which possibly is used in colleges more than any of his novels, another sign of the times.

Famous People He Has Known

Ars brevis, vita longus.

The Post-Modern Aura

Newman's work is very important, though, he too can't read all the contemporary fiction that is produced and subsequently finds theoretical criticism is much safer than practical.

Protesting N.E.A.; Artists Should Accept Grants from the Arts Endowment; Letters to Editors: The N.E.A. and the Loyalty Oafs

These were dispiriting pieces to write. The resounding silence from the ninety-seven writers who received grants to the general attack baffled and discouraged me: it did seem to point to a disturbing detachment from the fray from those literary novelists and short story writers most directly involved. Of course, I was not reading everything, so I might well have missed some manifestations in print. Was literature (or the writers deemed to attempt it) as superfluous in and to the culture as people contended? Though I am certain that the "loyalty oath" business was a slander, it is all too clear that, in our money-talks society, only refusing cold cash could one buy one's self a ticket to this particular cultural ball. Otherwise, it's wallflower city.

III. Fiction Times: America, England, Ireland

Craig Nova 1, 2, 3

Craig and I were classmates at Columbia University and buddies. Reviewing friends and acquaintances, I have found over the years, is more difficult than reviewing strangers; since I admire Craig's writing there isn't much critical conflict here. If you don't like what a friend writes, you have two problems, not just one. I have a suspicion you would get more honest—or accurate—appraisal of contemporary fiction if it were a requirement, not just a touchy circumstance, that only friends of the author be allowed to review a book. There is a philosophical problem here: should criticism spring from a feeling of generosity? Can you care for a person but not the work? If you don't like a stranger's novel you are his/her enemy. Should enemies be allowed to review books?

John Updike

Updike has reviewed over his long career almost no younger contemporary American male novelists, doubtless for psychological reasons, most likely of the Oedipal sort.

Nicholas Delbanco, Donald Marsh, Katherine Dunn, Rosalyn Drexler, Kenneth Patchen, Harry Crews, Robert Hemenway

While I was a student at Columbia I attended a party at Galen Williams's apartment and met Allen Planz, then the poetry editor of the *Nation*. Over drinks at a bar on lower Broadway (which collapsed, the building that is, some few years later), Planz suggested I drop by the offices of the *Nation*, since the magazine was looking for someone to do brief reviews for them, "and you're probably just what we're looking for," I recall him saying. I did that the next day; Planz barely recognized me through the haze of his hangover, but introduced me to Beverly Gross, the literary editor. She regarded me skeptically, but pointed to a shelf filled with books and told me to take a bunch and review a few. I did. I learned instantaneously the vagaries of getting a book noticed. I also realized the value of being in New York City; in fact, this is exactly why I wanted to be in New York City.

David Black

David Black and I were also classmates at Columbia. David's first novel had the bad luck to appear during the last long *New York Times* newspaper strike (1979). The ABA put out a book supplement which was carried by one of the still publishing tabloids to "make up" for the lack of the *TBR*. David published two more novels, a number of books of superior nonfiction, and, of late, has been writing and producing for television.

James Carroll

I was asked to do this review by *Commonweal*, doubtless because of my first book, *The Harrisburg 7 and the New Catholic Left*. *The Prince of Peace* sold well enough. Later, Carroll got a multibook million-dollar contract with E. P. Dutton, which had acquired my third novel, *Criminal Tendencies*, for $7,500.

Mary Gordon

Attacking the successful is a no-win situation. Since so few novels get any serious attention and criticism, those that do become important, not to the authors alone, but to the institutions that have made them well known.

Clark Blaise and Madison Jones

I was teaching at Rutgers University in Newark, N.J., when the *American Book Review* was launched (Rutgers has a stake in the *ABR*), but didn't review anything for them until I was at Mount Holyoke. Now, the *American Book Review* has expanded its coverage to the other "arts," thereby reducing the already shrunken space given over to books in our culture.

Hugh Nissenson

This was an assigned review. Nissenson wrote me a thank you note; I have mixed feelings about that practice, though I have written one such note myself.

Nissenson's book got a good bit of attention. Most book reviews, as I have written in a different context, are, since so few people ever read the book, eulogies for corpses no one has ever met.

John Barth

There is something to be said for not being too successful. There is a whetstone principle: authors need something hard to sharpen themselves, and a lack of success provides that hardness (though it may be too hard). Certain successful authors can indulge themselves, and Barth is one. What got left out of the review, though, is the statement that reading even this novel by Barth is going to be more rewarding than reading half of the other novels that would be published during the year. The reverence for the rich is laid on a bit thick in the novel; Barth should be forced to live in the Midwest, where the rich aren't as tasteful as their eastern shore counterparts. I coined a word in this review, *overread*; that is a new concept, since no one justly can claim to be overread. But readers, I fear, are breaking down into those two categories, under- and overread. The overread is often the "professional" reader.

Gordon Lish

All my reviews for the *Chicago Tribune*, save one, were assignments, though I was asked more pointedly if I was willing to do this book, the implication being some writers feared to consider someone as influential as Lish. I can't shake the notion that Lish's fiction is a psychological reaction to what he has brought to print of other authors over the years.

Thomas McMahon

It is always interesting to read a fiction writer who is intelligent and learned in some other field than fiction writing. They are rare in our culture.

James T. Farrell

This was solicited by a reference book publisher and I did it for sentimental reasons. Adhering to the publisher's "form" produced an odd result. Farrell's *Studs Lonigan* trilogy was one of the first adult books I read and the occasion of one of my father's few literary remarks: "So, you're reading that dirty book." My father and Farrell grew up in the same South Chicago parish. Farrell was later denounced from the pulpit. And I saw Farrell once: Craig Nova and I were sitting in the White Horse tavern when a large throng of what we took for tourists blustered in, in the tow of a short "tour guide" who was James T. Farrell. I suppose he needed the money; that was a few years before he died in 1979.

Joseph Caldwell and James Reid

Commonweal asked for this. I am not sure there was any logic to the pairing. Caldwell's book was serious; Reid's was genre stuff.

John Cheever

My interest in doing this review was sparked by Donaldson's earlier biography, *Poet In America: Winfield Townley Scott* (University of Texas, 1972). Scott was the omega to Dahlberg's alpha in my late adolescent world view of writers (since they were the only two writers I then knew—in the mid-sixties). Scott's situation, living well but unhappily in Santa Fe, New Mexico, was quite different than Dahlberg's; he was then living marginally on Rivington Street in New York City's lower east side. I was a friend of the Scott family when I worked for the Santa Fe Opera. Scott committed suicide in 1968.

Norman Kotker; Richard Elman and Robin Hemley; Nettie Jones; C. E. Poverman

These review were more or less arranged by me. Norman Kotker and Richard Elman are friends. See my earlier remarks on writing reviews of friends' books. Nettie Jones I had met. The Hemley and Poverman books were both urged upon me by friends. The literary world is paradoxically shrinking and expanding, insofar as the number of writers who are getting any attention decreases while a growing number, the overwhelming majority, of novels are cast off into deep space, retrived only by the most personal of interventions.

Douglas Unger; Richard Baush and Mark Probst; Howard Frank Mosher

These novels were assigned by Dianne Donovan at the *Chicago Tribune*. If any of them reveals a trend, Mosher's is the most disturbing.

Thomas Pynchon

I wanted to hop on the Pynchon bandwagon (and, given *Vineland*, it has sufficiently slowed).

Larry Heinemann

By writing an opera buffa, Heinemann avoided the trap fallen into by many authors who have written Vietnam novels and followed them with equally serious fictions, but ones that lack the commanding subject of Vietnam and are judged to fall short. The lesson of the *New York Times* episode (of skipping

Paco's Story for review until it was nominated for an NBA) was salutary, but not long lasting.

Adrian Mitchell

This review was done in the same aggressive spirit of the early *Nation* reviews. I recall Saul Bellow's remark about vitriolic reviews: they should be headlined by the reviewer, "I have written three unpublished novels!" (I had yet to publish—write—a book.) I certainly wasn't taking the long view. The *TBR* inserted a line of praise in the review; it's the only temperate remark in it.

Patrick McGinley, Bernard Mac Laverty, William Trevor, Fay Weldon, Iris Murdoch

All of these reviews were assigned. For some reason (my name, doubtless) I seemed an appropriate reviewer for Irish subjects—though, these were, in the main, Anglo-Irish authors. I felt towards them as if they were uncles and aunts whom I vaguely knew or heard discussed.

D. M. Thomas

I wasn't an admirer of *The White Hotel*, so I might have begged off, but I didn't.

IV. Nonfictional Times: Amnesty, Trials, Profiles, Censorship

Remembering to Forget

This was my only turn as a pamphleteer. I was asked by Leonard Boudin to do this, and it was originally to be published as a pamphlet. The National Emergency Civil Liberties Committee then decided to run it as an issue of their periodical, *Rights*. President Gerald R. Ford issued an executive order (September 16, 1974) early in his demi-term, that instituted a complicated "Clemency Program," which ultimately served roughly 27,000 applicants. On January 21, 1977, President Jimmy Carter pardoned most, but not all, Vietnam era draft evaders, the first major act of his presidency, an act which is not referred to in his 1982 memoir, *Keeping Faith*.

Jury Duty

Every writer, it is said, who does a stint of jury duty writes about it. The principal interest was the chimney sweep case and the odd circumstances of having Jason Epstein in the same group of juror candidates.

Michael Harrington

This was done originally on assignment for *Ramparts*. They decided not to run it and the magazine soon folded. The *Soho Weekly News* took it in this shortened form—and also shut down soon after. Harrington died of cancer on July 31, 1989. He had become for the American Left the Catholic version of I. F. Stone: the older, admired figure, a dignitary.

William Sloane Coffin, Jr.

This was assigned by *Politicks*, another periodical no longer in existence. Coffin stepped down from his post at Riverside Church in 1988 to become president of SANE/Freeze, an anti-nuclear organization.

Of Judges and G-strings; Will the Court Bare All?

This was another long article that turned into two. It surprised me that this case was so little written about (other than newspaper coverage). Nude dancing, I suppose, was considered so déclassé (as well as politically incorrect) that no magazines wanted to air the issues. I wouldn't have written about it, except that I lived in the town where the case originated and *Arts Indiana* asked for a piece. On June 21, 1991, the case was decided, five to four, in favor of Indiana's notion of public morality. Chief Justice Rehnquist, writing for the majority, held that enforcement of Indiana's public indecency statute, requiring dancers to wear pasties and G-strings, did not violate the First Amendment. The Seventh Circuit was reversed. Of the Seventh Circuit judges, the stupidest opinion, written in dissent, was by Judge Manion, who had some well-publicizied difficulty getting through his confirmation hearings and onto the Seventh Circuit's bench. But it was Manion's dissent that Rehnquist and Souter and Scalia most echoed: they held that Indiana's statute furthered substantial governmental interest in protecting societal order and morality and, Souter adding, in preventing secondary effects, such as prostitution, sexual assaults, and so forth. The *Nation* sat on the piece for a long time before running it; in that interim the *Rust* decision came down, and I should have changed the word *likely* to *possible*, when I predicted that the Seventh Circuit would be upheld, though even I was surprised by the obvious (which was that the Rehnquist court would not allow nude dancing enough First Amendment protection to be legal in Indiana).

Freedom at Risk

This appeared before Thurgood Marshall stepped down from the Court and his replacement ascended to it. To paraphrase Clarence Thomas on the subject of Coke cans, as quoted by Anita Hill, "Who put Clarence Thomas on our Supreme Court?"

V. Time for One Story

The Maggot Principle

Originally this story was published in the *Transatlantic Review* in 1972 with a subtitle: "The Indochina War as a Fish Factory." I removed it (and various similar headings in the story) when I included it in my anthology *On the Job: Fiction about Work by Contemporary American Writers* in 1977. This story was one incidental cause of the anthology. Why a short story concluding a collection of nonfiction? I suppose because I think of "The Maggot Principle" the way some critics think of George Orwell's "Shooting an Elephant," or "A Hanging"—existing somewhere along the margins where the two genres overlap.

INDEX